IN SEARCH OF
MIDDLE GROUND

Memoirs of a Washington Insider

Warren I. Cikins

DEVORA PUBLISHING

JERUSALEM • NEW YORK

IN SEARCH OF MIDDLE GROUND
Memoirs of a Washington Insider

Published by DEVORA PUBLISHING COMPANY

Text Copyright © 2005 by Warren I. Cikins
Cover Photograph: Fred Zimmer
Cover and Book Design: Benjie Herskowitz

ISBN: 1-932687-46-7

Email: sales@devorapublishing.com
Web Site: www.devorapublishing.com

Printed in Israel

To Sunshine, From Smiley

Contents

Prologue

I have had the temerity to work hard on putting together all the recollections of a busy life, although my loving wife of more than forty years has told me, "Why are you bothering? Who will read it?"

While much of my life has been conducted in a most modest manner, I must confess, however, that I am possessed of a similar ego to all of those who have held elective office (as I have). As Senator Alan Simpson has said, "Here in Washington the high road of humility is not bothered by heavy traffic." I do believe that much of what I have experienced often from behind the scenes may be of interest to many of those whose paths I have crossed, as well as those who have witnessed "the passing parade" in the Washington arena.

And so, what will you learn about in these pages? You will see a Jewish child born right after the Great Depression began, who attended school in an environment where the overwhelming Irish-Catholic student body was deeply anti-Semitic. That attitude was a reflection of the times, of course, and changed markedly as time passed by. The atmosphere in the neighborhood was in some ways analogous to living in a concentration camp. It wasn't until high school that I felt somewhat relaxed in the classroom, when I attended the famous magnet school, Boston Public Latin, the oldest public high school in the country founded in 1635, a year before Harvard. At this school there were many other Jewish students, as well as representatives of all other races and religions. Scholastically I was, as best I could tell, "first in my class" in my freshman, sophomore, and junior years, winning every award I was eligible for, including the Michaelman Mathematics Prize in my junior year. For reasons that will be explained later, I finished fourth in my graduating class of 1947.

The number one student at "Boston Latin" in those years always received a major scholarship to Harvard that included tuition, room and board, books, and a small living stipend. My own admission to Harvard, along with about sixty of my classmates, did include a scholarship (which about a dozen of us received) that covered only tuition. That meant I had to work a hectic schedule to raise sufficient funds to pay for room and board. I graduated "cum laude" in Political Science, with one of the readers of my undergraduate thesis telling me that document was close to "magna." If one considered the grades obtained as compared to the time and effort made, I was very efficient indeed.

I went on to the Kennedy School of Government (then known as the Littauer School) and ultimately settled in the Washington, D.C., area. My career has included service with six presidential or congressional commissions (such as the U.S. Civil Rights Commission, the U.S. Equal Employment Opportunity Commission, and the U.S. Advisory Commission on Intergovernmental Relations); senior positions with Congressman Brooks Hays (the hero of the Little Rock school-desegregation crisis), Senator Ed Muskie (a presidential aspirant), and Senator Clair Engle of California, and minor positions with Presidents Kennedy and Johnson. I also was involved in consulting with Chief Justice Warren Burger, Chief Justice William Rehnquist, and Justice Tom Clark on matters dealing with the administration of justice, while working as a senior staff member at The Brookings Institution. At the same time, I focused priority attention to criminal justice matters. Throughout this fifty-year era, I taught part-time at American University, George Washington University, and the Florida-based Nova University. I also served two terms as an elected public official in local government, in spite of a series of health problems.

All in all, I think it has been a remarkable experience. I have been a participant in many of the historic events of that period. It is true that in some instances, I was like the little old lady who confessed that she had seen Halley's Comet at the beginning of the twentieth century, "but only from a distance." It is also true that I played a significant role in both some key domestic and some key foreign affairs matters (I also served at the U.S. Department of State and the Agency for International Development). I followed the instruction of my Harvard political science professor V. O. Key, who observed that "survivability in Washington is inversely proportional to visibility."

As I complete these reminiscences, I recognize that I am a fossil of an earlier era. It was an era of bipartisanship, civility, bridge-building, concern about integrity, reaching for compromise, and an effort to control runaway greed. How different the present is! I have no regrets about my actions, as I have tried to do the right thing as best I could, during a more civil time, even when it meant severe negative reactions. I know that much progress in civil rights and other important areas has been made over the course of my life experience. In that journey, I have been blessed by a devoted wife, Sylvia, without whom I could not have functioned, two wonderful sons, Dean Franklin and Neil Winston, with the right sets of values, two daughters-in-law, Andrea and Traci, who share those values and three delightful granddaughters, Emme, Tori, and Maya.

I cannot conclude this introduction without expressing great thanks to publisher Yaacov Peterseil for encouraging me to write this autobiography and overseeing its completion in a kind and understanding manner. To Janet Greenstein Potter, my editor, whose insights and abilities were a great help to me. The constant give-and-take between us served to bring this work to fruition in a dynamic and inspiring way, creating exhilarating synergy.

Chapter 1

Shaped by Love, Overcoming Adversity

In Boston, Massachusetts, several hours into the fifth of July, 1930, I—Warren Ira Cikins—was born. My parents, Harry and Anna, and my two older brothers were living in the Dorchester section of the city, a neighborhood that was borderline upper-lower class—or lower-middle class, depending on your outlook. My parents conceived me about the time of the momentous stock market crash, and I've always wondered whether I would be here now if they knew then what lay just ahead. When I pondered that question, they always reacted angrily. Furthermore, they were really trying for a girl, and when I mentioned that fact, they would get angry all over again, saying, "We didn't throw you out, did we?" Wanting a third child was a brave act on their part, because my father ultimately lost his job as a civil engineer with Stone and Webster, a premier firm in Boston. Years later, that same firm graciously received me on a visit representing The Brookings Institution, agreeing to see me only after I related the family history on the telephone.

My mother's father, David Gallis, came to Boston in the 1880s from Koretz, Poland, a small town similar to the one in *Fiddler on the Roof*. I think it revealing that a Koretz Society was created and came to have thousands of members, since the immigrants and their descendants were anxious to preserve their association with their roots. My grandfather was only about fourteen or fifteen, but the Russian authorities who controlled the region often conscripted young Jewish boys into the army for many years of service, and he wasn't about to have any of that. He told me a hair-raising story about how he got across Europe to an English port, and worked his way across the Atlantic as a ship houseboy. He then settled in Boston. After getting a job as a butcher's assistant, he raised enough money to bring his mother and his brother Harry to join him. Ellis Island was not yet in service, and people were still cleared into the country at a mainland place called Castle Garden. In an amusing mix-up, the immigration officials thought Harry Gallis's last name was Gillis and that's how they noted it on his documents. And so Harry Gillis and all his children, grandchildren, and descendants on down the line carry the name Gillis—a wonderful Irish name in Boston—for a fine Jewish family.

My mother's mother, Sarah Gallis (née Kaufman), came from Odessa, Russia, as a girl of about eleven. She left her mother and father and eleven brothers and sisters to come with an uncle to the land of opportunity. I am named after two of her brothers, Wolf and Isaac. Her father was a supply officer in the Czarist army, so they lived a better life than most Jews in that region at that time. (I have a portrait of him hanging in my dining room that reveals very sad eyes, but a very determined jaw.) When my grandmother came to Boston, she worked many hours a day for very low pay as a seamstress in a sweatshop. Yet, she told me, all the girls sang songs of joy upon breathing the air of freedom. She married my grandfather at a very early age and they had five children (one of whom died not much beyond infancy), of whom my mother was the eldest.

While my grandfather never learned to read or write English (and the arrival of television in his old age opened up a whole new world to him), he was a successful kosher butcher and also became an impressive builder of tenements in the West End of Boston. His success reminds me of Somerset Maugham's book *Trio*, which has a section on the great achievements of an illiterate church sextant. His wife was not only a great mother, grandmother, cook, and housekeeper, she was the building manager for her husband. My own mother served as bookkeeper when she was still quite young, and she learned a great deal about the business world, while living a very elegant childhood and being somewhat spoiled. My grandfather was a great believer in self-education and street smarts, and he scoffed at those who felt the need to attend college. Thus none of his children did so, although they were all of above-average intelligence. He had many Jewish witticisms, which I put together in a draft of an article, but did not pursue—the expressions are funny only in Yiddish but were enjoyed by many of my family.

As for my father, he was born in Suvrene, Russia—another small town, this one near Odessa. His parents decided to seek their fortunes in the United States and arrived in Boston in 1903, when he was seven years old. My grandfather Abraham loved the world of commerce, and so he opened a market as soon as he could. My grandmother Lilian had the same maiden name as my other grandmother—Kaufman. While my dad had an entrepreneurial spirit as a youth—he built up a newspaper delivery service that earned him almost half as much as many adults earn—his father insisted that he work in the market as soon as he was old enough. Since his family was of modest means, my father never aspired to attend Harvard, (although a younger brother later did), but did get a degree in civil engineering at Northeastern University (NU) and a special graduate degree from the Massachusetts Institute of Technology (MIT). After a series of engineering jobs building bridges in New England, he decided to follow in his father's footsteps and open a market in Boston. As a practical joker, he enjoyed putting up a sign in the produce section that said, "Apples, 10 Cents Apiece and Two for a Quarter" and noticing how many customers bought two. He went back to engineering just before the Great Depression of 1929 hit, but when I was a baby he lost that job and went into selling insurance.

My father and mother met on a double-date with different partners, attending an annual outing of the NU Alumni Association. It was the spring of 1920. One thing led to another and they were engaged on her birthday in 1921 and married on June 20, 1922. They had a somewhat tumultuous life in the twenties, with my dad shifting jobs between his two loves, engineering and marketing, and two sons arriving—Milton in 1924 and Alvan (known as Abe, after our grandfather) in 1927. They moved about the city several times as the family grew, ending up in the same two-family house as my mother's parents in Dorchester. My grandfather was president of a Dorchester synagogue, where it so happened he mentioned that he was going to buy a nearby house. A member of the congregation overheard him and, immorally, beat him to it. Not being aware of the nature of the neighborhood and needing a larger house, my grandfather then bought a two-family house in the Irish, rather than Jewish, section of Dorchester, on Millet Street. This purchase was to have a very significant adverse influence on my family's life, especially on my brothers and me, since we lived on the first floor of that house for many years.

When I was born in 1930, the country was what Franklin Roosevelt would later call "one-third ill-clothed, ill-fed, and ill-housed." The people on Millet Street were quite representative of the nation. Coupled with economic pressure was the growth of latent anti-Semitism. Most of my neighbors became ardent supporters of Father Charles Coughlin, a great admirer of Adolph Hitler. He preached hatred of the Jews in a weekly radio program listened to by millions. When I started to go to school at the age of 4, I confronted that hatred among my peers. In most of my classes, from kindergarten through sixth grade, almost all of my teachers and fellow students were Irish Catholic. Interestingly, one exception was my fifth-grade teacher Miss Tanck, of German background, who treated me very kindly and gave me the role of Santa Claus in the school's Christmas play. It should be made clear that the atmosphere was a sign of the times, and when I returned to see some of my neighbors many years later, they were all very cordial.

The general climate in the 1930's, however, might be represented by a young man whom everyone called "Whitey." He had had the fingers of one of his hands severed in an accident and a piece of metal placed across the area where the fingers had been, or, in other words a readily available set of brass knuckles. When I saw Whitey coming, I crossed the street rapidly to escape him. I did not always succeed. Some of the neighbors had vicious dogs of the German Police variety, which made just the walking to school a difficult ordeal. My brother Alvan would not shrink from a fight, even though there might be ten antagonists arrayed against him, all calling him the proverbial "Christ-killer." I, on the other hand, had my share of fights, black eyes, and bloody noses; but when I could, I chose the option of being a good track man—abandoning the scene. (This training probably stood me in good stead when I became a mediator as an adult, trying to avoid a fight if there was any other, wiser option.) When my brother came home and my mother asked about his bruises and torn clothes, he just dismissed it as "some fun with the boys" and her concerns subsided.

This situation reminds me of the story told by columnist Art Buchwald, who grew up in somewhat similar circumstances. After he got a job as a correspondent for the *New York Herald Tribune* in Paris, he once saw one of the neighbors who had made his life miserable coming toward him, arms outstretched in greeting, and his nose started to bleed. A family in the Roxbury neighborhood adjacent to Dorchester known to us as the Hentoffs had a son Nat who became a great civil righter and music critic whom I admired very much. He wrote a book entitled, *Boston Boy*, where he described some similar experiences.

And so I spent these childhood years in an island that was surrounded pretty much by a sea of hatred. That problem was compounded by not having any close friends. The saving grace was having a loving family—parents and grandparents and other relatives who lived not too far away. The best pleasures came from the great cooking of my grandmother.

As the Depression deepened and our financial circumstances worsened, it was clear that we could not move away from the very inhospitable environment. My parents emphasized that education was the way to escape my plight. While I wasn't particularly scholarly, I spent many hours at the local library, without much structure to my choices, starting at one end of the library and gradually reading just about every book the library had. It became clear that I was bright enough, since my grades were mostly As, but I yearned for a more normal well-rounded life.

To keep ourselves amused, my brothers and I played many games at home that we had invented ourselves. We designed a home baseball game using a monopoly board, with the roll of the dice determining what kind of hits or outs took place. When we went outside, we managed to get some boxing gloves and used the garage during the times it was empty as the boxing ring. I think I was knocked unconscious more than once. We created another baseball game—played with bat and ball in our narrow driveway—which we came to call $2.50, since that was how much it cost to replace the windows we smashed.

I had a brief window of opportunity to have a somewhat normal life when I went to the Oliver Wendell Holmes School for the seventh and eighth grades. It covered a wider area than my previous schools, and many of my classmates were Jewish. There were a number of pretty girls I got acquainted with, and I enjoyed the association very much. The boys and girls of the Jewish section of Dorchester already knew each other quite well, and so I was pretty much frozen out of any social contacts after school. But it was a great leap forward for me to simply be in a school where I was not singled out for mistreatment. I remember having an excellent English teacher named Nellie McNair, who took a real interest in me and constantly lectured me on manners, grooming, and proper behavior. She especially berated me for not combing my hair. She said I would be dating soon and should care more about my appearance. How wrong she was about my dating! Another teacher named Miss Sullivan startled me one day by saying I was only a mediocre student; but I knew that I was far smarter than she was and I thought her wacky. She in no way shook my confidence in my intellectual abilities.

During this period I contracted an ear infection that got quite serious. It was necessary for me to have a "mastoid operation," which meant the mastoid bone behind my ear had to be scraped of infection. I can still remember the pounding on my head, although I must have been sedated. Later in life, I learned that the year after my surgery, penicillin was given wide distribution and would have cured me.

While I was recuperating, my dad asked me if I'd like something special to eat and I said—knowing that the hospital was carefully regulating my food intake—"a hot dog." The next day he brought me a hot dog in a roll, and when I bit into it, it bounced! It was made of rubber. On a serious note, sharing the room with me was a boy very seriously ill, who may not have survived; and I was deeply affected by his moaning and groaning. It made me commit to trying as an adult to improve the quality of health-care research and delivery.

Before this time, I had been attending Hebrew school to prepare for my bar mitzvah—the religious ceremony in which a thirteen-year-old boy fulfills the commandment to become responsible for following Jewish law. My schedule had been quite challenging. Public school went from about 9:00 a.m. to 3:30 p.m. and Hebrew school began at 4:00 p.m. and ran until 6:00 p.m., which constituted a very full day, supplemented by evening homework. After my ear operation, I was a Hebrew-school dropout, until a very charismatic ultra-Orthodox rabbi arrived in Boston. His name was Avram Hecht, and he rounded up a number of young boys to learn Talmud—a collection of revered fundamental writings related to the Torah (the Five Books of Moses).

Since he taught in Yiddish—a language with which I had only a passing acquaintance (mostly my grandparents using it in private conversation)—I had a mighty struggle to keep up with the classes.

My brother Alvan had become quite caught up with the mystical Hasidic movement. Several years earlier, when he was thirteen and I was ten, he had moved to Eastern Parkway in Brooklyn, New York, where the Lubavitcher yeshiva (a school associated with the movement) was located. He wanted to train to be a rabbi. Although I became quite devout under the influence of Rabbi Hecht, I think my commitment was far less than that of my brother, and that difference partially contributed to my sense of loneliness. I did give thought at the time to becoming a rabbi, which Rabbi Hecht encouraged.

Although my folks were barely making ends meet, they wanted to have a big party for my bar mitzvah, but I really didn't want to. Since I had no real friends, it was mostly for family and friends of my parents. But it turned out that the religious service fell during the time when the destruction of the Temple in Jerusalem is mourned, and it was not appropriate to have a major celebration. A more modest one suited me just fine. All I remember about the ceremony was that I somewhat flubbed the speech that the bar mitzvah boy makes in effect announcing, "Today I am a man."

Most of the guests gave me checks as gifts for the occasion, which I was pleased to apply to the cost of the event. When one relative gave me a comb and brush set, my mother insisted that I put it aside to use at some later date. I don't think I ever used it until I was about thirty years old, and I still have it. I owned very few toys, which I lovingly cherished and preserved as a small boy; but when I outgrew them, I gave them to some cousins who were in more favorable financial circumstances, and they quickly destroyed them.

Chapter 2

Schooling in the World of Hard Knocks

After turning thirteen in the summer of 1943, I entered Boston Public Latin High School (BLS), founded in 1635— possibly the finest public, college-prep institution at that time. I started in the ninth grade with some 600 classmates, but by the time we graduated four years later, some 450 had left to attend less demanding regional high schools and only 150 of us remained. This was a wonderful group of young men (no women back then, unfortunately, because there was a separate Girls' Latin School), who were all oriented toward academic study. Just about everyone later attended first-rate colleges. While I continued to miss the pleasure of contemporary female companionship, at least my classmates were stimulating group of mostly Jews, Irish, Italians, with some WASPs and a few Blacks.

The teachers at BLS were generally superb, but their job was made easier by the atmosphere of intense scholarship. My best teacher, Mark Russo, was a fantastically good trainer in grammar, who taught me that grammar was not static but an always evolving and debated discipline. Everyone wanted to succeed and there was plenty of competition. I soon discovered that I could compete with the best of them. My first year was a smashing academic success. The most prestigious prize for each class was the Classical Prize which I won handily.

19

I also won the 1885 Prize given to two or three of the most promising freshmen.

World War II was raging, and the family was concerned about my brother Milton, who was in the U.S. Army Air Force as a weather observer. I became quite a student of airplanes and could identify the planes of all the Axis nations—in order to help sound a warning should they fly over Boston. The system for identification was called WEFT: Wing, Engine, Fuselage, Tail. People teased me about my brother. They said I missed him as much because I had relied on him to help with my homework as because he might come in harm's way. As it turned out, I was capable of handling my high school assignments alone—very well indeed. My brother came back from war unscathed.

You might say I was pretty much what today is called a nerd. It was an externally imposed categorization, however, since I yearned to do everything the typical teenager would do—and I'm proud to say my sons later were able to do—but there was no opportunity to do so. And so I focused on clubs at BLS that were within my reach, such as the chess, history, and poetry clubs. I became an outstanding chess player, vice president and number-two player of our chess club, which became citywide champion for several years running.

A particularly exciting moment took place when I went to downtown Boston alone one day, and with some time to kill, I went to the Young Men's Christian Association to play chess. While I was watching others play, I challenged an older man to a game. He reluctantly agreed. We sat down at an empty table, and he quickly dispatched me with a brilliant attack. He then even more reluctantly agreed to a rematch. Then we had a battle of the titans. As the game went on for some time, it attracted many kibitzers; and I began to realize I was playing a nationally recognized figure, possibly Sam Reshevsky (I can't be sure), who had been American champion. I finally won the game! He immediately challenged me to a third game, where he wiped me out again rather rapidly. But for a brief moment, I had reached great heights in the chess world.

During this period I made friends with four classmates—a friendship that has endured for some sixty years. (We were even roommates at Harvard College.) The four were Dave Bloom, Michael Bucuvalas, Joe Rosen, and Eddie Schlossberg (later changed to Shore). Michael was Greek Orthodox and the rest of us were Jewish. Michael's father was a prominent lawyer, and his financial success gave Michael considerable economic advantage over the rest of us. In no way did he attempt to manifest this favorable situation. Dave and Joe had started delivering newspapers at an early age and after awhile gained considerable stature in that area. Since work for teenagers was hard to obtain, I don't think Eddie had a job, and I know I didn't have one.

One school year, as the summer approached, I asked my father to help me get a job. He responded beautifully. As an insurance salesman, he had met some people of consequence who might be in a position to offer me employment. One of his clients was in the movie industry and he agreed to meet with us. When we got to his office, the movie official had three or four colleagues with him for the interview. I was asked many questions about my qualifications and interests, and it looked like I would be offered a job. Then they asked me if I could work six days a week, including Saturdays. At that time, I was strictly observing the Jewish religious requirement that one rest on the Sabbath (Saturday for Jews) and not work. While it was likely that most of these men were Jewish, albeit not observant ones, I shrunk from explaining that while I would work long hours on Monday through Friday, and even on Sunday, if that were feasible, I did not want to work on Saturday. My dad stepped in to save me embarrassment and said he thought I should only work five days a week. I have long regretted my cowardice in not being forthright and have often wondered what might have been. The men expressed their regret and I was not hired. To think, I might have ended up a movie mogul, if I had persuaded these men and prevented my father from intervening.

The next year I had a somewhat different experience. In anticipation of taking the college boards and hoping to gain admission to an outstanding college, just about all the seniors stayed after school for months of drilling with every possible examination question we might face. As the school year was ending, we were told we would be released a month early if we had a job. I responded to a *Reader's Digest* ad and signed up as a magazine salesman. The only subscription I sold was to my dad. And so I continued to look. I saw another ad in the paper—this time for a mail clerk at a local insurance company—and went in for an interview. I did not admit that I was available only for the summer because I hoped to be part-time during the school year. They asked me to take an intelligence test, which I raced through rapidly, as primed as I was to take exams. I outfoxed myself, however, because the personnel officer was shocked at how well I had done—better than the company president himself. She lectured me on the need to go to college, and, saying I was way too qualified, refused to give me the job.

My four years at Boston Latin were very intense. I had practically no social life, just about no money, and only the fervent desire to excel academically so that I could escape my plight. I remember watching enviously as my peers attending proms and other functions for boys and girls, all of which were way beyond my grasp. Later in life, when my circumstances had changed, I was still somewhat socially crippled by the lack of normal human relationships, which had created in me an enormous social inferiority complex. I don't rule out the possibility that there was some personality defect in me that contributed to this condition.

Studies at BLS were enormously challenging, but each year I got all As and won a series of prizes that put me in the running for being first in my class. I had a wonderful English teacher, Mr. Benson, for my first two years at BLS and he praised my work giving me straight As. (I had been saddened to learn that he had lost his only son in the invasion of Tarawa during World War II). By my junior year I won the Michaelman Math Prize, which meant I was the best mathematician in my class. This led me to make an unfortunate decision in my senior year—to choose the only BLS track that was scientifically oriented, aimed at MIT, rather than classically focused, aimed at Harvard.

When I began my senior year, my homeroom teacher was named Sheehan, who would also be my English teacher. He had some injury to one of his legs, which caused him to drag it as he walked. That led the students, with typical cruelty, to call him "Swifty Sheehan,"—behind his back, of course. This infirmity might well have been responsible for his rotten disposition. He also reeked of anti-Semitism. I did not realize this until I got a B in English on my first report card. I had never gotten a B at Boston Latin, and my English grades had been superlative. Since the grades at BLS were number grades, translated into A through F by ranges, getting an average B with mediocre number grade could have a devastating impact on my quest to be number one in my class at BLS.

When I confronted Sheehan with the fact that I was being treated unfairly, he just said that that was my tough luck. While a math grade can be challenged very easily, because numbers don't lie, it is much harder to challenge an English grade, since so much of the student's work is judged subjectively. It was also obvious that Sheehan was giving the Irish kids the highest grades. I should have immediately transferred out of the science track and changed homerooms, which would have given me a different English teacher and a Latin class instead of an advanced science class. I made the unfortunate mistake of not changing because I never liked Latin, even though I always got As and won several Latin prizes.

And so when my senior year ended, I had one B on my record—the only one I had I ever received in four years of high school—and it was from Swifty Sheehan's English class. It meant that my ranking dropped from first to fourth in the class, although only because the third and fourth years of high school grades were considered. I would have been first if all four years were counted (I was told), and I've always wondered if some hanky-panky was involved in the school's decision. Avram Goldberg, the son of a prominent judge, came in first; he later married the daughter of the owner of a major food chain, Stop & Shop. Second was John Rexine, a dedicated Greek scholar, who made a career in academia. And third was a young man named John Mulhern, who became a prominent lawyer and died at an early age. As number four, I received one of the six Franklin Medals awarded to the top students. (Mine—the Pennypacker Award—was named after a distinguished headmaster.) Harvard usually gave a complete scholarship to number one, which included room, board, tuition, and expenses. The other five were eligible for full tuition scholarships, one of which I was later awarded by Harvard.

When I had signed up to take the college boards, I had listed Harvard as the only school to receive the results. (I was being rather arrogant, I guess.) As for the testing date, I was concerned that the exams came on a Saturday, the Sabbath, and in the middle of Passover, to boot. When I inquired, I was told I could take the exams after sunset that day, meaning from about 9:00 p.m. to 3:00 a.m. I therefore spent the holiday at the home of a prominent Orthodox Rabbi Twersky, along with his son, Isadore, who later became a Harvard professor and a boy whose last name was Feuerstein, from a distinguished business family. Of the many thousands of Jews in Boston, we were the only three to ask for this treatment. The rabbi had a synagogue attached to his house, and it was quite an experience participating in this process. Being very sensitive to the residual anti-Semitic atmosphere at Harvard (a former president, A. Lawrence Lowell, had set a quota for Jews), I knew my choice of the exam time might jeopardize my chances for admission; but I was a feisty kid on this front, if not on the social front. As an example, when I was later at Harvard studying philosophy under Professor Henry Aiken, he said the Jews contributed justice, the Greeks rationality, and the Christians love, and I responded in a term paper that he was full of malarkey. His response was not kind. In any event, I was admitted to Harvard, with that full-tuition scholarship—a wonderful day, although short of what

I had hoped for. It meant that I had to work my way through Harvard. to earn room and board, rather than being able to give full attention to my studies or to have the wherewithal for a full social and activities-oriented life.

When I was about seventeen years old, I had my first taste of being active in politics in Boston. I was approached by a young man named Jerry Rappaport (possibly the same one I read about recently in an issue of *Boston* magazine, May 2004), who was anxious to have Mayor James Michael Curley unseated. Rappaport was among those who created the "The New Boston Committee ." Curley was a great orator who was also somewhat unethical, but a politician with a great loyal following. As I recall, he had even been reelected, or at least not ousted, while sitting in a Federal penitentiary (incarcerated on bribery charges, I believe). The electoral system of Boston was nonpartisan at that time, with no run off if no one obtained a majority. Thus, Curley, who was always good for at least 40 percent of the vote, won many elections. If he had a strong opponent with a good Irish name like John L. Sullivan, he often would find a lesser person with the same name to put on the ballot, thus diluting the opposition vote.

Many stories are told about Curley, but I'll just mention two. When Franklin Roosevelt was running for President in 1932, he would have liked to ask Curley to nominate him for president, but he could not risk doing so because of Curley's reputation, which also related to Curley's not being chosen as a Massachusetts delegate. At the convention, when the time came for Roosevelt's nomination to be seconded, the gentleman from Puerto Rico, "Jaime Miguel Curleyo" was recognized to speak. Another story, possibly equally apocryphal, but quite plausible, tells that when a potential contractor for a city project came to see the mayor to apply for the contract, Curley would ask the person to guess how many people there were in the picture of the huge crowd that hung in his office; and when the "appropriate" number was suggested, that amount was paid to

Curley "under the table" above the basic cost of the project.

To get the electoral process to be modified, I assisted in establishing the New Boston Committee through outreach to a distinguished bipartisan group of leaders, who were willing to promote the adoption of a new charter for the city. Such a charter would provide for runoff elections to require that a candidate receive a majority vote to be declared the victor. I believe this new charter was adopted at the next election in 1948. Curley was then defeated in the 1950 election, with his usual 40 percent of the vote. Our reform effort had succeeded. Reform candidate John Hynes, the city clerk, was elected mayor. As a lesson to reformers, I am told that he turned into a mayor not much better than Curley. In the typical Boston tradition, however, a great auditorium was built in his honor in the city, bearing his name.

College

My first year at Harvard was a dismal one. Since it was in 1947, the college had limited dormitory space–much of it being used for the flood of veterans returning after the war. People living within commuting distance of the college were required to live at home. And so I did not escape from dismal, hateful Dorchester that year, but rode the subway to school. For the commuters, there was a place to stay during the day called Dudley Hall, which was equally dismal. About all one could do rather than study was play Ping- Pong. Just about all of the commuters became excellent Ping- Pong players, including me. While 1947 was the first year Radcliffe students were allowed to take classes with Harvard students (before that time, professors gave the same lecture twice at each institution), there was no way I could figure out how to get acquainted with the females. The ones in my classes certainly didn't seem to give me the time of day, which didn't surprise me at all.

The year mercifully passed quickly, although I didn't study very hard, suffering from low morale and knowing that I could easily make the B average necessary to keep my scholarship. I lacked courage to make the outreach necessary for gaining a real college experience, so I didn't join any clubs or other on-campus activities. I had much free time during my freshman year because I lived at home and was not working at any jobs to provide the funds for room and board at college, That situation would change, of course, when I lived at school the rest of my undergraduate career.

Looking back on those days, I grow angry at myself for not having the curiosity to explore what college life had to offer, even to a commuter. Nor did I have the confidence to approach any of my professors, to explore further any of the topics from the courses I was taking. My advisor, a young instructor named Rogers, seemed of little assistance. That judgment was confirmed by an article in the college newspaper, *The Harvard Crimson*, which evaluated all the instructors and had Rogers listed at the bottom of the list with the comment, "and Rogers was pitiful." Surprisingly, the only course that I excelled in was the natural sciences, where I got an A. I got only a B in political science, my major, which I had decided on as preparation for a career in public service. I did recognize that getting my degree from Harvard would certainly serve as the "union card" for accomplishing that objective. (Teddy White, the great chronicler of John F. Kennedy's presidential election and later presidents' elections, grew up in a neighborhood near mine, was known to my family, and had some similar childhood experiences to mine. It is interesting to note that he mentioned in his autobiography, *In Search Of History*, that he viewed his Harvard experience in much the same way, simply as preparation for whatever career he might have.)

That spring I made another effort to find a summer job. This time I had a modicum of success. I was offered a job as a dishwasher at a resort hotel in Maine. This was not exactly the kind of job I had in mind, but it was better than nothing. Shortly thereafter, I approached the Liggett-Rexall chain in Boston and was offered a summer job as short-order cook, sandwich man, and busboy at a drug store with a food section on Boylston Street, across from Bonwit Teller store. They also said they would send me to a school to learn how to do the job. That sounded like a better opportunity than the resort-hotel assignment, so I turned that one over to my friend Eddie Shore, even though the hotel manager wasn't too happy about the switch. I was also required to join the union, then known as the Retail Clerks, which I was proud to do, since I had always been pro-union. And the thought of having a lot of Bonwit Teller models crowding in for lunch was also a pleasant one.

While I was never able to get a date with any of the models, many were very friendly, especially if they wanted some special attention. Some had very little time for lunch, and they needed a dish of their favorite food as quickly as possible. That did give me some feeling of self-worth or even power, since I could play favorites. All in all, being surrounded every day by some very attractive women was a pleasant way to spend my time, and the work wasn't onerous. I worked hard and gained the approval of the manager of the food section. This led to his putting me completely in charge for one Sunday evening. That was a big mistake. For some reason, unfathomable to me, the small oven used to prepare the BLT sandwiches caught on fire, and it took some quick action by me with the extinguisher to put out the flames. I was careful to lock up when the store closed, but forgot to put the keys in their special location. When I got to work on Monday morning, all the doors were off the hinges—done by the manager to get the section open. My employment was not all a fiasco, however, because I got much praise for the quality of the coffee I served. I later figured out the reason for my skill: I thoroughly cleaned out the large urn in which I prepared the coffee—the first time the urn had been cleaned for a long time.

In the spring of my freshman year, I had signed up to live at school for the next year. It was an act of faith, because the amount of money I needed for room, board, expenses, and books far exceeded what I expected to earn that summer. I hated the idea of working in the dormitory kitchen, an assignment that would possibly be available, but I would have done it if there were no alternative. I hoped that I might get a job as a student librarian, which I felt would be much more suitable. The situation at home was very tight, so I did not expect, or even want, any financial support from that direction. Harvard had the "House" system, with separate small collegelike communities of dormitories, where there were a whole range of activities and separate dining halls. My friends Joe Rosen, Dave Bloom, and Eddie Shore applied to Leverett House for a five-man suite, since we expected to have Mike Bucuvalas join us. While my brother Milton had stayed in Dunster House, such sizeable suites did not exist, or so I was informed. My reason for wanting to consider Dunster House was that living in the same House as one's older brother gives you status with the Housemaster. Living at Dunster would have, indeed, helped me later, I realize with regret.

I remember arriving earlier than my colleagues so that I could move in at a convenient time on that September day in 1948. The apartment looked dark and gloomy, and such furniture as was present consisted of standard desks and chairs, with a few battered armchairs and sofas we had bought for a small sum from the prior residents. It was a desperate time for me, because I had very little money to cover my costs, no real idea about where I could get the sizeable difference, and little expectation that I was going to have a happy academic year. I wandered Harvard Square in some despair, but decided that I would not let my mood overwhelm me. I went into a delicatessen in the Square, known as the Wursthaus, which had a wonderful special sandwich. It was known as a "hot-and-a–half" of pastrami on rye bread (one-and-a-half sandwiches) for only sixty-five cents. Thus reinforced, I went back to the apartment to unpack with renewed confidence. There were two double bedrooms and one single bedroom in the suite, and we had been informed that a holdover had first claim to the single. That roommate turned out to be Bill Healy, a senior of Irish Catholic faith, who on the whole was an amicable roommate. Mike and Dave did not join us that semester, so Eddie, Joe, and I were the only three of us to move in that fall. (Mike later went to a different suite and Dave replaced Eddie whose finances were too limited to enable him to stay with us, and he became a commuter.) The fifth roommate was Don Brick, of the Jewish faith, from New Jersey. Once everyone had moved in, my gloom ended, because having the opportunity to leave Dorchester and move in with good friends was a wonderful change of lifestyle.

I arranged to take courses that met Monday, Wednesday, and Friday, but was forced to take one or two that met on Tuesday, Thursday, and Saturday. Since I usually went home on Saturday to observe the Sabbath, I arranged with Joe Rosen, who also took the courses that met on Saturday, to immediately copy his notes when I returned Saturday night or Sunday. I was angry that I was forced by idiotic university policy to pay for twenty-one meals a week, although I often had only fourteen or fifteen—missing many breakfasts, also. Missing my breakfast was my own stupidity, because I often played contract bridge until the wee hours, with our apartment living room having one or two tables going regularly. Meanwhile, I was still panicky about getting a job. I started to haunt a senior librarian at Harvard's Widener Library about hiring me. He kept telling me that there was no opening, but I would not take no for an answer. Finally, he said to me that he did need someone, thinking he would get rid of me because my class schedule made it impossible for me to be available at the times he wanted. But I thought, "Aha, I've got him!" So I said that I would be available whenever he needed me. Some two weeks into the semester, I changed every course on my schedule to build my classes around the library work. I figured that I could ultimately get all the course work I needed, but without a job, my status would be tenuous indeed. This was the great breakthrough in my college education, and I was grateful.

After a year of working in a departmental library I was accepted to work in the newly-opened Lamont undergraduate library in the fall of 1949. The head librarian was Phillip McNiff, a wonderfully kind person who treated me most graciously. This library was open only to Harvard undergraduates; Radcliffe students, being females, were not allowed to use the facility during the regular school year. The only women in the library were library personnel. It turned out that many were quite attractive and in my age range, so that working in the facility was a pleasant experience. My job was generally to do whatever was required of me at any particular time, mostly shelving books and keeping the library in good condition. I had the opportunity to familiarize myself with thousands of books assigned in a wide range of courses, all of which were of interest to me.

I was amused when another employee of the library, who happened to be a high school student, told of a surprising experience he had in his English class. He admitted to me that he was a mediocre student, at best. But the teacher had tried an experiment to see how widely read the different class members were. She asked if anyone knew the authors of series of great books she mentioned. The only one who raised his hand when she called the book titles was this colleague of mine, and he knew the author of each one. She was flabbergasted! His status rose enormously. She did not know that he worked in a library. She did not know that he could tell her the color of the cover, the number of pages, and the nature of the book's binding, but that was about all.

Working in the college library was an almost perfect job for a student, since one could put in many hours of work between classes, time that otherwise might well have gone to waste. While the pay was only minimum wage, it took practically no time to get to work, the work environment was very pleasant, and I learned a great deal being exposed to so many great books. While I worked hard and achieved a high reputation with the library hierarchy, I still had time to review many of these books, an education equal to all my course work. Later in my experience I was named curator of the Poetry Room, where I learned a great deal about the poetry world and also had much time sitting behind a desk to do much of my homework. An added bonus was that I got to know about a half-dozen of the young women who worked at the library well enough to ask them out on a date. While I was too socially inexperienced to make much headway in that regard, it was at least a step in the right direction—getting me to become comfortable with female companionship.

The five-man suite in Leverett House was D-42 in the D entry. Across the hall was another five-man suite. And on the fifth floor there was what I recall as a four-man suite. While there were changes in occupancy over my three-year residence there, we had a core group of wonderful young men who interacted very well with each other. Some of us were fresh out of high school; some were battle-hardened World War II veterans. Among the veterans was Lou Nordlinger, a ballet-loving U.S. Marine. His father was a colonel who helped arrange the surrender of the Japanese to the Americans and French at Hanoi, Indochina. Roger Newton, who came to the U.S. in the 1930s, was of German origin, I believe, and joined the Army to expedite his full integration into American society. He became a brilliant theoretical physicist and went on to get a Ph.D., and go to the Princeton Institute. Hank Booth and Al Paulsen were delightful companions, who revealed some residual effects from their wartime experiences, suffering what we now often refer to as post-traumatic stress disorder (an affliction that hit many fellow student veterans). One example relates to Hank. We often played the card game of Hearts to kill time, especially during school recesses. Being hit with the "Queen of Spades" was a serious setback. Being hit with the queen three straight times so upset Hank that he got up from the table and went to his room, and didn't socialize for days.

Al Paulsen was very creative in a technological way, often diabolical, and he arranged the creation of an outlaw radio station. During the study period before midyears, I was up late studying when Al came into my room expressing great alarm. He tuned in a radio frequency that had an announcer reporting that Soviet troops had invaded West Berlin. General Lucius Clay was mobilizing Allied troops to resist. Back at that time, the Soviets had blockaded Berlin and Truman had ordered the Allied sector to be supplied by air, so tensions were very high. One could hear explosions in the background The announcer said that *all* U.S. reserve soldiers should report to their units. One of our roommates was a reservist, and he was the most upset human being I think I had ever seen. As for me, I threw my textbook across the room figuring exams were not very relevant at this time. I woke up all my roommates and went across the hall where Paulsen and his roommates were wringing their hands. All of us were in a state of hysteria. The announcer said that it looked like World War III had begun. He then said that President Truman had appointed General Nudnik to take overall command of the European theatre. When I finally got the significance of this, I stared in amazement at my colleagues and relaxed. What an incredible hoax had been played on those of us in our suite! Al Paulsen and those in his suite had far outdone Orson Welles and his radio program dealing with the invasion of Martians that had so panicked Americans. I only regret that this effort was not recorded so that it could demonstrate the creativity of those with whom I was living. One of my roommates nearly had a heart attack, which was not so funny.

Another one of our housemates, Al Thompson, was the rebellious son of a senior executive of a New York life insurance company. Although he was a member of one of Harvard's "final clubs," the exclusive domain of the sons of the leading families in America, he was a very democratic person and enjoyed being one of us. He concocted several activities designed to ridicule some of Harvard's sacred traditions. Adjoining Leverett House was Lowell House, a much snobbier place, named after the anti-Semitic Harvard president. I learned about President Lawrence Lowell quite early in my college life when a fellow student at Harvard, Al Cella, told me about Lowell's championing the WASP effort to execute Nicola Sacco and Bartolomeo

Vanzetti, who were tried for allegedly holding up a bank and committing murder to fund the anarchist movement. Cella told me he
was going to devote his entire life to clearing the executed Sacco and
Vanzetti, which he did, with limited success. They became symbolic
figures to almost all Italians in the United States—almost as symbolic as the early-twentieth-century lynching of a Jew (Leo Frank) in
Atlanta. My awareness and sympathy certainly helped me bond with
many Italians.

Al Thompson learned that Lowell House had adopted the British tradition of having "High Table"—a Friday evening dinner where
select students dressed formally and sat at a special table with resident faculty members. Thompson obtained some lumber, and we
built a high platform in the middle of Leverett's dining room and
placed a table on top.. The ten of us who lived in the two adjoining
suites got ourselves tuxes and top hats. On Friday evening, we
mounted the platform, sat down, and hooked our canes on the edges
of the chandelier just above us. We pretended to smoke our fancy
cigars and proclaimed that we had created Leverett's Highest Table!

Al Thompson was a handsome, loveable person who certainly
had a way with women. We occasionally double-dated and I learned
a lot from him. His great success made us all envious of him in an
admiring way. He was equally comfortable with the daughter of a
Rockefeller or the waitress at a local café. His major vice was alcohol, which he occasionally imbibed to excess. When he was sick one
day, he went to the college infirmary, where the doctor told him, "Mr.
Thompson, I have found traces of blood in your alcohol stream!" He
often stayed out late at night and had trouble getting to class in the
morning, but he eventually got control of himself and finally graduated.. He was such a breath of fresh air that we all forgave him his
foibles and wished him well. The last I heard, he had become a very
successful insurance salesman for his father's company.

One example of his total lack of anti-Semitism or any racism of
any kind was that he did not mind inviting me to his final club to

play poker when his colleagues needed another participant. The players were very friendly but I was a little disconcerted to find an occasional anti-Semitic expression written on the chips we used to play poker. Most students were hardly aware of the final clubs and their 400 members did keep a low profile. We did know that they were likely to contribute significantly to the nation's leadership in the future. Jews at Harvard during this time were still quite wary, because of the legacy of President Lowell, and I think *The Harvard Crimson* reported that about one-third of them did not identify their religion. In Al Thompson's case, as was true of all the Christian roommates we had, there were no traces of anti-Semitism at all, which was quite an enormous change from my childhood.

I find the recent Supreme Court deliberations about the constitutionality of affirmative action to be somewhat hypocritical, when I remember the many sons of the wealthy who attended Harvard during my time whose qualifications were at least suspect. When I went to the financial aid office one time when I needed just one hundred dollars for a short time, I found the office director surrounded by football players and other jocks, who were probably admitted because of athletic prowess rather than academic grades. While I obviously had fine grades, he gave me a hard time and was very unfriendly. I also remember what I did one semester when I had a slate of very difficult courses and had one elective opening to fill. I wanted that course to be a very easy one, so I went to the first meetings of several possible courses, and, in each one, I counted the number of pairs of white shoes–worn mostly by wealthy students. I then chose the course that had the most of what we called the "white-shoe boys." There were plenty of white-shoe boys at Harvard, who were admitted because they had rich alumni fathers. I was not wrong in my choice of course, because I breezed to an A while doing hardly any work. So much for college admissions based only on merit!

As a senior, one had to write a thesis or dissertation to get honors at graduation. Because I expected to go to Harvard Law School, I wrote about the role of precedent in Supreme Court decisions. It was a great opportunity to review how the judicial system works and learn how rife it is with the potential for hypocrisy. While many who participate in the system are dedicated and well-intentioned, the miracle is that the system works at all. Although the walls of the Supreme Court building say "Equal Justice Under Law," that goal is far from current reality and sometimes seems to be receding. The focus of my study was the Sherman Antitrust Act, passed in 1890 to stop businesses from colluding against the public interest. "Doesn't it sound familiar!" The first case to come before the Supreme Court to test this law was brought *against* several labor unions for collaborating in bargaining, rather than the many corrupt corporations, whose actions had inspired the phrase "the era of the robber barons."

I consider myself to have been a moderately liberal person, who thought the Americans for Democratic Action a little too liberal for my taste at that time. Nonetheless, I was appalled at the actions of many corporate leaders of the 1880s–1920s: The Rockefellers, the Morgans, the Vanderbilts, the Carnegies, as well as many others, who raped the country, to an extraordinary extent. With such unions as existed then being very weak, it is incredibly ironic that the Sherman act was used to terrorize labor. In my study, I noted how the Supreme Court sought every opportunity to cite precedent to avoid going after corporate wrongdoing and only very reluctantly began to accept cases focused on big business. This situation changed under Presidents Theodore Roosevelt and Woodrow Wilson. During the time I wrote this 150-page document, I got an infected tooth that required a root canal job, leaving me in great pain when I wrote the last chapter. The faculty reviewer later noted that the last chapter was by far the best part of my paper, and that I would have graduated *magna cum laude* if the rest had been as good, rather than the *cum laude* I received.

I had always assumed that I would go to Harvard Law School, but circumstances have a way of intruding on life's plans. In my senior year at college, I had changed locations in Leverett House from McKinlock Hall to Mather Hall (later part of another House) to join with Mike Bucuvalas, whose roommate had moved on. This roommate had come from Hungary, fleeing the Communists and was ready to be a doctor, but U.S. rules required that he take some undergraduate courses he had not needed in his country. He was a wonderful young man, a great tennis player (beat me at squash right after I taught him how to play) and had earned needed funds working for Harvard President James Bryant Conant. Sadly, he died in Korea serving as a doctor, when he stepped on a land mine. My joining Mike meant I could have solitude more easily when I wanted it, yet plenty of companionship when I wanted that instead, by visiting with the old gang.

In December 1950, my oldest brother, Milt, who had abandoned Harvard Law School after two years, at the same time split with his wife, to whom he had been married for three or four years. Those last couple of years had been tumultuous for him. Until he got himself together, he came to stay with me and Mike, living on the couch in our parlor. He finally did find other accommodations and moved out. But his long struggle with law school had a profound impression on me, even though there were many forces at work on him that were not relevant for me. By December 1950, I had applied to Harvard's Littauer School of Public Administration (now the Kennedy School) for admission. Since my grade average was about a B+ to A-, I knew it would be a close call regarding my acceptance to law school. I met with Acting Dean Charles Cherington and convinced him of my serious desire for a career in public service. I was accepted by Littauer shortly thereafter, and agreed to go, still in December. I, therefore, abandoned submitting the law school application, which would have been laborious and costly. I think that Mark Cannon and I were the first students to be admitted straight out of college. The school had only about 100 students at that time, and other than the two of us, all were government employees or other civil servants.

My grades were not good enough for a fellowship, so I had to rely on my librarian earnings, savings, and the borrowing of about $300 to cover the costs of the year, 1951–52.

During that summer, I worked full-time at the library, where it so happened some classes were taught because that building was one of the few air-conditioned places at Harvard at that time. I used the opportunity to sit in for free— in my spare time, of course. It was amusing that many students came from all over the country not only to take summer courses at Harvard but also hoping to meet Harvard students. Very few Harvard students actually took courses during the summer, except those who weren't doing very well or who wanted to take required tough courses when the competition was weak. Although young women were allowed in Lamont during the summer, my being a lowly library employee didn't enhance my status very much. I did meet one fine person—a graduate student from New York who shared some pleasant time with me. But she kept the relationship platonic.

Of my four Boston Latin pals, who shared my college life, one went to Tufts Medical School, one went to Harvard Business School, one went to Harvard Law, and one went to graduate school in Connecticut. This was Eddie Shore, who got married on the weekend after we graduated from college, and I was proud to be his best man. Getting married was the last thing in the world I myself was thinking of at that time, being still twenty years old when I graduated—without any acquaintance that could be called a girlfriend. (I didn't marry until I was thirty-four.)

Graduate School

While the number of Jewish students at Harvard was growing substantially, there was little evidence that the university was at all interested in whatever minorities were in its midst. The message one got was very Darwinian—survival of the fittest, a pattern of life I had become quite familiar with in my childhood. When I challenged professors on their philosophical or theological views in courses on political theory or religion, their responses were often very hostile. I think if they behaved in such a manner in today's climate, charges of discriminatory behavior would be brought against them. There was an atmosphere of propriety in the air that made today's experiences of concern over political correctness seem quite overblown. Everyone was taught to follow the rules of the WASPs. I called the Jews that did so JASPs, the blacks that did so BASPs, the Hispanics that did so HASPs, and the Chinese or other Asians CASPs. Those that conformed did splendidly; those that did not were at risk. That certainly motivated me to challenge the system. I don't think the school's president, James Bryant Conant, was as aware of this situation as I might have expected him to be—considering his many great achievements. He really did what a college president should do but rarely does: he spoke out vehemently on many public issues. He challenged universities not to accept so much federal money that their scholarship and integrity were compromised. He led in the establishment of community colleges; he served as ambassador to Germany; and he served as an important conscience of the nation. Another champion of mine was Professor Carl Friedrich, who was a great political science scholar and promoter of human rights. After World War II, he helped write the constitution of newly formed West Germany.

My first year of graduate school was an unusual one for me. I made some wonderful friends, along with having much academic success. But there was one serious setback before the year started. Every undergraduate House had a House librarian—a plum job, since it provided a free apartment which would have helped my finances enormously. Phil McNiff, a top library official, said I was in line for the job, because no one else had a better professional librarian background, and I had previously lived in Leverett House. I was told no library system nominee was ever turned down. The Leverett housemaster, Leigh Hoadley, however, was a WASP in the tradition of former President Lowell, reflecting a genteel variety of anti-Semitism, of course. He was pretty much a failure as a housemaster, who did the minimum to help make the House a more enjoyable place to live, even though he had an ample budget for that purpose. When Harvard finally caught up with him, I was told that he was dismissed as housemaster, long after I had left. I'll always remember my only social contact with him when he invited me to his quarters for "*a* beer and *a* sandwich." I felt that I might get my hand slapped if I reached for a second sandwich.

When I was summoned to see Hoadley about the library job, he informed me that I would not get it. Lying through his teeth, he said that since I would only be in graduate school one year, he wanted someone who would stay longer. I had never said I would only be in graduate school one year—I planned to get a Ph.D! In a beautiful WASP move, he gave the job to someone named Lorington O. Weller, a name I did not know but will never forget. (Ironically, Weller left Harvard after one year.) The Harvard library authorities were shocked at Hoadley's behavior and sent word that I should try to get the open librarian job at Dunster House, where my brother had resided and where I was known to Professor Arthur Maass. They sent the message, unfortunately, through another Lamont Library employee whom I have always suspected of being jealous, and he didn't inform me for several crucial days. I went to Professor Maass, who seemed very coldly disinterested. Maass later informed me that the matter had been resolved in favor of another and I was out of luck. Phil McNiff, director of the Lamont Library, was still in my corner, however, and he sent me to the chairman of the Harvard Philosophy Department, who hired me as chief librarian of the philosophy library in Emerson Hall. While the housing bonus wasn't available, this job saved my life. I was in charge of a 20,000-book library—I read many of its volumes—and I met many philosophy majors and distinguished professors. My Harvard library experience taught me many things: (a) that, during the course of my life, I would probably always run into mean-spirited people who would harm me; (b) that I would also meet wonderful people who would help me; (c) that I could learn a lot from the jobs I held; (d) that being an employee at Harvard, rather than a teacher, definitely put you into the "hired hand" category; and (e) that anti-Semitism would probably always crop up in my life, genteel or otherwise.

A new graduate center had been built at Harkness Commons near the Harvard Law School and the Littauer School, and I shared a suite there that fall in Richards Hall with a Canadian agricultural scientist from Saskatoon, Saskatchewan, named Jim Hay. He was a tall, taciturn guy who went about his business in a determined manner. It was difficult for me to understand his Canadian accent. He told me he was working on some experiments to develop a "wheat killer," which puzzled me very much, and it wasn't till months later that I learned what he said was a "weed killer."

All of the people in Richards Hall majored in fields other than mine. Subjects ranged from geology to philosophy to Sanskrit to economics. There was also a mix of nations represented—from Australia to Europe to the Philippines. Bridge and bowling were unifying factors. I became very fond of my hallmates and learned a lot from them. I became chairman of the Graduate Political Science Club and invited both scholars and practitioners to be guests at our monthly meetings. While I took courses in political theory and on the planning process, I started a precedent by getting approval to take a course in public finance at the Harvard Business School and also audited a course on taxation at the Harvard Law School. All in all, however, I felt very lonely and lost confidence in my ability to really excel in my studies. The strain of trying to make ends meet was also beginning to tell. My mood changed, of course, when one of the most prestigious professors of political science at Harvard, Carl Friedrich, said he wanted to publish my planning-process seminar paper about the Council of Economic Advisers in the Harvard Public Administration Yearbook, *Public Policy*. This was an enormous honor for a first-year graduate student (I was only twenty-one years old when I wrote it and twenty-three when it appeared in print in 1953).

Meanwhile, I found out about a program supported by the Ford Foundation that involved a summer job at a Southern government agency and attending three southern universities: the Universities of Alabama, Tennessee, and Kentucky. It was known as the Southern Regional Training Program (SRTP) in Public Administration, and one would earn a degree analogous to a masters' degree after completing one semester at each university. I didn't expect too great an intellectual challenge, and I was anxious to have some kind of social life. By February of 1952 I had been awarded the Thomas E. Upham Fellowship at Harvard and also had been accepted by the SRTP. Quite to my amazement, I had gotten all As in the fall semester, and even more mind-boggling was the previously mentioned publication of my paper on the Council of Economic Advisers to the President. But by the time this all happened I had fallen into a deep depression over the course of my life. I went to see the new acting dean of the Littauer School, Professor Robert McCloskey, and told him I thought I needed a change of scenery. He was very understanding and agreed to a year's leave of absence (keeping my fellowship available for the following year). And so, with some adventuresome spirit, but with much trepidation, I arranged to leave New England for the first time in my life (I had not applied for a Fulbright fellowship to England, because I wanted to learn more about my own country first). Fortunately the Cambridge draft board agreed to this academic shift. One had to remain in a strong academic setting to keep one's deferment. (I soon enlisted in an Army Reserve unit, in any event, one that would not require active duty.)

While I had read a great deal about racism and was briefed on what I might expect on my first stop—Tuscaloosa, Alabama—I really had no idea on what I might confront. It was June 1952 when I arrived. I got off the train, after what seemed like a very long ride, and went to the nearest waiting room to find out where I might pick up my suitcases. After a while, I noticed that no one would come to the window to assist me. I looked about the room and realized that all the other people were black. Welcome to the South! It never had occurred to me that waiting rooms would be segregated.

After checking in at my accommodations at the University of Alabama, I attended the first briefing session. I found that the five students with whom I would be sharing the academic year were very congenial, but I realized I had very little in common with them and would have to carve out the kind of experiences I wanted on my own. I then met the faculty members who would be directing our program. They included Dean York Willbern, a most distinguished public administration expert, and Professor Albert Lepawsky, a widely respected political scientist. Others that I recall now were Chester and Valerie Earle, who became lifelong friends when they came to Washington to teach at American and Georgetown Universities, respectively. As I encountered additional impressive faculty members, I became reassured that my learning experience would be a good one.

I was quite taken with the charm of the University of Alabama, and the school layout was an interesting contrast to that of Harvard. I was later to experience another contrast between the two schools, with the Alabama Crimson Tide contesting for the national football championship, while the Harvard Crimson was lucky to win one game per year during my undergraduate days.

After receiving an orientation on the year's agenda, which would first be my summer internship at the Tennessee Valley Authority (TVA), and then one semester each at the Universities of Alabama, Tennessee, and Kentucky. (I would return to the University of Alabama the following summer for another research assignment.) I was on my way to Knoxville, Tennessee, which was TVA headquarters. The only accommodations I could afford were at the local YMCA, which proved to be adequate and was close to the TVA building. The supervisor of my work was Elinor Carr, who proved very gracious and very professional. I was to have three different assignments over the three-month period, one on TVA-Federal General Accounting Office (GAO) relations, one on TVA-steam power generation, and one on forestry economics (at Norris, Tennessee). I was quite excited about learning more about this great New Deal innovation: a regional body that covered as many as eight states (depending on the activity involved) and that brought irrigation, navigation, flood control, recreation, and power to the people of the area. I knew from my studies that the citizens of the region had been very suspicious of TVA at the start but had become very supportive of it in time.

As an intern to the director of the TVA, I had a great opportunity to meet the chairman of the board of directors, Gordon Clapp, which happened my first day on the job. He was about to fly on a TVA plane, a Beechcraft twin-engine plane, throughout the entire TVA region, to check on the status of operations, and he invited me to join him. This was to be my first flight in an airplane, at the age of almost twenty-two. What an exciting experience it was for me to see all the great new facilities of TVA, both from the air and the ground, and have my tour guide be Gordon Clapp himself!

My summer in Knoxville was a very pleasant one. I was fascinated to discover that it was a Republican area, with the people having a very independent character. During my stay, I made a one-day trip to Cherokee, North Carolina, in the Smokies, where the Cherokee Indians had an outdoor theater on the side of a mountain. Here they put on a play for the general public called "Unto These Hills." Much to my surprise, it was a condemnation of Andrew Jackson, who, as president, rounded up as many native North Carolina Cherokees as he could and moved them to Oklahoma, with many dying in the process. The descendants of those who hid out in North Carolina were now attacking Jackson for cruelty. This was a very valuable lesson for me, because I had practically minored in history at college, especially American history, and had never heard of this aspect of Jackson, whom I had always admired very much (and still do, with reservations).

I discovered that the only synagogue in Knoxville was a Reform temple, which I decided to attend, although the experience was an unusual one for me. I met two families that welcomed me into their midst, one which ran a hotel and had a son about my age who befriended me and became my companion. The head of the other family had started as a small businessman but had built a large scrap-metal operation.. It was the first time I ever watched an entrepreneur making calls to many places in the world. This family had a beautiful daughter who was only a senior in high school, but was very mature for her age. While I was about five years older than the daughter—and being a Harvard grad gave me some additional status—I really was unprepared to reach out to her in any meaningful way. I remember most painfully to this day what happened when I asked her out on a date and she accepted. She came by the YMCA to pick me up in an elegant convertible and moved over so that I could drive. This was a challenge in itself, because I hadn't done much driving and certainly was not accustomed to using a gear shift rather than an automatic transmission. In hindsight, I should have declined the offer and let her drive, but the macho in me wouldn't let me confess my discomfort. She guided me to her family's country club—the first time I'd ever been in a country club—and it was a real challenge to know how to behave. All in all, it was another feeble effort. We spent some additional time together that summer, which went somewhat better, probably because her parents were very gracious to me, and we always went out in groups, not on individual dates.

On the brighter side, my work at TVA was very exciting. I wrote a study of the battle between GAO and TVA to determine how the cost of producing and distributing electric power was determined. This was a crucial matter in the ability of TVA to provide low-cost power to the region, thereby raising the standard of living of its customers. The private power industry tried very hard, but unsuccessfully, to stop TVA from defending its methodology for providing low-cost power, thereby setting a pricing standard that the private sector had to respond to in its southeast market area. I found TVA's battle for low-cost power a dramatic example of the virtue of competition between the sectors.

The second area I examined was the TVA's growing use of steam plants to augment its hydroelectric power. I was concerned that TVA would become so caught up in power issues that it would lessen somewhat its concentration on delivering services to the environmental, recreational, and transportation needs of the areas it covered. During my stay at TVA, it became clear to me that steam plants were becoming the basic source of regional power, with hydroelectric only as the backup for peak periods. I had the temerity to express some reservations about the trend, and my supervisors were quite offended and took a great deal of time to try to convince me of the error of my thinking. Actually, long after I left TVA, it has continued to have considerable difficulties with the very balancing of its commitment that I had observed. This excessive focus on power delivery means there is a reduction in priority attention to irrigation, navigation and transportation, recreation, and environmental protection—all parts of TVA's mandate.

My last assignment was at the Forestry Economics Section of TVA in Norris. The Director had the beautiful name of Bill Jolly. He told me that TVA had developed an approach for determining how much timber was used to produce a ton of coal. The formula was to add up all the tons of coal and divide that number by the amount of wood used for such things as shoring up the mines and providing for railroad tracks. Bill Jolly sent me out in a TVA car for several days— a great adventure—to visit coal mines in Tennessee, Kentucky, and southwest Virginia, with special emphasis on Virginia areas such as Dante (the Chesterfield Coal Company), Big Stone Gap, Norton, Wise, and several others. I remember how difficult it was negotiating those roads and finding the mines. I stayed in Norton on a Saturday night and Sunday, and heard some women playing bridge in a private conference room. They told me that they would be chastised if their neighbors knew they were desecrating the Lord's Day. When I returned to the Forestry Division, my final report revealed that more timber was being used per ton of coal mined than had been earlier believed. Bill Jolly congratulated me for doing a fine job, especially for "a city boy who didn't know a sycamore from a hackamore."

The rest of the year went by quickly, traveling to the University of Alabama again for a semester, going home to Boston for Christmas vacation, returning to Knoxville for a quarter, and then completing the program by participating for a semester at the University of Kentucky, in Lexington. I found the faculty at all three universities to be of a much higher quality than I anticipated, and I learned a great deal about state and local public administration. Despite the racial segregation that I found very offensive, I generally found the people to be pretty progressive otherwise. Having the opportunity to attend the Kentucky Derby in Louisville was quite a memorable experience, especially to see the long-shot Dark Star defeat the heavy favorite Native Dancer in a dramatic finish. As I completed this year by being awarded a graduate certificate signed by the presidents of all three universities, I felt that the time had been well spent, because I had escaped what I called "the cosmopolitan parochialism" of my home city of Boston. What I also learned was that the old expression was quite true "you can take the boy out of Boston, but you can't take Boston out of the boy." Most of the associations I had developed were with the faculties of the three universities, and I barely got to know any of the students there. The five other participants in the program were not very relevant to my lifestyle and I only saw one of them again, when he worked in Washington. Rather surprisingly, he was working for a firm headed by Robert Bennett, who is now a Utah senator, and who also employed a number of other persons who were later involved in the Nixon Watergate fiasco.

As for my wish that I would be able to establish the kind of social life that I had never been able to achieve at Harvard, that ambition was never realized. That huge gap in my life remained. While at the University of Alabama, I did attend one reception at a Jewish sorority, but there was no follow-up. I also attended the temple in Tuscaloosa on the Sabbath. A couple of times, members invited me to dinner, where I always found that an eligible daughter was present. These young women and I had zero chemistry. One time the mother of the household told me that she was originally from New York City, but had lived in Alabama for some twenty-five years. In my honor, for the first time in these 25 years she had made gefilte fish, a type of chopped fish "delicacy" shaped in balls, which I loathe. She placed two huge balls before me on a plate, and I felt that politeness required that I eat them. I managed to down them, while drinking copious glasses of water. I then turned to talk to the man of the house, who sat next to me and was anxious to learn what I thought of the South. When I turned back to my plate, I found my hostess had placed two more huge balls in front of me!

My visits to Knoxville and Lexington during the school year were even less socially eventful. The one saving grace was my ability to play quality contract bridge, which I did at the local bridge clubs that met weekly. Anyone who played well was always welcome. This expertise made life bearable because I met some very interesting people from all walks of life.

At the University of Alabama, I went to socials at the Hillel House that were not particularly eventful but helped pass the time. I met a young instructor named Paul Rigby, who I understandably thought was Jewish, but who turned out to be a very ecumenical Christian (he later married a Jew). Paul and I seemed to have very much in common, and his work at the University Business Research Bureau coincided with my experience in the world of electric power production. He later suggested that I return to the university next summer so that we could work together on a project examining the Southern Company, especially the Alabama Power Company.

While I had decided to return to the Harvard Graduate School of

Public Administration in the fall as the Thomas E. Upham Fellow, I did accept the offer to return to the University of Alabama for the prior summer as a research fellow at the Bureau of Business Research to work on power production matters in the South. I shared a duplex with Paul Rigby at his invitation, and we attended many social and intellectual gatherings together. I was impressed by how many different churches he went to on different Sundays. As a lay theologian, he was at home with many denominations and could pinch-hit for vacationing ministers. Our joint study was another great learning experience for me because I observed how the private sector functioned as compared with TVA. Both approaches had strengths and weaknesses. Paul and I produced a book on the matter, published by the University of Alabama. I remember that public-administration expert Professor Albert Lepawsky was upset with me, because he was a dedicated public-power advocate and did not appreciate my even-handed approach. During that summer, Paul made a vacation trip to Boston, and my folks took him to a concert. When he returned to Tuscaloosa, he commented on how strange it was to attend a musical event where he knew no one else who was there, as compared to university-sponsored concerts where he knew *everyone* who was there.

Back at Harvard for the 1953-54 school year, I activated my Upham fellowship. I completed the course requirements for the Ph.D. in Political Economy and Government in May of 1954. That month I also passed the oral examinations which were a requirement before you could write your dissertation. During that school year, I lived in a graduate dormitory and returned to work at the university library system. I invited the young woman I had dated at Knoxville (who was now at Sarah Lawrence) to attend a Harvard football weekend, but it was another unsuccessful experience. But, on the positive side, I met a young fellow student who was a Mormon from Utah, Mark Cannon. While he was a conservative Republican and I a moderate Democrat, we hit it off right away and became lifelong friends. I returned as chairman of the school political science association and once again held a number of seminars with distinguished professors and visiting public officials addressing the group.

Meanwhile another option opened up to me. A couple of years earlier I had joined the U.S. Army Reserve in the Army Security Agency, where I had learned to break codes and to read Russian. This meant two weeks active duty in the summer and a meeting one night every week. I was a good code cracker, but a lousy soldier. (I ultimately served out an eight-year reserve enlistment and was honorably discharged as a private.) Every time I was considered for a promotion, I was guilty of some infraction and the orders were torn up. It was great fun tweaking the Army, so long as no national security matters were endangered. For example, much to my amazement I turned out to be a very good shot with a carbine and an M-1 rifle. They made me a coach, and one time on the firing line I had to oversee a young soldier who was terrified by the experience. I knew he couldn't hit the side of a barn, so I instructed him to fire off his bullets as fast as he could to prevent him from killing someone else along the line. I then scored him all 4s and 5s, which represented bull's-eyes. I would not have done this if the Korean War was still raging, but that war was over. (I later found out he spent his active duty time as a clerk.)One of the great moments of my Army life was when he was awarded an "expert" medal (I myself only rated "sharp-shooter.") Watching the look on his face when the commanding general called out his name as one of the only three members of our division who rated the expert medal—I found that was worth all the hardships of my Army experience!

My First Washington Adventure

With some frequency, I had considered a break from my academic experience. The Federal Government had established an elite corps in the civil service known as the Junior Management Assistant (JMA) program. I may have been one of very few who took the extremely difficult written and oral exams—three years running—and passed each time without then taking a position. By May of 1954, though, I decided I might finally accept something appropriate and worry about the Ph.D. situation later down the road. Harvard told me that the Upham fellowship was mine to use again for working on my dissertation, whenever I was prepared to do so. The hitch was that government agencies weren't anxious to hire someone who might be drafted, and it wasn't clear whether my Army Reserve status would exempt me from being drafted. While I would have preferred the Bureau of the Budget (now the Office of Management and Budget), the agency that offered me a job was the U.S. Civil Service Commission (now the Office of Personnel Management) and I accepted, starting in June 1954.

While the group of "JMAers," as we were called, was a splendid bunch, I never felt very comfortable with the format that the Civil Service Commission provided. The Executive Director was John Macy, who was highly respected by most, but I personally was not too impressed. He seemed to be a company man, who strove to be admired by his superiors but didn't care too much for the common man. I saw so many things at the Commission that I would have done differently, but, obviously, I was not in a position to do anything about. All in all, I found that this experience in government service paled mightily in comparison with my time at the creative and energetic TVA. In addition—on the creature-comfort level—this was a period when air-conditioning was still in its infancy; most government buildings did not have it. And so by mid-August, when the Washington, D.C., heat became unbearable, I jumped ship and resigned from the Commission. I contacted Harvard and was told I would be welcome to come back that fall as the Upham fellow. I was to have the Upham fellowship from 1953–4, 1954–5, and from 1955 to January 1956. I was on my own financially at Littauer in 1951–2 and had the Southern Regional Training Program (SRTP) fellowship for 1952–3. Finances were always a near-crippling challenge.

One professor who greatly disappointed me was Arthur Maass. He had been an advisor to my brother Milt, which led me to rely on him also. He was friendly to me, but not too supportive. I asked him to be my Ph.D. thesis advisor and he accepted only if I would write about natural-resource issues, not about the Council of Economic Advisers—the topic that would have been my choice and one that would have been easy for me to expand upon. I was very pleased that Professor Friedrich was quite kind to me, but I was intimidated by his gigantic scholarly stature. He would certainly have been my Ph.D. advisor if I had asked, and I should have dropped Maass like a hot potato. Instead I embarked on a futile effort to appease Maass. That meant that I struggled with a public versus private power thesis for more than two years but never completed it nor got a Ph.D. (I did use the natural-resource material for two journal articles and a small book, and the academic training helped me get a part-time job at the university level for fifty years.)

Toward a Return to Washington in a New Capacity

Back in September 1954, Professor Brad Westerfield, who had been my undergraduate tutor, told me that a U.S. congressman had asked him to recommend someone to work as his legislative assistant. It was a short-term position, possibly six months. Westerfield had himself served as a Political Science Fellow, one of the first under a new program of the American Political Science Association. He had spent an outstanding several months as assistant to this same distinguished member of the House Foreign Affairs Committee— Lawrence Brooks Hays, who had been representing Arkansas since 1943. Brooks Hays, as he was called, had so enjoyed having Westerfield in his office that he expressed the desire to have someone on his staff in the same capacity, but on his own payroll, not as a fellow. At that time, not many members of Congress had legislative assistants, as Congress was in the early stages of professionalizing the legislators' staffs. The objective was to lessen the dependency on information from the executive branch. There was a considerable lack of trust between the branches, regardless of party affiliations, when it came to enacting legislation and providing congressional oversight.

My initial reaction was delight at the opportunity and gratitude to Westerfield and Hays for making it possible. Westerfield send word that I had accepted and would arrive in Washington in January 1955. I began to have some misgivings, because I feared that if I left Harvard before completing my doctorate I would never obtain the Ph.D—a prophetic fear. With much trepidation, I told Westerfield that I would prefer to wait a year and then start working for the Congress. Westerfield reluctantly notified Hays of my decision. "Warren Cikins still expects to be able to work for you next session. If there should develop any hitch on this in the fall, I will look for another graduate student for you." Much to my relief, Congressman Hays accepted this arrangement. Ironically, I did not finish the dissertation in the intervening year, and, in fact, never did.

Chapter 3

Youthful Transition to Congress and the White House

I arrived in Washington in January 1956. I came at that point because Hays asked me to do so. He had been spending some of his time, the preceding fall, in New York at the United Nations, as a delegate appointed by President Eisenhower, for one session as was the tradition with Members of Congress. When I heard that news, I regretted that I had not joined him a year earlier so that I could have participated in that experience. I later heard that he had been a great success in that forum, not only because of his wisdom but partly because his outstanding sense of humor was put to great use. When the Soviets wanted to have Outer Mongolia admitted as a separate nation, Hays had the proposal laughed out of consideration when he replied, "I think we should have a package deal, with Texas admitted to the UN as well as Outer Mongolia, as long as its name was changed to Outer Arkansas." One of the valuable experiences of his service was becoming a friend of fellow delegate Colgate Darden, governor of Virginia and the former president of the University of Virginia.

By a wonderful coincidence, a colleague of mine from Harvard, Mark Cannon, notified me that he too was going to work for a congressman, Henry Aldous Dixon of Utah, at the same time as I was to work for Hays, and we agreed to room together. Our friendship ripened because of this experience and continues to this day. He is a Mormon and a Republican, and I am a Jew and a Democrat, and so we naturally had wonderful conversations about religion and politics. Mark had discovered an apartment on Capitol Hill which we rented and later found out had been the house of the great African-American orator and leader Frederick Douglass. Each day we walked to work past the Supreme Court, little realizing that Mark would one day be administrative assistant to Chief Justice Warren Earl Burger from 1972 to 1986, and I would be a consultant to that court on Mark's recommendation.

Our friendship deepened as we both learned more about our respective religions and found that our political differences could easily be reconciled. Since the Mormon Church had many social functions, I often went along with Mark to enjoy the occasions. I would joke that if the church restored polygamy, I would be quick to propose to one of the splendid young women I met on these occasions. If I was allowed to practice polygamy, I would still be able to marry a Jewish girl later. At one point, another Mormon, a military officer, lived with us. He was a fine young man and he shopped for us at the PX—meaning that our food bills were reasonable. Mark and I would take turns preparing meals and cleaning up afterwards. For a while I talked Mark into flipping a coin on who should wash the dishes, but after he lost seven straight times, he refused to continue, saying the Lord was punishing him for gambling.

Mark and I agreed we would follow each other's religious dietary restrictions. That meant, for example, that I would not drink coffee and he would not eat pork products or shellfish. I noted that he had a whole array of activities at the church on Sundays, and I would tease him about Sunday supposedly being a day of rest. As for me, I found an Orthodox synagogue in Georgetown where I felt comfortable (Kesher Israel, later attended by Herman Wouk and Joseph Lieberman). While I would drive there on regular Saturdays (contrary to traditional Jewish law), I did walk there on Jewish holidays, which was quite a challenge since Capitol Hill is quite a distance from Georgetown.

Because of our friendship, Mark and I wanted Congressman Hays and Congressman Dixon to get acquainted and they did. This association would later have a particularly touching dividend. In the 1850s, part of a group of Arkansans on their way to California was murdered (leaving only children alive later returned to Arkansas) by a band of renegade Mormons (disguised as Indians). Hays and Dixon arranged for a reconciliation meeting between descendants of the survivors and the marauders. They also collaborated on a number of bipartisan pieces of legislation, such as one promoting a program that enabled career civil servants to have job-training sabbaticals at relevant schools and, another, an intergovernmental job-training effort that had different levels of government involved.

At Hays's office, as legislative assistant, I was given a desk in a perimeter office by the window, a most desirable location as evidence of my being treated graciously. The three other staff members—the administrative assistant John McLees, the receptionist Kitty Johnson, and the Hays's personal secretary Lurlene Wilbert —were all wonderfully welcoming. The congressman and I had an instant rapport. This man from Russellville, Arkansas—in the Ozarks—who was old enough to be my father (and who did become a sort of second father to me) and I, a Harvard graduate student who grew up in Boston, had the same values and the same outlook on life. He was a prominent Baptist and I was a devoted Jew, and yet we had religious convictions that were quite analogous. While I didn't know it at the time, I had launched a relationship with someone of incredible experience and breadth of vision who would influence my thoughts and actions for the rest of my life.

Unlike many leading religious figures who are active in public life, Hays kept his commitment to the Baptist doctrine of the separation of church and state. He was very probably the most admired member of Congress for his genuine piety and integrity, but he did not flaunt his piousness. Brooks Hays was the chairman of the Christian Life Commission of the Southern Baptist Convention at that time. He told of the time he was having lunch with the director of the commission, Foy Valentine, a quite handsome young man. The waitress asked Hays in a very friendly tone, "What'll you have, honey?" and turned to Valentine and said gruffly, "and what'll you have?" When Valentine asked Hays why the waitress had acted so differently, Hays responded with a twinkle in his eye, "Well, some got it and some ain't!" He was equally at ease with waitresses and presidents. He had developed wonderful relationships with other Protestant denominations as well as Catholic leaders (including the Pope) and reached out to many world religions. Members of the House loved to tease him about his ecumenicity, and when he was elected president of the Southern Baptist Convention in 1957, Congressman Eugene McCarthy came up to him on the House floor and said, "Well, Brooks, now that you're pope of the Baptists, I'll bet you're now a whole lot more congenial with the doctrine of papal infallibility." Ever quick with the witty response, Hays put his hand forth and said, "Yes—but you don't have to kiss my ring."

Getting Adjusted to Capitol Hill

Evidence of Hays's commitment to the less fortunate came to me early on. The first week of my service he asked me to research the situation regarding migrant laborers—who, obviously, don't vote— so that he could introduce legislation to improve their condition. Incidentally, I wrote a paper on the topic, and Congressman Hays liked it so much, he said he was going to put it in that day's *Congressional Record*. That remark kind of shocked me, because I realized that everything I wrote from that day forward might well see the light of day and should be especially carefully researched.

Over the years I often heard Hays mention with pride his 1930s work gaining passage of the Bankhead-Jones Farm Tenant Act, which helped farmers who only rented their land become owners instead.

And during my service to him, he championed the creation of a Country Life Commission. On July 8, 1958, accompanied by the
co-sponsors, Senators Flanders of Vermont and Cooper of Kentucky
(evidence of his strong bi-partisanship), he offered testimony to the
House Agriculture Subcommittee on Family Farms. He emphasized
the need to strengthen the institution of the family farm and called
for the creation of a two-year study to review "what happened to country life, what has happened to human values that are involved, and
what might be done to correct this unhappy trend in the deterioration of rural life in some parts of our country." The debate on this
legislation had great influence, even though it was not passed.

Congress at that time was a far more congenial place than it is
today, and I soon became friendly with just about every other legislative assistant in the House of Representatives, both Democrat and
Republican. I really felt I had found a professional home. Hays paid
me what was left in his payroll account, which was about $5,000 a
year (soon raised to $6,000) not very much even then, but enough to
cover my needs. I was able to send home $1,000 a year to help my
parents manage a difficult situation: my middle brother Alvan was
quite ill. He had given up his ambition to be a Lubavitcher rabbi and
returned to Boston. Soon thereafter he was hit by a car in front of
the house and was having a difficult time recovering. My dad had
never really recovered financially from the Great Depression, and my
folks were barely managing on his earnings as an insurance salesman. He was very knowledgeable about the complexities of the
various policies he sold, but he was not too successful as a salesman. He had been a great civil engineer; and when World War II
began, many of his former colleagues urged him to return to that
profession, but my mother was fearful and discouraged him.

In many ways, the Congress of the late fifties was the "Camelot"
Congress of the last half of the twentieth century. After the
Eisenhower victories, many of the finest scholarly Democratic poli-
ticians came to work on Capitol Hill. It was a transitional period,

because up until this time, the legislative branch had not attracted such "career professionals." The progressive LaFollette-Monroney Legislative Reorganization Act of 1946 had stimulated the change. To the best of my knowledge, Mark Cannon and I were the first two graduates of Littauer to work for Congress; all the rest were oriented toward the executive branch of government. There were not many legislative assistants in the House, and, while the Senate had more, there were far less than would staff the Senate in later years. There was great camaraderie between the two houses and I spent much time getting to know my counterparts in the Senate, especially brilliant staffers for Senators Paul Douglas of Illinois and Joe Clark of Pennsylvania. This situation was strengthened by the fact that both houses worked much harder from January to the end of June, not going home on weekends, and then adjourned from about the end of June to the end of the year, meeting constituents at home and making fact-finding trips abroad.

Unlike today, most Members of Congress were not career politicians and had other jobs at home, such as lawyer or professor or farmer. Many would only stay for a few terms and would then return home to their "real" jobs. They did not feel so dependent on getting reelected. I believe that the atmosphere reflected far greater integrity—despite potential conflicts of interest—as well as civility than is the case today. There were far more friendships that crossed party lines. Voting patterns were enormously different, since there were many Republican liberals (such as Javits of New York and Case of New Jersey) and many Democratic conservatives (such as Russell of Georgia and Stennis of Mississippi). While the media seem to enjoy the greater party-focused, ideological purity of today, I believe it is doing great harm to the objectives of the Founding Fathers.

For me the next few years were some of the happiest professional years of my life. The Hill was a relaxed and socially convivial place. It was great working for a man who was probably the most admired House member on both sides of the aisle. As a gracious and gentle person, he radiated kindness. He was deceivingly very intellectual (Phi Beta Kappa at the University of Arkansas) and very involved in many legislative challenges, well beyond his senior status on the Foreign Affairs Committee. As a caring person, he looked out for the disadvantaged of his district, black and white. Because racism was still predominant, though, he was careful in his progressive steps. As he liked to remember, "A British philosopher said an elected official should lead his people, but not get so far ahead of them that he breaks the bond that ties him to them." Hays was blessed with the talents of a great storyteller in the tradition of Will Rogers, and he used this ability to emphasize the policy positions he supported. At the same time, he played a most significant role in the national religious scene, devoted to fundamental Baptist doctrine, but anxious to reach out to other faiths.

His administrative assistant John McLees was also a remarkable man, who knew all the inner workings of the House so well that he made the Hays agenda much easier to achieve. Lurlene Wilbert, Hays's secretary, was a most efficient worker who "called them as she saw them." When I didn't laugh very hard at a joke the congressman told, and Lurlene prodded me to explain why. I said, "I give them what they're worth," and she responded, "Well, you won't be around very long." (In actuality, my association with Hays continued in one capacity or another until he died in 1981.)

Being the person he was, Hays attracted all the odd characters who would come to the Hill to get a hearing. Since the rest of the staff was as kind and considerate as Hays, I was selected as the "bouncer." It was my assignment to ask these folks to leave after a reasonable period. And our receptionist, Kitty Johnson, was always extraordinarily polite. When some constituent phoned to berate the congressman, she was very courteous in her responses; and after the person had hung up, the worst epithet Kitty could utter was "the old goat." I always chuckle when I recall a response Kitty gave someone who called to talk to Hays and was not conversant with Hill terminology. Hays had been called away to help a colleague embattled in a floor debate on foreign policy. Kitty told the no-doubt dumbfounded constituent, "I'm sorry, the congressman can't come to the phone; you see he's on the floor with Mrs. Kelly." We had so much fun together that, while we all worked very hard, it did not seem like work at all. I researched a great many areas and wrote articles and drafted speeches for Hays—assignments that both helped him and enlightened me.

Broadening My Experience

While I had done a little college teaching before coming to Washington, I was anxious to get more experience. Brooks Hays was on the board of trustees of George Washington University (GW), and he introduced me to the school's president, Cloyd Heck Marvin, who hired me as a part-time instructor in the College of General Studies. I was under the direction of the assistant dean—a man also named Hayes, spelled with an *e*. (Brooks Hays used to say, tongue in cheek, that anyone who spelled Hays with an *e* was either Republican or illiterate or both.) Over the years, I taught GW courses at the main campus, at Quantico Marine Base, Virginia, at the Pentagon, and a range of other GW university outposts around the city. At the military institutions, I had students ranking from general to private and called them all Mr., Mrs., or Ms. Several outstanding students went on to get graduate degrees and became professors. As for my own scholastic education, Hays arranged for a stall at the Library of Congress, where I could continue to work on my doctoral dissertation, in the event I might decide on an academic career.

Of course there was also much on-the-job education. When Hays and Bill Fulbright were both elected to the House in 1942, Hays had deferred to Fulbright for choice of committee. Fulbright served on the House Foreign Affairs Committee, while Hays went on the House Banking Committee. In the next election, Fulbright became a United States senator, and Hays subsequently switched to his first choice, the Foreign Affairs Committee. By the time I joined him, he was a senior member of the committee, but never became chairman because the delay in joining the committee had cost him seniority. He was also a member of the powerful three-person House Patronage Committee, which involved many hirings and firings of the permanent staff of the House; and that gave me some stature in my relations with all the employees.

I found out that Hays had a deep interest in many topics on the House agenda, and that meant that he would assign me to do research in these areas. I would review such matters as the status of the underprivileged in Arkansas, both black and white; immigration, legal and illegal; the national economy, federal budgets; federal aid to education; national health care; separation of church and state; improvements to the criminal justice system; and many more. He relied on the staff of the Foreign Affairs Committee for most of his needs regarding world affairs, and I got to know the staff members very well, especially the director Boyd Crawford and Dumond Peck Hill, specialist in Inter-American Affairs—a subcommittee that Hays chaired. Congressman Hays always encouraged me to attend hearings of the Foreign Affairs Committee—and any other committee hearings in both the House and Senate that interested me. I probably learned more about the U.S. government and the Congress during those first months than I ever had before.

At the same time, I was getting to know Congressman Hays better and better. He was incredibly kind and gentle. His wife Marion said, "Brooks loves everybody; he even loves some of my relatives that I can't stand." I gradually learned of his very remarkable, but difficult political career, as well as his significant role in the Southern Baptist Convention. Hays had championed many social-service causes as a young man, had been very active in his church, and had been involved in many political activities. He was unsure whether he wanted to make his career in religious service or in politics and finally determined to straddle the two. His father, Steele Hays, had set a fine example for him as a courageous lawyer who championed the causes of the disadvantaged. It was 1924 when his father ran for Congress and lost, partly because he would not join the Ku Klux Klan. Father and son were about the only prominent citizens in the area who weren't pro-KKK.

Brooks Hays combined his passions in an oft-preached sermon, "The Ministry of Public Service." I also used the same title in sermons I preached later in life when invited to do so at many Christian churches. Hays preached many sermons during my first year with him, and I attended the services with him frequently. I became very comfortable in the Baptist Church, as I saw many similarities with the Jewish Orthodox outlook, related to a fundamentalist and literalist approach. The Baptists focused a great deal on the Old Testament, and I found that Hays knew chapter and verse better than I did, using quotations to make key religious points in his sermons.

Back in 1928, at a mere age thirty, Brooks Hays ran for governor of Arkansas on a reform platform. He took on the Establishment, which never was comfortable with him throughout his whole career. Arkansas was not unlike a number of the border states of the Old Confederacy, whose crooked elections were not uncommon. And so Hays was counted out, with some precincts turning in more votes against him than there were registered voters. He knew it was futile to challenge the results in the courts, because the Establishment ruled there as well. He ran again in 1930 with the same result. By this time he was married with two children, and these defeats not only were very politically disheartening but also put a great deal of financial stress on his family. He managed to make ends met by various means, such as teaching Dale Carnegie courses on public speaking, which sharpened his oratorical skills at the same time. The biggest heartbreak was losing his bid for Congress in 1932, during the depths of the Depression. But his persistence paid off when he was elected Democratic National Committeeman in 1933.

During that difficult decade, Hays went to work for the U.S.

Department of Agriculture to help impoverished farmers survive the Depression. Rexford Guy Tugwell, Undersecretary of Agriculture, was a giant of the period, and he inspired the department to reach out to both whites and blacks. Hays was associated with an agency of the department, the Resettlement Administration, and its dedicated leader Will Alexander who worked to help tenant farmers. Alexander became director of the Farm Security Administration after the Bankhead-Jones Farm Tenant Act was passed in the mid-1930s, and he and Hays helped many hundreds of thousands of such farmers obtain farms of their own. Hays loved to tell the story of the black woman he called to say he was coming over to her house so that she could sign papers making her a farm owner. Over the phone, she told Hays how much she admired him and trusted the U. S. government to help her. When he arrived at her door, however, she looked him up and down and said, "You know, Mr. Hays, my trust is really in the Lord!"

Things never seemed to go smoothly for Brooks Hays. A question was raised about whether it was appropriate for a Democratic Party National Committeeman to work for the federal government. The debate raged on until Franklin Roosevelt himself resolved the matter in Hays's favor. By 1942, Hays had strengthened his political roots in Arkansas so greatly that the Establishment could no longer deny him his just due, and he was finally elected to Congress. He was a natural politician in the best sense of the word, and he soon became very popular with all his colleagues. His Arkansas stories were his signature card. He told about his lawyer father having to supplement his income by being a census enumerator during that every-ten-year undertaking. One time his father walked up to a modest home in the Ozarks and asked the man who came to the door what his name was. The man replied, "Hearn, Randall J. Hearn!" When he asked the man to spell his name, the response was, "Spell it yourself, stranger, I'm a non-scholar!" So later, during hearings of the House Foreign Affairs Committee, when distinguished public officials were testifying, such as the secretary of state and the secretary of defense, Committee Chairman Dick Richards of South Carolina would ask Hays, "What do you think Randall Hearn's opinion would be." Hays would answer appropriately, presenting the average citizen's views. I chuckle when I think of today's scholars, looking back on that period, reading the hearings, and wondering who that apparently distinguished 1950s scholar Randall Hearn was.

As in the present, there were serious confrontations between Arab nations and Israel. Hays was highly regarded as fair-minded by both sides. Matters were complicated by the fact that the Cold War was on, with the Soviets arming and supporting the Arabs. To ward off conflict in the mid-fifties, President Eisenhower drafted a proposal for American intervention in the Middle East. The proposal was referred to the House Foreign Affairs Committee, and Brooks Hays took an active role in the Committee's deliberations. He offered many modifications to the proposal to accommodate suggestions made both by Israel's representatives and ambassadors from Arab countries. (Hays benefited from being a regular on the diplomatic cocktail- and dinner-party circuit—which Marion Hays enjoyed—and being on friendly terms with many ambassadors.) The Eisenhower Doctrine, which, after much wrangling, Congress finally passed, had many Hays elements in it, and the president called to thank him for his role. The troops Eisenhower sent to Lebanon helped create conditions for about ten years of peace in the Middle East, however uneasy that peace was.

While a close friend of Adlai Stevenson and Southwest coordinator of Stevenson's 1952 campaign for president, Hays operated in a very bipartisan basis in the House, which gave him great influence. Eisenhower was destined to thank Hays many times for building bridges between the two parties. Another occasion that comes to mind is passage of legislation to extend the terms of loans made to Great Britain during World War II. The Brits were struggling in a recession and just didn't have the money to make the payments. But then the Queen did a silly thing by going on a visit to Paris, with the papers claiming that she took many dozens of pieces of luggage and many, many staff with her. This upset the Congress very much. Hays was out shopping with his wife, when we got an urgent call from Speaker Sam Rayburn that the situation on the House floor was deteriorating. We managed to track Hays down. He rushed to the House floor and saved the day. Eisenhower was on the phone again, and our staff listened in on extensions to his prolific expressions of gratitude to Hays.

Among the other advantages in my working for Hays were invitations to many diplomatic receptions. I remember going to a very impressive tea party at the British Embassy, where I bumped into an old friend from Dorchester, Mike Rashish. Mike's father was a struggling Hebrew teacher in the 1930s; but Mike, a friend of my brother Milt, was bright enough to go to Harvard. By the time we met at this party, he was a professional staff member on international trade matters for the House Ways and Means Committee. (He later became an undersecretary of state in the Reagan administration.) Wanting to tease me in this very august surrounding, he walked up to me and asked in a stage whisper in Yiddish, "What are you doing here?" I answered him also in Yiddish asking him what *he* was doing here. We both had a good laugh about how far we had come from Dorchester.

During the middle of my service with Congressman Hays, I became aware of an interesting problem confronting the U.S. after World War II. When the war began, the Americans had frozen the assets of German corporations. By 1957 the value of these assets had increased to billions of dollars. Each chamber of the Congress created a committee to consider disposition of the assets. Practically every major law firm in Washington was put on retainer by the West German government to help them get these assets back. The lobbying was intense. Hays was on the temporary special House committee and became acting chairman when the chairman got sick. Senator Olin Johnston of South Carolina was chairman of the Senate committee and known to be strongly supportive of the Germans. Hays was very leery of proceeding hastily and moved slowly to find a resolution. During this period I was approached by someone involved in the matter, and it was made clear that if I tried to persuade Hays to support the Germans, "it would be worth my while." Of course, I did not do that. There was no resolution until the Kennedy administration, when Attorney General Robert Kennedy decided to split the difference, restoring half the property to the Germans and putting the rest in the hands of the U.S. government.

Teaching at George Washington University part-time also gave me the opportunity to invite distinguished Washingtonians to be guest lecturers in my classes. They included Members of Congress, diplomats, government officials, judges, and noted scholars. In this way, I began a lifelong development of associations with people of stature related to government activity, which stood me in good stead throughout my career. In the same vein, I became active in the Congressional Staff Club, the Hill Bowling League, the Hill Bridge Club, and the Staff Prayer Breakfast. Not only were these activities of great interest and relevance, my ability to socialize improved greatly and I finally felt I was getting out of my shell. I observed Brooks Hays carefully, and slowly I learned how to reach out to people of many different backgrounds, so that compromise could be achieved and bridges of understanding built. As Hays put it, "Half of something is better than all of nothing." I muted a tendency to be self-righteous and pugnacious, and was pleasantly surprised to find that, with enough work, it is possible to change one's personality. While I had the natural tendency to want to talk about my achievements, Hays often reminded me that "there's no limit to the good you can do in this world if you don't care who gets the credit." The world I was living in was quite a heady one, and I look back on it as the most satisfactory of my professional experiences.

Off to Little Rock

When the Congress adjourned on June 30, 1956, Mark Cannon and I closed our apartment. I packed up all my belongings (which fit into my car) and headed for Arkansas to Hays's state office. It was to be my first time across the Mississippi River. I went through Virginia to Tennessee, visited my old stomping grounds in Knoxville, and went on to Nashville On the open road to Memphis, I went 100 miles per hour, for the first and the last time in my life. Memphis was a most impressive city, even in the 1950s, and I could hardly wait to see West Memphis, Arkansas, across the Mississippi. But before I knew it, I was back on the open road and West Memphis had turned out to be a few stores and homes along the highway. The drivers on the road to Little Rock drove like the wild Arkansans I was familiar with, and so I settled behind a big truck to ensure my safe arrival. After I checked into my rooming house, run by a kindly woman named Thelma Blessing, I walked past the Sam Peck Hotel where Hays was staying and stopped by the Hays office in the Federal Building. There I met Dick Emerson, who was Hays's Little Rock representative, a man I'd only known as a phone voice before. He was a gruff, outspoken person, but very warm-hearted. Hays was in the office and he suggested we go out to lunch. As we sat in a nearby restaurant, he passed me the cornbread that had been served us, and I said that I really didn't like cornbread. He responded, "Son, I could be defeated for less than that." So while I was in Arkansas I ate cornbread.

I slowly acclimated myself to Little Rock and found it to be a very welcoming city. The people were certainly friendly, and I found the racial situation to be quite progressive for the South. At that time, Governor Orval Faubus projected himself as a moderate as did the mayor, Woodrow Mann, and the school superintendent, Virgil Blossom. Certainly Hays was viewed as the essence of moderation. Southern Baptists admired him greatly and the Second Baptist Church had a Bible class called the Brooks Hays Bible Class. When I arrived in Little Rock, Hays was already involved in a campaign for reelection. His opponent in the Democratic primary was a young lawyer who was attacking Hays for the obvious reasons—too progressive for Arkansas, too supportive of American involvement in world affairs, too concerned about the poor and minorities, and too committed to "tax-and–spend" policies. In the Fifties, there was no real Republican party in Arkansas, and so the primary *was* the election. The November election was pro forma. Hays represented five counties in the center of Arkansas—Pulaski County which included Little Rock, and four rural counties. A day or two after I arrived in Little Rock, Hays took me with him as he traveled his district, in the old Southern tradition, to address a series of political gatherings. I met hundreds of Arkansans that day, and they were all very gracious to me. When they asked "Where are you from, son?" I answered "Boston, Massachusetts, Arkansas!" And they all laughed. While I gradually began to talk like an Arkansan, I wasn't about to try to pass myself off as a genuine native.

In the middle of his campaign, Brooks Hays got a call from Speaker Rayburn urging him to come right away to the Democratic National Convention, which he was chairing in Chicago. It appeared that the Platform Committee was in the middle of a major debate on the language of the civil rights plank. Back in 1948, that plank had not been strong enough for the liberals, and then-mayor of Minneapolis, Hubert Humphrey, stampeded the convention floor in enthusiastic support of him when he offered a very much tougher civil rights plank than the one that was originally proposed. In his famous words, he said "It's time for the Democratic Party to get out of the shadow of states' rights and get into the bright sunshine of human rights." Humphrey prevailed and the convention adopted his language. That led Strom Thurmond, then a racist, to bolt the Democratic Party and create the Dixiecrat Party to contend in the election. Four years, later, in 1952, Brooks Hays and Hubert Humphrey wrote a plank that all sides could live with, preventing a repeat of 1948.

Sam Rayburn was calling Hays now to come to Chicago to do the same thing. Even though his own reelection was at stake (because in the South at that time the Democratic primary *was* the election), Hays agreed to leave his campaign and head for Chicago. And so in the summer of 1956, this Jewish Yankee Bostonian, very new to Arkansas, hit the campaign trail and filled several speaking engagements for Hays that had already been scheduled. We were excited to learn on election night that Hays had won one of the biggest victories of his political career.

I immediately took off for Chicago to join Hays. I watched as he and Humphrey drafted an outstanding civil rights plank in the closing sessions of the Platform Committee. When it was taken to the floor, it was accepted easily, although most Southerners, including Hays, voted against it. It was not so controversial that they were offended. I was very excited to be at my first national convention and later in the week Governor Faubus, who chaired the Arkansas delegation with an iron hand, gave me the credentials of an alternate delegate. Being on the convention floor was a special treat. Adlai Stevenson was easily nominated again to be the Democratic candidate for the presidency. Then Stevenson did a remarkable thing, throwing the convention open to choose a vice presidential candidate.

From my seat in the Arkansas delegation, I watched this fascinating contest. I recall Senator Lyndon Johnson of Texas being a candidate, as well as Senator Stuart Symington of Missouri, Senator John Kennedy of Massachusetts, and Senator Estes Kefauver of Tennessee, and possibly several others. Our delegation was located between the Texas and the Tennessee delegations, an ideal spot to observe the drama. Kefauver had challenged Stevenson in the primaries but Stevenson clearly had the inside track for the presidential nomination because he had made the same run in 1952. Kefauver was now the favorite for the vice presidential nomination, even though he was not too popular with his own delegation. After a round or two, it became clear that Kefauver was likely to be the nominee, except the young upstart Jack Kennedy seemed to be captivating the delegates. More and more states, including Arkansas, switched to Kennedy, and it looked like he would sweep to victory. But, at the last moment, Chairman Rayburn recognized the chairman of the Tennessee delegation (Senator Albert Gore, Sr., father of the later Democratic presidential candidate), and he threw his state's votes to Kefauver—stopping Kennedy in his tracks, just a few votes away from the prize. This was the most exciting event of my political experience up to that time.

My old roommate Mark Cannon was going to the Republican convention at the Cow Palace in San Francisco the next week. He agreed to get me two tickets to the convention, in my capacity as a part-time professor at GW. Another dormmate at Harvard Graduate School, Carl Potter, who had some time earlier invited me to visit him at Berkeley, said he would welcome me to stay with him at his family home, even though he had three other house guests. And so I traveled from Chicago to San Francisco to attend the 1956 Republican Convention. Carl's dad was a professor of English at Berkeley, and the family was extremely hospitable. Carl had a grandmother who was very Republican, and she teased me about my politics. Then Mark called to tell me that he would need my second ticket on the last day, Thursday, when President Eisenhower would arrive to accept his re-nomination. That would be the only interesting day, because the convention—with its predetermined outcome—would be otherwise boring, I had already promised Carl and his guests that I would find a way for them to attend the last day of the convention with me, and I tried to solve my now even-more-complicated problem, since I now would only have one ticket.

On that Thursday, Carl, his three guests, and I piled into his car and drove to the Cow Palace. Mark had asked me to leave my second ticket at the box office in an envelope addressed to a prominent Utah Republican who would not be arriving until late in the day. I had a little time to play with. I noticed the tickets had stubs that would be torn off upon initial entry, with the ticketholder keeping the body of the ticket to be used for reentry. So using the two tickets, just Carl and I went in; and I told him to give me his ticket and wait at a designated place. I went out, got one of his guests and reentered a different door and brought that person to join Carl. I did that two more times, until I had everybody in the convention hall. I then went out one more time and left the second ticket in the envelope for Mark's political colleague at the box office and went back in one last time. Thus, five of us were in, and I still had one ticket in my hand.

All the seats were taken. As we stood blocking the aisles, ushers kept telling us to go to where our seats were, and we kept moving. Finally, I found an usher who was very friendly and allowed us to remain in his section. We then had a fine time watching the proceedings that built up to a fever pitch as the time came near for Eisenhower to arrive. I, of course, worked to solidify my relationship with the usher who responded very well. Just before the big moment, he turned to me and asked to borrow my ticket so he could go out and bring a friend of his in! *He* had been cultivating *me*! A good time was had by all, and I brought back to Carl's grandmother a huge pin that said "Ike & Dick—Sure to Click."

After the Republican convention was over, I decided to return to Arkansas by train so I could see much of the nation. We passed through a number of states I had never been to before. I stopped in Utah, where Mark Cannon entertained me royally. I visited the auditorium where the Mormon Tabernacle Choir performed, the home of Brigham Young, with its many gables representing bedrooms for his many wives, and several other historic sites. Mark arranged for me to have an audience with the head of the Mormon Church, David O. McKay. We had an interesting conversation about which people are the "chosen people," and he referred to me as a "gentile," which is what all non-Mormons are in Salt Lake City.

When I returned to Little Rock I got into the rhythm of a life that involved meeting many of Hays's constituents and helping them with their problems. In addition, Hays and I agreed that it would be a good time for him to write a book about his career, and I offered to help him put it together. We actually had two books in mind. One was to have a greater focus on his applying his Baptist philosophy to his everyday life and the other was to emphasize his lifetime focus on improving the lot of the little guy, black or white. Both of these books were later published. The first was titled *This World: A Christian's Workshop* , from the Broadman Press, and the second, *A Southern Moderate Speaks,* from the University of North Carolina Press.

Review of Status of Race Relations in Arkansas

Hays and I were not too concerned about the ability of Little Rock to adapt to the 1954 Supreme Court decision about school desegregation *(Brown v. Board of Education)*, since the people of Arkansas seemed prepared to provide a gradual transition. Daisy Bates of the National Association for the Advancement of Colored People was prodding the authorities to move at a faster pace, but her efforts using the court system did not seem to have much success. A September 20, 1956, issue of *U.S. News and World Report* cited Little Rock as one southern city that seemed ready to comply with the courts. The story was entitled, "How One Southern City Plans to Integrate." The mayor, the superintendent of schools, the school board, the chief of police, and, of course, Congressman Brooks Hays preached acceptance of the law of the land, however opposed to integration an individual might be. Hays was quite comfortable having me at his side, even though I was a native Bostonian. In speeches I made, I publicly preached the same moderation that Hays counseled, to reassure constituents that I shared Hays's views. The many hundreds of people I met were generally quite moderate also, with little evidence of last-ditch opposition, but rather quite resigned to the inevitable. I spent much of the rest of the summer doing a substantial amount of book research for Hays, all on my own time, while using office time to help constituents on the many problems they were having with government agencies.

I remember one example of my ability to help resolve matters that seemed hopeless at first. A woman came into the office saying that she was making a living publishing a newspaper datelined Jacksonville, a suburb of Little Rock, and delivering it to families at the nearby U.S. Air Force base. However, she actually produced the paper in another suburb, Morrilton. She came to see us because the post office had turned down her application for a permanent mailing permit. The postmaster said the paper had to be datelined where it was published, Morrilton, not Jacksonville. The base commander was equally adamant that the paper had to be datelined Jacksonville, the place where it was distributed. I talked to the postmaster and I talked to the commander and neither would yield. The woman was desperate. I finally had a brainstorm and suggested that the dateline be "Printed in Morrilton for Jacksonville." Both the postmaster and the commander agreed! And so this woman—who had been blocked by people rigidly interpreting regulations—was again able to earn an honest living. I have used this example hundreds of times when giving lectures for the Civil Service Commission. This true story helps civil servants understand how to accommodate the public by stretching their imaginations in a lawful, satisfying way.

There were very few Jews in Little Rock, maybe five hundred as far as I could tell, and two synagogues—a reform one in the heart of the city and a conservative one in a quieter area. I attended the conservative synagogue and was well accepted as a participant. Unlike my experience in Knoxville, however, the Jewish community was quite a closed society that did not extend the same type of embrace. I got the impression that they were worried about their acceptance and tried hard to blend in with the rest of the society. On one or two holidays, Brooks and Marion Hays accompanied me to the synagogue; and on a number of other occasions, I attended prayer services at the Second Baptist Church. I met the son of one of Hays's strongest supporters in the Christian business community, Whitney Dyke, who was somewhat younger than I, but was a very bright graduate of the University of Chicago and a very pleasant companion.

The Congressional Session of 1957

In the late fall of 1956, I returned to a new (to me) furnished apartment I found in Washington near GW for $75 per month. I was still back early enough to teach an evening course or two at GW. At the same time, I prepared for the next session of Congress, which would begin in early January. Congressman Hays asked me to research several topics: federal aid to education; assistance to migrant laborers, improving American–Canadian relations (he and Congressman Frank Coffin of Maine wrote a major report on the subject for the House Foreign Affairs Committee which was issued in 1958); and strengthening American foreign aid programs (a project he worked on with Congressman Walter Judd of Minnesota).

This session of Congress was the period when Brooks Hays and I really bonded. He had not really known much about Judaism, but was deeply concerned about the persecution Jews had suffered throughout the history of Christianity. His status in the Southern Baptist world was growing stronger by the day, and he served as chairman of the Southern Baptist Christian Life Commission, doing great work in outreach to the world's less fortunate. He also became widely known for building bridges from Southern Baptists to other faiths, working one on one with all other branches of Christianity, with Moslems, with Hindus, and with Jews. The Jews he knew in Little Rock were generally socially conscious, caring to improve the lot of less fortunate whites, but they feared being identified with Zionism, as though it represented being something less than 100 percent American. While friendly to me, they feared that I was a conventional Jewish "Yankee" who would complicate their lives with their Christian neighbors, and what's more, would reach out to blacks in the community, something that would hurt their relations with whites.

As for Hays the individual, he was his usual open-minded self. In our early conversations, he seemed to think that as Christians embraced Jews more and treated them as full equals, the barrier between them would drop. I got the impression that he hoped that Jews would consider Christianity more favorably as an option for themselves. Of course, being Hays, he was not about to promote some evangelistic effort. I think one of the most important contributions I made to his understanding was when I demonstrated, by my actions and convictions, that my Judaism was as deeply rooted as his Christianity and that the best road ahead was having the two faiths come to understand each other better and embrace each other as fellow religions. One measure of the greatness of this man was his willingness to completely modify his perspective and welcome Jews as full equals for all time.

By the spring of 1957, Brooks Hays had been elected president of the Southern Baptist Convention (SBC). This was a most remarkable event, because he was clearly more progressive than the average Southern Baptist and a layman, a very rare phenomenon in that organization. He was accepted not only because of his deep devotion to the Baptist faith, but also because of sheer force of personality. He was also blessed with a wonderful speaking ability, which he used to great effect. As an outstanding humorist, he utilized this humor to reinforce his beliefs in a most congenial manner. This approach was what had enabled him to get elected to Congress in the first place, since he was also more progressive than was the average voter in the Fifth Congressional District. And so he captivated the SBC of that year and was elected, over considerable opposition and disbelief. Surprisingly, this development strengthened our bond, as he reached out to me even more than before to find a universal moral code. I in turn became even more protective of his reputation and his influence.

During this period, white Members of Congress from the South were getting more and more restless about the Supreme Court's desegregation decision. Hays was struggling with the situation because he hoped to find middle ground on the matter—not challenging the Supreme Court, but enabling his constituents to gradually accept the inevitable. The more extreme members of Congress drafted "The Southern Manifesto," which called the Supreme Court decision unconstitutional and urged the South to adopt the doctrine of "interposition." This would mean the use of states' rights to block the enforcement of the court's decision. Hays and other moderates found this development quite distasteful. After softening the most inflammatory language, most Southern members signed the document. Hays explained to me that he felt he could do more good reaching out to his colleagues than breaking the bond, and I assured him I understood this approach. He was in a difficult position, because his Northern colleagues found his actions puzzling, while his Southern colleagues were not too convinced of his allegiance.

During this period, Wellesley College sent a group of students to Washington for a period of internship. Hays agreed to have one who happened to be Jewish serve in our office. She was an attractive undergraduate and we naturally started dating. Because I was twenty-seven years old and she was about eighteen or nineteen, I think Congressman Hays might have been attempting some matchmaking. We did grow close over the several weeks she was in Washington, but it did not amount to anything in the end. Proof of that came when I visited her at Wellesley sometime thereafter, and she seemed quite indifferent. By that time, in any event, I was in a regular dating pattern, which certainly was long overdue, although I was still governed to a considerable extent by the conservative, religious outlook on dating that had controlled my behavior.

And so the session passed, and we headed back to Little Rock for the summer. We started meeting with many people in need. I remember being with Hays when constituents would request actions to help them that would have brought him to the brink of impropriety. He would sit and listen and be polite—and offer no encouragement. After a while they would almost always apologize for the request, reassure Congressman Hays that they understood his reluctance, and indicate that they would seek this unsavory help elsewhere. Traveling with the Hays through much of his district, I met hundreds of people from the Ozarks whose genuineness led me to identify them with the old phrase "granitic integrity." I learned that higher education does not necessarily lead to higher integrity, since these rural people demonstrated an honesty that few college graduates could match.

Orval Faubus represents one Arkansan who lost whatever connection to integrity he might have had after he had been elected to his second two-year term as governor. The voters retained him as a moderate who had carried out a reasonable agenda of state accomplishments, including educational improvements. When confronted with the realization that the tradition of a two-term limit would probably preclude his reelection and having no fallback occupation, he slowly allowed the opportunistic elements of his personality to dominate his behavior. He had always evidenced such elements, which had made him suspect from the beginning. A previous Arkansas governor, Sid McMath—a progressive who had been elected in a post–World War II surge of reform, gave Faubus his first opportunity to serve the state in the late 1940s. McMath was later known to have observed, humorously, that his greatest mistake as governor was building the road to Madison County that "let Faubus out."

Little Rock Erupts

Despite what we knew about him, it was still a shock when Governor Faubus called out the Arkansas National Guard in September 1957 to block the integration of the Little Rock Central High School, in the name of "public safety." The major risks to public safety that I saw around the high school early on were organized generally by a character named Jimmy Karam, understood to be one of Faubus's "dark-side" agents. The national media had put Little Rock way down on the list of cities where school integration problems were expected in 1957. The *New York Times*, for example, sent its best reporters to other cities in the south, such as Nashville, Memphis, and Atlanta. The *Times* sent Benjamin Fine, its education editor, rather than a reporter; and he tended to stir up "the mob" at Central High. He wrote stories for the *Times* that were quite different from what I saw with my own eyes. He was ultimately dismissed by the *Times*. By the time the "big leagues" of reporting had arrived in Little Rock (most of whom spent many hours camping out in Congressman Hays's office), the national confrontation was well underway.

For a series of complex and unique reasons, no one seemed to be in a position to serve as an intermediary between Governor Faubus and President Eisenhower. Former President Truman did try to get Governor Faubus to reconsider, but nothing came of it. To put it bluntly, no one had the stature and the courage to enter the fray until Brooks Hays called on an old friend, Sherman Adams, who was serving as Eisenhower's chief of staff, and offered his assistance. This was an act of great bravery, since Hays could gain nothing political from it, and there was considerable political risk involved. As Sherman Adams put it in a book he wrote in 1961 entitled *First-Hand Report*, "Hays was a man of deep convictions and was hurt and disturbed by the disrespect for the Constitution being shown... He felt a moral obligation to do something about it, even if it meant political suicide. I still think Hays showed one of the greatest exhibitions of sheer courage in modern political history when he walked into the line of fire at Little Rock."

When asked about his courage later, Hays responded with a famous phrase widely attributed to Martin Luther, "I could do no other." As an Adlai Stevenson kind of Democrat, he put politics aside to help his nation in a time of difficulty. Harry Ashmore, a reporter for the *Arkansas Gazette*, began bitterly challenging the legitimacy of the governor's actions, which caused a huge negative reaction to Ashmore in Arkansas. (He would later win a Pulitzer Prize for these newspaper stories about the Little Rock unrest.) In his 1994 book, *Civil Rights and Wrongs: A Memoir of Race and Politics*, Ashmore, contrary to Sherman Adams, states that however worthy Brooks Hays's intentions were, he was the wrong person for the job because he was too trusting of Faubus and not tough enough to take the governor on. His very words are "a sad case of miscasting." While I generally respect Harry Ashmore, this is revisionist history at its best (or worst as the case may be).

Harry Ashmore was a conventional knee-jerk liberal, albeit a skillful writer, who was fortunate to have found himself working for a newspaper publisher supportive of his views, in an environment that had been generally moderate but was deteriorating rapidly. During the Little Rock crisis, I saw with my own eyes how hundreds (even thousands) of people who had previously been moderates were now turning bitterly racist, as Governor Faubus gradually moved down the racist path and outrageously fanned the flames of hatred.

Quite contrary to Ashmore's 1994 "recollections," Hays's own book, *A Southern Moderate Speaks*, written in 1959, makes cogent and accurate observations about what happened. The racist Georgia governor, Marvin Griffin, and the leader of the Georgia White Citizens' Council, Roy Harris, had come to Little Rock to meet with Faubus and stir up trouble. When he and Griffin got back to Atlanta and learned that Faubus had called out the National Guard, they were puzzled about which side Faubus was on. As Harris said later "I sat there . . . just scratching my head and wondering if he called 'em out *for* us or *agin* us." Thus Ashmore was much too simpleminded and glib when he said that Faubus was already a lost cause when it came to moderation and that Hays was too innocent to detect that fact. Ashmore's account reminds me of philosopher John Dewey's whimsical definition of history: "Man's recollection of what he'd like to think happened in the past."

While my observation may seem like a mean-spirited aside, I do think Ashmore was eager to have the unchallenged title of best white "good guy" in the Little Rock crisis, and this required him to dimin-ish the image of Brooks Hays. The green-eyed monster of jealousy reared its ugly head (much greater jealousy than I was aware of until I read his books on Little Rock). I have lived long enough to see people I have otherwise respected behave in an ugly way to demean those they believe are in some way their competition. Others have unfor-tunately attempted (unsuccessfully in most cases) to do this to Brooks Hays in the Kennedy State Department and in the Kennedy White House. Hays always accepted this disgraceful behavior in good grace.

While Harry Ashmore was able to win the applause of the na-tion for his pieces in the *Arkansas Gazette* attacking Orval Faubus, he was risking very little compared to his publisher or Brooks Hays. Many people canceled subscriptions to the *Gazette,* and the paper went deep in the hole. I believe its ultimate demise can be traced directly to its economic woes in the fifties. Meanwhile Ashmore went on to greater recognition at a research institute located in Santa Bar-bara, California, funded by the liberal Ford Foundation, doing fine work that did little to heal the wounds of Little Rock. He saw his role as an attack reporter, "telling it like it is" in a most extreme fashion. His attack mode may well have contributed to Hays's later electoral defeat. Hays would never renounce the extremist writing of Ashmore, which had so alienated the public; and because of Hays's silence. many thought Hays agreed with Ashmore. It is outrageous for a reporter to write extremist and inflammatory language in the midst of a huge uproar, in his own community, no less, regardless of what his views might be. The bottom line in Little Rock is that Ashmore ultimately contributed to a huge setback for civil rights in Arkansas and the political demise of his presumed dear friend, Brooks Hays.

As the mediator and healer at the time (and in all times), Brooks Hays tried desperately to get the governor to behave responsibly early in the confrontation. He went to see him at the mansion every day for a week as he set up the arrangements for the famous confrontation

between Faubus and Eisenhower in Newport, Rhode Island, that occurred later that month. He made progress reports each day to
Sherman Adams. I often went to the mansion with Hays, but either
stayed in the car or the entrance hall, because I did not want to be
viewed as a participant in the deliberations. Hays later told me that
in probing for conscience with Faubus during that time he came to
the realization that "there was no there there" and that Faubus was
the consummate opportunist and charmer, but not an ingrained racist. We shuddered each day as the latest Ashmore blast was issued
by the *Gazette* because we knew it inflamed the situation. Hays was
too kind to ever say an unkind word about how Ashmore was making his job that much harder. When northern liberals called on Hays
to do more at that time, he shrugged his shoulders and continued on
his moderate course.

As an experienced veteran of Boston's political wars, I can assure the world that Brooks Hays was no innocent and was fully aware
of the challenge he faced, but was nonetheless totally committed to
his moderate approach. Unlike Harry Ashmore and possibly myself,
he was incapable of utilizing a combative approach. He was deeply
wedded to the truth, but he often quoted the Bible as his guide; and
in this situation he cited Paul's letter to the Ephesians in Ephesians
4:15, "to speak the truth in love."

It is important to note here that Orval Faubus's opportunism
led him ultimately on a slow slide into complete racism. The words
Faubus used at the beginning of the crisis were far more conciliatory
than those he used a year later. At Newport he made what appeared
to be a firm commitment to use his good offices to assist in admit-
ting the black students to Central High. He agreed to an appropriate
law-abiding statement that he and Hays prepared after the meeting
with Eisenhower. But he later completely recanted under the influence of his equally opportunistic staff led by the Svengali figure
Claude Carpenter—making the wonderful statement, "Just because
I said it doesn't make it so." As Brooks Hays so cogently put it, "The

mask worn long enough becomes the face." As Faubus slid into greater and greater racist utterances over time, he did indeed become a genuine racist.

As the world should recall, President Eisenhower finally felt it necessary to send the 101st Airborne to establish law and order at Central High. Harry Ashmore, who rushed quickly to disclaim any personal responsibility for the sending of the troops, offered no other recommendation to break the deadlock once the troops arrived. Brooks Hays and I had felt that gathering several hundred federal marshals might have been a better solution to avoid demagogic references to the Reconstruction period, but Hays respected the president's decision and provided full cooperation. Integration of Central High by "The Little Rock Nine," as the students were called, was achieved, but the situation remained tense.

My mother called me from Boston to express concern and urged me to keep off the streets. Actually the situation was rather calm except for the area around the school, although the Little Rock Jewish community of that city began to bear some of the brunt of the hate campaign fostered by such groups as the KKK and the White Citizens' Councils. One Friday morning, officials of the conservative synagogue that I attended notified me of a bomb threat they had received by phone. The anonymous caller had said that the synagogue would be blown up that evening. When informed, the police said that they would do what they could, but they could guarantee nothing.

I discussed the situation with Congressman Hays. He agreed with me that to close the synagogue would constitute a victory for the forces of evil. I conveyed our opinion to a small group of synagogue leaders, who decided to keep the matter quiet and go forward with the services. They took all precautions, including floodlighting the premises and hiring private detectives to search and guard the building. While this matter had been very closely held, and normally only about twenty-five to thirty people attended Friday evening services, that night more than one hundred people suddenly appeared. Nobody was going to stop them from worshipping! The very next day Brooks Hays expressed his great satisfaction to the Jewish community that they had not bowed to this cowardly threat of an act of religious hatred. He recalled that he and his father had stood up to threats of the Ku Klux Klan in the 1920s, even though it most likely cost his dad a seat in the U.S. Congress.

School Matters Continue to Fester

By early October 1957, the situation in Little Rock had stabilized sufficiently for me to return to Washington to prepare for the next congressional session and resume my part-time college teaching. I certainly hoped that the people would calm down and that Governor Faubus would not further inflame the situation.

But after numerous meetings trying to build bridges with the governor, Hays told me he still "hadn't found any there, there." It looked like Faubus was preparing to back a racist opponent of Hays in the 1958 congressional primary.

I continued to use some evenings and weekends to gather data on Hays's life so that he could write his autobiography. The fall of 1957 and the spring of 1958 went by somewhat uneventfully. Hays was reelected president of the SBC after a spirited convention full of challenges to his position of moderation on race. He and Mrs. Hays made overseas trips to visit Baptist churches in Moscow and made plans for a later visit to see the Pope in Rome through Monsignor Ligutti, the papal representative in Washington. (These plans did not culminate until 1963, when Pope John XXIII greeted Hays warmly and called him a "brother in Christ"—a historic meeting between the Pope and a leading Southern Baptist.)

Election of 1958

When Hays and I arrived in Little Rock after the Congress adjourned for the year, about June 30, 1958, Hays was faced with a reelection challenge for his House seat from Amis Guthridge, a well-known racist who had challenged Hays before. Since Governor

Faubus would be involved in a first primary with several opponents, Hays did not want to wait till the runoff period, when a candidate would run for the first time if he had only one opponent. Faubus would, if Hays waited, feel free to work against him in a second primary. We therefore encouraged another candidate to run, who would not be a threat, and he did so, putting Hays in the same first primary as Faubus. Thus Hays would not have to fear a Faubus involvement, if Faubus won a majority on the first go-around and Hays had to wait until the second round. And so Hays and Faubus both won their nominations by comfortable margins on the first go-around, July 1958. It is important to mention again that, in Arkansas at that time, a Democratic nomination was considered tantamount to election, with the November election itself being pro forma. On September 10, 1958, Faubus wrote Hays a congratulatory letter saying, among other things, "I also want to congratulate you upon your victory, and wish you continued success as a member of our Congressional delegation." Obviously, Faubus meant final-election victory not simply a primary election victory.

Even though Hays had no Republican opposition, I was still worried about leaving Arkansas too prematurely before the November "election;" but GW had my teaching schedule set to begin, and Hays was his usual considerate person in urging me to go back to Washington. When I returned in early fall, John McLees and Lurlene Wilbert were already there. That left in Little Rock only Kitty Johnson and one other person, Dick Emerson, Hays's district representative—an extremely loyal assistant who was, I say complimentarily, a "good ole boy." About ten days before the November election, the news came out that Little Rock school board member Dale Alford was going to run as a write-in candidate against Hays. Unbeknownst to us, Faubus and Claude Carpenter had been raising substantial sums of money and lining up racist supporters for this sneak attack. Closer to election day, Governor Faubus started making midnight visits to political leaders in the several counties of the Fifth Congressional District to ask them to support

Alford. Many racist politicians had always been opposed to the progressive policies that Hays championed, but they had laid low for many years. They now welcomed the opportunity to do battle.

It did not seem that a write-in candidacy could have much success, because there had only been one or two write-in election victories for Congress in the history of the country. What I didn't understand was the control over the election machinery that Faubus had established. He had replaced a man on the election board who was fair-minded with a man who was an avowed Faubus lackey. There was an old southern motto that "It don't matter who does the votin'; it matters who does the countin'." Faubus was fanning statewide antidesegregation emotions to a fever pitch. From Washington, we talked to Hays every day, and he seemed quite calm and in control of the situation. He did not want any of us to come to Little Rock, even though we always asked if we were needed. One thing did worry us. Several weeks before the write-in was announced, Hays had accepted an invitation to speak at the annual convention of black Baptists in Chicago; and pictures of him with black church leaders were being circulated over the Fifth District to major racist centers. As election day neared, we were concerned that in our phone conversations with Hays, his tone had changed, and he talked about the possibility of an upset. But we still couldn't believe that was really possible.

Early on election day, we heard that many poll workers were pasting stickers with Alford's name on the ballots, with an X already on the sticker. This was, of course, blatantly illegal, but not surprising. Hays had already lost three elections in his life—two for governor and one for congressman— of questionable legality. To add insult to injury, we found out later that some election officials had thrown out ballots where voters had scratched out the Alford X and placed their own X beside the Hays name. The officials "explained" that these ballots had now been tampered with!

And so we were startled when we heard that the "official" results of the election were that Hays had lost by about 1,000 votes. Because the November election had only the Hays contest on the ballot, far fewer people voted than had in the summer primaries; and if the same number of people had voted, Hays would have won handily, despite whatever tampering had taken place. Many people didn't come out to vote because they didn't take the Alford challenge seriously. Also, one woman came up to Hays after the election and said, "Oh Brooks, if I had known you were in any trouble I wouldn't have voted against you." It was clear that some people had voted for Alford only as a warning to Hays not to be too sympathetic with integration. Many people now wanted Hays to challenge the obviously crooked nature of the election—Hays most likely was the winner by at least a couple of thousand votes— but he did not want to be involved in another battle at this already divisive time.

Back in Washington we received a letter from then–Vice President Richard Nixon which startled us all. It said something to the effect that Nixon felt Hays's loss was the most devastating thing that had happened in this election, because Hays was such a role model for the Congress. That a Republican vice president would write this letter to a Democrat in a year when the Republicans lost a great many seats in the House and Senate was remarkable. While I was already seasoned in dealings with the press, I made a big mistake when talking to a reporter from the *Baltimore Sun.* In what I thought was an off-the-record remark, I said, "I do not want Brooks Hays to become the darling of Northern Republicans of the Nixon ilk." Naturally, I made the front page of the *Sun* the next day. It was very embarrassing to Hays, and he called Nixon when he got back to Washington to thank him for his letter and to apologize for his staff member. Characteristically, he never chastised me.

Soon Hays got a call from Majority Leader John McCormack, saying that the crooked election was an outrage and that every effort would be made to unseat Alford. The whole nation seemed to be in an uproar about Hays's so-called defeat. Reporters were calling from all over the country and from much of the world. When Hays held a press conference, some of the hardened press members were moved to tears. Trying to put a light touch to the event, Hays told two stories. In the first, Hays mentioned the fact that many of his northern liberal colleagues had called him during the yearlong Little Rock confrontation and urged him to do more to obtain community acceptance of the *Brown v. Board* decision. He said they reminded him of the hypochondriac who had put on his tombstone: "I told you I was sick."

The other story was told when a reporter questioned Hays about the role of Orval Faubus in this matter, and how much he should be blamed. Hays answered that he was embarrassed to have succumbed to Faubus's machinations. He said his current situation reminded him of the farmer who had been kicked in the head by his mule. When the doctor arrived, he told the farmer that the blow was lethal. The farmer pled with the doctor to keep him alive long enough so that he might die of pneumonia. When the doctor asked him why that was so important, the farmer replied, "I don't want it on my death certificate that I was kicked to death by a jackass."

Chet Huntley of the *Huntley-Brinkley Report* was at the press conference and retold the jackass story on the NBC newscast that evening. His partner, David Brinkley, broke up so much in hilarity that he almost couldn't finish the program. On the same date (November 10), "Herblock" (Herbert L. Block) drew a famous cartoon for *The Washington Post* that gained wide distribution. It bemoaned Hays's defeat and ridiculed Orval Faubus. Edward P. Morgan of ABC News devoted his entire program to eulogizing Brooks Hays. He quoted his own colleague, Benjamin A. Franklin, who attended the Hays press conference and noted, "Hays was gloriously, militantly, tolerantly right about everything... He knew he was right even in bitter defeat and it radiated from him almost blindingly." Bill Moyers was later to say, "Brooks was the first Baptist hero I met face-to-face. Brooks's courageous stand during the 1958 school desegregation crisis cost him his seat as congressman from Little Rock, but it won for him a place in legions of hearts."

A congressional farewell dinner was organized to honor Brooks Hays, with many distinguished Washingtonians serving on the organizing committee. One of them was Congressman Eddie Hebert of New Orleans, a prominent segregationist, but an honorable man whose office was next door to that of Hays, and he was Hays's good friend. When segregationist constituents complained to Hebert about his role on the committee, he blew them away. Hundreds of people of all walks of life came to the dinner, and it was a very emotional evening. The Reverend Billy Graham made a great speech praising Hays for his courage and his Christian concern for the disadvantaged. Several senior Members of Congress also addressed the audience, reflecting the fact that Hays had probably been the most popular and courageous Member, on both sides of the aisle.

At the same time, a congressional committee convened to review the results of the election. Hays had not challenged the outcome, to avoid exacerbating racial tensions, John Wells, however, a conservative publisher and editor of *The Little Rock Arkansas Recorder*, who was a friend of Hays and a decent man, had filed a protest about the crooked results; and he was deemed to have standing as a citizen of the Fifth District. After extensive hearings that fall, the committee voted 3–2 to have Alford stand aside until the next Congress investigated the election. The vote would have been close to unanimous, but one moderate Southerner did not think it wise to join the majority, since the fifth committee member, Congressman Davis of Memphis, who was known as "Judge Davis," was an ardent segregationist and would only vote for an investigation that would occur after Alford was seated. I attended those hearings and recall that Judge Davis appeared to be drunk throughout the process. The committee could not have functioned without the expert leadership of the Committee Counsel Gillis Long, who later became a Louisiana congressman himself. The leader of the majority vote was Tip O'Neill, who was a senior member of the House Democratic leadership and would later succeed McCormack as Speaker of the House. He was supported by the two

House Republicans on the committee, Ken Keating and David Dennison.

The Congressional Whitewash

Sometime between the issuing of the investigative report by the congressional committee and the convening of the next Congress in January 1959, the fix was put in. The repercussions throughout the South and the nation remained great. Many white Southern congressmen feared for their futures if they were moderate. The powerful chairman of the House Ways & Means Committee, Wilbur Mills of Arkansas, had become the agent of Orval Faubus, and he implored Speaker Rayburn to seat Alford. Rayburn agreed and convinced Minority Leader Charlie Halleck of Indiana to go along. I was sitting in the gallery when the Congress opened. I was nauseated to see the entire Arkansas delegation sitting together prepared to vote for Alford—gutless wonders, all of them. They had purported to be good friends of Hays for years, but would not refuse the bidding of Faubus. When Speaker Rayburn started the process of swearing in the new Congress, Tip O'Neill rose to offer a motion asking Alford to stand aside until after a full investigation of his "election." Only four other members supported his motion, including, interestingly, a newly-elected congressman, John Lindsay of New York, later to be New York City's mayor. As O'Neill's committee had asked, Alford was sworn in separately and a follow-up investigation was initiated. The only good thing that came of this fiasco was that John Wells was awarded the 1959 Elijah Lovejoy Award for Courage in Journalism.

In following years, Brooks Hays strengthened his ties with outstanding civil rights leaders such as Arkansan Wiley Branton and Washington lobbyist Clarence Mitchell of the NAACP (National Association for the Advancement of Colored People). Decades later, Bill Moyers would recall that at a civil rights gathering, the Reverend Martin Luther King introduced Hays to a friend, saying, "This is Mr. Hays. He has suffered with us." (Moyers made this remark on January 19, 1993, at the First Baptist Church in Washington, on the eve of President Clinton's first inauguration. The speech was later issued by Harvard Divinity School in the spring of that year as a document entitled "Forum on Religion and Values in Public Life.")

Not too long after Hays's 1958 "defeat" for his seat in the House, *The Washington Star* carried a story that, the Reverend James O. Duncan, editor of a Baptist publication, suggested that the Democratic party seriously consider Representative Hays for its 1960 vice presidential nomination. Duncan drew a parallel between Hays and Abraham Lincoln, who lost a Senate race to Stephen Douglas, one hundred years before the Hays defeat, and was elected president just two years later. In Duncan's view, each lost his congressional election "because he dared to stand on principle rather than on what was popular."

Hays Adjusts to Life after Congress

Hays was only sixty-one years old and prepared to move on with his life. President Eisenhower so admired Hays that he told him he could have any position he wanted in his administration. Hays told Eisenhower, "I would like to stay in my beloved South, the land which has nurtured me." And so Eisenhower nominated him to serve on the three-person board of the TVA. Hays was unanimously confirmed by the Senate, with many senators praising his fortitude and integrity. The African-American community in Knoxville was delighted to have Hays in its midst. The *Knoxville Journal* reported that the paper didn't know how much Hays knew about flood control, navigation, recreation, or power production, but it did know that the Baptists now had access to the largest baptismal pool in the world. I would frequently visit Hays in Knoxville, but, despite my admiration for him, I wasn't interested in going back to TVA, because I had been there once and was well situated in Washington. The appointment was just for one year, but Eisenhower then named him to a full nine-year term. He was still able to travel about the country making speeches, which he loved to do. He also kept a hand in politically. John Kennedy was running for president at a time when the country wasn't quite comfortable with the idea of a Roman Catholic leader. Hays gave him a boost by helping organize a meeting in Texas, where Kennedy convinced a group of Baptist ministers that he was devoted to the doctrine of the separation of church and state.

Hays would only serve at the TVA for about two years. Kennedy was elected president in 1960, and, being aware of Hays's great accomplishments in Congress, he named him Assistant Secretary of State for Congressional Affairs (of course, a handful of Southern segregationists tried—unsuccessfully—to block his confirmation) and then Special Assistant to the President. I heard Kennedy say directly to Hays that, if he were to write a sequel to his book *Profiles in Courage*, the story of Hays's courageous actions in Little Rock would be Chapter One. More will be said about Hays's and my experiences in the Kennedy Administration in due course.

Over time, I got some personal satisfaction at witnessing the downfall of two Members of Congress whose actions would not have earned them places in Kennedy's book. Both of them had been involved in the destruction of Hay's career in Congress. Back when a House committee was whitewashing the crooked election in Little Rock, the investigatory committee feared that one of its members— Frank Thompson, a liberal Democrat from New Jersey—would expose their chicanery. The leaders arranged for Dale Alford to vote against a bill that would have harmed the union movement, Thompson having a strong pro-labor position. (This was the only union-friendly vote Alford ever cast.) In return, Thompson supported the whitewashing, thereby making the committee vote unanimous. In the 1970s, Thompson was caught taking a bribe in what became known as the Abscam scandal. He was thrown out of Congress and served time in a federal penitentiary.

A few years earlier, Wilbur Mills—who had taken the lead to see that Dale Alford was promptly seated in the 1959 Congress —was in a car stopped for speeding,. The police found he was intoxicated and bloodied from a scuffle with his companion, ex-stripper Fanne Foxe, who then leapt from the car and jumped into the Washington Tidal Basin (and was rescued). That incident effectively ended Mills' congressional career. I've always viewed Fanne Foxe as an emissary of the Lord. It isn't often that one sees two people who have sold their souls for material gain get their comeuppance so soon afterwards.

Setting the Record Straight

I am distressed, however, by the continuing efforts by some Arkansans and their colleagues in the local media and elsewhere in the country to diminish the significance of Brooks Hays's courage during this major crisis in America's racial history. (This event was also a very rare case of state insurrection against the federal government.) Roy Reed, a native Arkansan and a former reporter for the *Arkansas Gazette* and for *The New York Times,* wrote a feature story in the *The Times* of September 6, 1992, about progressive Arkansans. I sent a letter to Jim Powell, a senior editor of the *Arkansas Gazette,* registering my shock over Reed's article. Powell responded to me, in strong rebuttal to Reed, "It is pretty bad on two counts, the ones you cited— the omission of Hays as a great progressive Arkansan and the resuscitation of OEF [Orval Faubus]." He went on to say, "Roy is falling into the revisionist trap—trying to do something new by doing it differently. Earlier I had some clues that he was trying to scrub up Faubus's record, or maybe explain it, in his biography. The article in *The Times* errs fundamentally in suggesting that Faubus cleaned up his act in the 60s. It isn't so." He concluded by writing, "Brooks Hays was one of the great progressive Arkansans—and my good friend."

The following year saw publication of David Halberstam's book *The Fifties.* I sent a letter to Halberstam in which I reproached him for omitting Hays from his chapter on Little Rock, and I also inundated him with evidence of Hays's major role in the crisis and his outstanding national status. Halberstam took the trouble to respond which I appreciated. As Halberstam put it, he saw Little Rock as simply part of an evolution of "an increasingly audacious black leadership and an increasingly powerful national media instrument, the synergy of both creating what came to be known as 'The Movement' ... Brooks Hays is, I regret, a relatively minor figure in this context."

The fact that there was a growing black movement is certainly true, but that phenomenon had little, if anything, to do with the Little Rock crisis, where the black movement was minimal. The significance of Little Rock is the challenge to national authority by a governor whose primary motivation was staying in office, raising racism as the method for that purpose, and providing "leadership" to drive a state backward instead of forward, in its acceptance of desegregation. While Daisy Bates of the Little Rock NAACP and her colleagues are to be commended for their effort to integrate Central High School, they were extremely "minor figures" in "The Movement" (to throw Halberstam's words back at him) of that time; and Little Rock would have been a blip on the scale of black audacity if it were not for Orval Faubus. It was because of Brooks Hays and many other moderates in Little Rock who had led the city into greater racial harmony over the years that the shock of the crisis was so great. Having spent much of three years in Little Rock at that time, from early 1956 on, my entire experience before the "crisis" was of great appreciation of the moderation of the people. Until Orval Faubus, Little Rock was *not* an area of civil rights confrontations because Brooks Hays and others had taken the leadership to further the cause of improved civil rights. (In all honesty, I have to confess that Harry Ashmore had been one of those valuable leaders—my concern about him was his intensely confrontational mode later in challenging Faubus, which made it just about impossible for Hays to bring Faubus back to middle ground.) The brewing confrontations were in other parts of the Deep South, where heroic black citizens had challenged intransigent whites who were not about to yield—states such as Mississippi and Alabama, among others.

The Arkansas picture after the Little Rock eruption is not entirely clear, because the people's election of Hays's son Steele to a position on the Arkansas Supreme Court, several years after Hays's defeat, could be interpreted as reflecting a feeling of remorse about Brooks, in addition to respect for Steele's abilities. Steele held that position for many years thereafter, election after election.

I regret to have to a make a disparaging set of comments about a senator I have long admired, but it is relevant to the jealousy of others over Hays's honorable civil rights activities. In a profile, in *Time* magazine, January 22, 1965, Senator Bill Fulbright of Arkansas very defensively spoke of his evasion of responsibility in dealing with Governor Faubus, as follows: "What could I have done to control the governor? What did Brooks Hays accomplish? Hays was lauded as a statesman—but he isn't a statesman any longer. I'm in politics. This is the sentiment of my state. I would not like to retire from politics with the feeling that I had betrayed them."

I am saddened to see this distinguished senator be so craven in his willingness to accept racist behavior on the part of his constituents, which he knows to be wrong, using the convoluted reasoning that attempting to help his constituents to understand that racism is wrong would be to *betray* them. It is also surprising that he said that Brooks Hays was no longer a statesman, at the very time when Hays was serving as a major spokesman for Presidents Kennedy and Johnson to the religious world and to the intergovernmental world. It is interesting to note that not long after Fulbright's comments in *Time*, among the young staffers who came to work for him were Bill Clinton and Jim McDougal. It is ironic that Brooks Hays, the essence of moderation, could possibly have been interpreted as having attempted to do too much in the Little Rock crisis. Supporting the Supreme Court decision on school desegregation as "the law of the land" had once again in some respects become an extremist position in the eyes of some Arkansans.

Hays Promotes Baptist Outreach

After Hays's defeat for reelection to a ninth term in Congress, he received many national awards and honors, including several from the National Conference of Christians and Jews. After his service at TVA, the State Department, and the White House, he would become a "visiting distinguished professor" at several universities. He wrote five books about public affairs and religion, in the last of which he referred to me as his "spiritual son."

But his proudest achievement was the 1966 establishment of the Ecumenical Institute at Wake Forest University in Winston-Salem, North Carolina. When then-President Ralph Scales (who had formerly served at the University of Arkansas) asked him to undertake this venture, Hays threw himself into the effort with great energy and dedication. He was in his element—building bridges of understanding between different faiths. With the assistance of Professor Bill Angell and others, he arranged numerous ecumenical conferences and exchanges among Protestants, Catholics, and Jews. I was pleased to make many visits to Winston-Salem to help with the conferences and to serve as the point of contact with the American Jewish Committee (AJC), on whose Washington, D.C., chapter board I had served for many years. Rabbi Marc Tannenbaum, AJC's national religious leader, responded beautifully to these overtures, and much good was accomplished in the exchanges between Baptist and Jewish leaders. Brooks Hays became referred to as an "ecumaniac," dedicated to a course of religious outreach consistent with his profound Baptist roots.

It was in this context Hays reacted so strongly to the 1980 words of Reverend Bailey Smith, who stated, "God Almighty does not hear the prayer of a Jew," Brooks Hays was very disturbed. He issued a public statement immediately after Smith's appeared saying the following:

> As a former SBC president, I feel an obligation to disassociate myself from the statement of the present

president that God hears no prayers unless they come from Christians who invoke the name of Christ. That would be to shut out from God's love and care the largest part of the world's population, and to abrogate to ourselves alone His mercy and favor, something Jesus never intended...

He elaborated on his views, concluding that "... the way to God should be, and is, open to everyone, saint and sinner, Jews, Moslem, and Christian."

Hays later cited for me a statement from one of the greatest of Baptists, Roger Williams (1604–83), who was run out of Massachusetts by Puritan theocrats and founded the first American Baptist Church in Providence, Rhode Island, in 1636. On one of his trips back to England he said, as Hays paraphrased the statement:

On this boat returning to England, there are men and women of diverse views; we have Protestants and Catholics and Jewish adherents and a small number of Moslems, and the composite should give us assurance, since each has captured an important truth and I feel safer with the cross-section of religious devotion.

Reactions such as those of Brooks Hays made at least a short-run impact on Reverend Smith and, in the long run, contributed to better Baptist-Jewish understanding. The Jewish community has been the beneficiary of good deeds from Hays and other Christians who would not remain silent. One would hope that this spirit will prevail.

Brooks Hays had always wanted to be Governor of Arkansas and he made another effort to win that office in 1966, after first trying to get elected in 1928. Orval Faubus was leaving office after twelve years and assured Hays that he would not stand in his way. Hays was pitted against Jim Johnson, an arch-segregationist, and the first readings in the state were that Hays had a strong chance. Just before the filing date closed, however, Attorney General Frank Holt entered the race, a person who was something of a moderate but one who was viewed as being Faubus's candidate. His entry in the race was widely interpreted as another example of Faubus's treachery. As an interesting footnote, Bruce Lindsey, often cited as Bill Clinton's alter ego, tracks his interest in politics to his involvement in Hays's 1966 campaign. Bill Clinton, by the way, supported Holt, *not* Hays.

Ironically, when Jim Johnson then won the primary, all decent Arkansans turned to the Republican candidate, Winthrop Rockefeller, who organized a very professional campaign and, while he was not too impressive a candidate, he succeeded in being the first Republican-elected governor of Arkansas.

In 1972, Hays was the Democratic nominee for Congress from his North Carolina District, running against the Republican incumbent, Vinegar Bend Mizell, who had earlier made his reputation as a major-league baseball player; but the disastrous results of George McGovern's race for president against Richard Nixon made success impossible. Nonetheless, the campaign was a great time for Hays, and he enjoyed himself immensely. I joined him often, walking across almost the entire congressional district; and we had great fun talking to hundreds of constituents. Shortly thereafter, the governor appointed Hays to the state human rights commission, where he was very effective helping people promote better race relations. Hays would now remain based in the world of academia and a widely respected national lecturer until he died in 1981 at age eighty-three. Brooks Hays will be remembered as a giant in the congressional pantheon, who put principle above personal success.

My New Life

Let us return now to what happened to our careers, mine and that of Hays, right after the Little Rock defeat. After Hays lost the congressional election in 1958, he worked hard to see that his staff was swiftly and properly placed. He helped Kitty Johnson get a job with Senator Fulbright. Lurlene Wilbert ultimately became associated with Congressman Oren Harris, another Arkansan, for several years, and later worked for me in a senatorial office. John McLees did not want to risk taking any of the offers he got for short-term positions on the Hill. He did ultimately get a job with the U.S. Chamber of Commerce, which he held for a number of years. As for me, I would have stayed with Hays in the Congress till the end of time, but I was now interested in working for the United States Senate. After Hays's lost election, he raised the salaries of all the staff, with what little was left in his official expense account, to help our bargaining positions when we looked for other jobs. This increase would only last, of course, for the remainder of his term, about two months. He was able to raise mine from $6,000, which had been a huge underpayment for the position I held (because Hays had a very limited budget at the time I was originally hired) to $9,000, which was about right.

There were many Democratic senators elected in 1958, and I considered applying to a number of them for a job; but I finally narrowed the choice to Senator Ed Muskie of Maine or Senator Clair Engle of California. As a New Englander, my first choice was Muskie, but I was told he was slow to make decisions. I interviewed with his top staff, and they said they wanted me. The administrative assistant for Clair Engle told me I was the first choice for that office. When Senator Engle then offered me the job of legislative assistant and press secretary at $10,000 per year, I was sorely tempted. Meanwhile, Muskie hadn't come to any conclusion. I had already gone off the congressional payroll and was feeling a little nervous. A Maine congressman, Frank Coffin, had been friendly to me when I worked for Hays. Because he was close to Muskie, I thought I would discuss the matter with him. He repeated the old saw, "A bird in the hand is worth two in the bush." And so I accepted Engle's offer—and then Muskie offered me a job two weeks later. I regretfully told Senator Muskie I was already committed, but hoped to keep in touch about future options.

Working for Senator Engle turned out to be to be quite a challenge. I was the sole legislative assistant, the sole press secretary, and the sole supervisor of the constituent mail on substantive matters. We were inundated with such mail because California was the most populous state and its citizens sent us thousands of letters each week. The administrative assistant, Tom Bendorf, hired many case workers, but few staff to help me. The senator, as past chairman of the House Interior Committee, also maintained a small staff for that special area. Gertrude Harris was his general speechwriter and an outstanding one at that whom I grew to have great admiration for and became close friends with, Addy Krizek was the legislative secretary, and Doris Naumann was my personal assistant. Stephanie Reid (later Floyd) handled many assignments for me, especially the mail.. I felt somewhat overwhelmed at first, because thousands of letters had piled up before I came on board. It took me six months to create the machinery necessary to get current in our responses. There was little time to file the letters after they were answered, and so I "streamlined" the system: I put the letters in file drawers chronologically until the drawers were filled—and then threw them out from the rear. In only two or three cases did we get a follow-up letter, and I simply contacted the writer to say that the first letter had been misplaced, which worked fine, until Senator Engle found out what I was doing. It was several months into the congressional session, and he ordered us to make every effort to file the letters by subject matter, and keep them all.

One of my first assignments had an amusing consequence. A major group of constituents from Whittier College had put together an intriguing proposal: They wanted the federal government to lease them, for one dollar, a former cruise ship (converted to troop ship) that was in mothballs. They would use it to create a "University of the Seven Seas"—enrolling students to sail around the world for a semester with the students taking courses related to stops made along the way. Senator Engle, at that point, was giving high priority to his assignments on both the Commerce and the Armed Services committees, and he thought this school-ship idea was somewhat frivolous. Since we were getting a lot of pressure, however, I kept reminding him of the proposal, until he reluctantly gave it the go-ahead. It "sailed" through the Congress. The launching of the University of the Seven Seas received headlines throughout California and the nation, while some of the senator's other early initiatives got little attention. Senator Engle really grumbled about that turn of events.

Soon after I came to work for him, Senator Engle told me he wanted to address two significant issues that were confronting the nation. One was the disarray in the organization of the Defense Department and the other was the lack of communication between the U.S. and what was then called Red China. His Republican predecessor in the Senate, Bill Knowland, was known as the "Senator from Formosa," because he had prevented any outreach to the mainland Chinese. I immediately began to research that situation with the assistance of senior staff at the Congressional Research Service (CRS) of the Library of Congress, especially Clem Lapp. At the same time, I also began to put together much data on the need to bring order to our defense structure, again with the help of CRS, especially from an exceptionally knowledgeable Defense Department alumnus there, Colonel Donovan.

Within six months of his taking office, Engle went on the Senate floor on two different occasions to make "maiden" addresses, as first major addresses by new senators were called. It was pretty exciting for me, since he asked me to sit next to him on the Senate floor, to be of assistance. Because I was only twenty-eight years old, I really felt this was a highlight of my professional life. The senator's remarks received rave notices in the press and from his colleagues, and he was credited with opening up meaningful outreaches to the People's Republic of China. His effort was courageous, because the United States had been paralyzed on this matter, and his speaking out took place long before election of President Nixon, who was hailed

for similar actions some ten years later. Senator Engle referred to the
area that California faced beyond its coast as the "Pacific Basin,"
(which included all countries in the Pacific region), and he wanted
it to become the economic engine of the world. As a member of
the Senate Commerce Committee, he wanted Chairman Warren
Magnuson to emphasize Engle's and Magnuson's contributions to
greater international commerce, including the outreach to China.
This led to my becoming a good friend of Magnuson's key staffer on
the committee, Gerry Grinstein, who would play a significant part
in my life. To promote his vision, Senator Engle toured the Pacific
Basin—a tour I could have gone on, but I sent the Library of Congress expert, Clem Lapp, instead, who could better serve the senator.

With regard to defense matters, many of Senator Engle's recommendations were adopted and led to a far more efficient operation of
the Defense Department. His most controversial suggestion—that
the branches of the service be folded into unified regional commands
around the world—was regarded as being too radical and therefore
not accepted. But here, too, he established himself as a senator whose
ideas needed to be reckoned with, as a key member of the Armed
Services Committee.

Being heavily involved in the senator's work on defense matters,
I faced another significant challenge. The U. S. government was
working with the Soviets on the first treaty to create a nuclear-free
region, in this case Antarctica. While it would not make a significant difference with regard to international public safety, it would be
a very symbolic treaty setting the stage for other more significant
treaties. Most mainstream foreign policy experts recognized the significance of such a treaty signed between the two superpowers.
Senator Engle, however, was close to the U.S. Navy, which opposed
the treaty as detrimental to U.S. defense needs. I decided to marshal
all the information I could gather in support of the treaty, and I met
with Engle to try to persuade him. Ultimately, I failed, and he decided to lead the floor fight against Senate approval of the treaty. He

then asked me to write his major Senate presentation since I knew so much about the subject. I did as he asked, and he made a dramatic presentation to the Senate. I held my breath when the vote was taken and sighed in relief when the treaty was approved by a narrow margin. I was very pleased when the senator thanked me for my excellent support, even though I personally held a different view. I responded that I was happy to be of assistance so long as I agreed with his policy positions at least 80 percent of the time, which was indeed the case. This exchange between me and the senator served to solidify our mutual respect.

An amusing event took place about this same time. I decided to move to a much nicer apartment on the Senate side of Capitol Hill, rather than where I was living near GW. A new apartment building was just about to open, and I signed a lease to move in on August 15, 1959. Since this efficiency apartment was unfurnished, I needed to buy some major furniture, such as a sofa bed, a desk, a dresser, a dining room table and chairs, and bookcases. Knowing nothing at all about furniture, I enlisted the assistance of my cousin Ida Brown. She joined me at Lansburgh's Furniture Store and helped me pick out all the items I needed. The salesperson was an attractive young woman, who must have been delighted at the large sale, and responded favorably to my light banter, including my invitation to see the furniture once it was set up in my apartment. I kept calling the resident manager of the new apartment to learn if the furniture had arrived, but had no affirmative report. When I returned home on the evening of the 14th, an extremely hot day, I was astounded to see that movers, let in by the superintendent, had shoehorned all of my new furniture into my fully furnished old apartment. Apparently, the salesperson had been so flustered by my attention that she reversed the location of the old and new apartments on the sales slip. It was past the store's closing time, so I had to make arrangements to spend the night elsewhere. Early the next morning I called the furniture store, and they said all their trucks were busy and it would take several days to correct the error. I responded that my lease was up that day, and if they didn't move the furniture immediately I would throw it out on the street, stop payment on my check, and let them try to collect from me. They relented, hired a truck not in their fleet, and moved my furniture to the new apartment. Needless to say, I did not live up to my commitment to have the salesperson come to visit.

Since I was a distance from the Kesher Israel synagogue in my new location, I decided to continue my active membership there, but would also sometimes attend an Orthodox synagogue located on 8th & H Streets, N.E. This was within walking distance, but the area was a mixed one, with some good and some bad housing, and some good and some bad people, both white and black. I opted to take my chances during daylight hours and never really had any serious confrontations. The rabbi there was a dynamic person who put on a good show, to hold onto his dwindling congregation. The area was clearly on the decline and it wasn't too long before the synagogue was no more. My primary focus was on the Kesher Israel congregation which was in Georgetown, and there I became quite a regular, making many friends and winning the confidence of the rabbi, Philip Rabinowitz.

As we moved into the presidential election year of 1960, I became particularly interested in the outcome. I did not think at that time that I would ever have a chance to hold elective office, and the Executive Branch bored me, except for the one place I had always dreamed of working—the White House. My work for Senator Engle was very interesting, but I wasn't too happy with the anonymity required. I also had some significant management differences with the senator's administrative assistant, Tom Bendorf, to whom the senator delegated the whole operation. I liked Tom—he was a gracious person. But I thought he had the office completely wrongly structured and functioning at a very low level of performance. I worked extremely hard with a handful of assistants to cover the whole field of legislation; to interface with the representatives of hundreds of newspapers, radio stations, and television stations; and also to over-see the substantive responses to thousands of constituents. Most other Senate offices, many from states much smaller than Califor-nia, had different staff assistants to direct each of these functions. I thought having many independent assistants to simply handle the letters involving individual problem cases made no sense at all. The small interior-affairs shop also was a drain, and its work was very difficult to coordinate with the rest of the office. Thus, of a total of about twenty-five staffers, I had only five to handle the vast bulk of the work of the office. When Tom compounded the problem by re-fusing to give any of us the routine pay raise generally given to all Senate staffers, I decided it was time for me to go into high gear in preparation for leaving.

Senator Engle seemed oblivious to the discontent that was rising all around him. I checked with Senator Muskie's office, but they had no opening at this time. Careful exploration of other offices did not produce any immediate results. I still kept in close touch with Brooks Hays and saw him on his frequent visits to Washington, but I did not want another experience with TVA. One thing that kept me at-tracted to Senator Engle was his great dedication to his job. He had me make a scoreboard for the wall, where we kept track of the status of all the bills he had introduced or cosponsored. The result of his hard work was evident—more of his legislation gained Senate atten-tion than that of any other senator. In promoting this legislation among my contemporaries in the Senate and with the press corps covering California, I had learned a great deal and had become a somewhat significant player in the Senate. In hindsight, I should have continued to pursue another position in the Senate or asked the sena-tor to get me on the staff of one of his committees, but I looked for other opportunities elsewhere. I did not want to wait for the out-come of the 1960 presidential election.

In the meantime, I invited Senator Engle to speak to my class at GW. The day he was to speak, he went out beforehand for one his recreational flights about the area (he kept a plane at an airport near Bailey's Crossroads, Virginia). Piloting his plane usually helped to clear his head before voting on a crucial issue. But this time he over-ran the runway when landing and banged up his head pretty badly. (When he later developed a brain tumor, a nurse I knew well said that he might have saved his life if he had gotten medical attention quickly, but he was too macho to do so.) And so I had to find a sub-stitute at the last minute. A good friend of mine, the administrative assistant to Senator McNamara of Michigan, suggested I call a new House member who was very knowledgeable and very accommodat-ing. Congressman Jim O'Hara had just come back from a trip to Michigan on Congressional matters, and he agreed to pinch-hit if I got him home early. He did a wonderful job explaining to my stu-dents exactly how he saw the Congress functioning. This was the beginning of a beautiful friendship, which benefited me in the 1970s, as well, when I got into local politics. This whole experience con-vinced me to redouble my efforts to leave Senator Engle's office.

When I first came to Capitol Hill to work for Congress in the fall of 1955, Brooks Hays introduced me to Delphis Goldberg, who had worked for him on the Kestnbaum Commission, informally named for its chairman, Meyer Kestnbaum, president of Hart, Schaffner, and Marx. a clothing manufacturer. The bipartisan commission was cre-ated during the Eisenhower presidency to improve federal–state–local government relations. Hays had been named to the Commission by President Eisenhower. When the Commission finished its work, Del (as he was called) went to work for a subcommittee of the House Government Operations Committee, chaired by Congressman L. H. Fountain of North Carolina, which was tasked with implementing the report's recommendations. Hays maintained his interest in this area and urged me to support Del. It was the beginning of yet an-other beautiful friendship.

One thing led to another, and legislation was introduced to cre-ate a permanent Advisory Commission on Intergovernmental

Relations (ACIR). When I had gone to work for Senator Engle, that legislation was pending in the Senate, and I helped push it through. The commission got underway with twenty-six members representing the Congress, the president's cabinet, state governors, state legislators, county officials, mayors, and many others. It was chaired by a great public servant, Frank Bane, who had been the first head of the Social Security Administration in 1935, knew more governors than any other living person, and was remarkably bipartisan in his outlook. The commission had hired another great public servant, Bill Colman, as the director, and an outstanding economist Laszlo Ecker-Racz, as the deputy. They were looking for a third senior staffer and I decided to apply. Backed by Del Goldberg and Brooks Hays, I got the job. (I'd like to think Senator Engle was sorry to lose me, since, after I told him I was leaving, he wrote letters of praise about my work to all twenty-six members of the commission, stating how highly he thought of me.) So in the middle of 1960, after only a year and a half, I left the Senate and would come to miss it very much. Everyone at ACIR was very kind to me, but the atmosphere of a research agency was hard to adjust to after the excitement of Capitol Hill.

At ACIR, I had three assignments: reviewing the urban planning process and urban development; assessing the quality of the fifty state constitutions; and considering the pros and cons of creating a department of urban affairs. For the first one of the three, I showed Laszlo my draft of the urban planning recommendations and he said, "Warren, this report is surprisingly well written." We were preparing this document in conjunction with the North Carolina Institute of Government, then headed by the legendary Albert Coates, who came to Washington to review the report with me. He said, "Warren, this is the finest report of its kind I have ever seen." He then proceeded to tear the report apart and completely rewrite it. I have since then referred to his comments as the "Albert Coates system of evaluation." This study influenced urban development in North Carolina and many other states.

I was overwhelmed by the complexities of the fifty different state constitutions, which was my second assignment. The states had such different procedures for amending their constitutions that I could not find any commonalities that could be identified and evaluated. As for the third component of my work, the full commission adopted my report on the pros and cons of enacting legislation to set up a Federal Housing and Urban Development Department (HUD). It was used in the congressional debate by both proponents and opponents of creating HUD, with the proponents obviously winning out. It gave me great satisfaction to have been a major architect of the congressional consideration of this matter. And I had nipped in the bud the alternative of creating a White House Office of Urban Affairs. A White House Office would have been the wrong place to give priority attention to a substantive program to meet national housing needs.

Despite the very pleasant environment, (the office having been recently vacated by The Brookings Institution, which moved to its own building, where I was later to be employed), I still felt somewhat at a loss over what the future held in store. My sense of the purpose of my life hadn't matured very much, other than being elevated to knowing that I wanted to make a difference through public service. I had already rejected becoming a rabbi or a doctor or a full-time professor or a lawyer or a number of other professions, but I was still working on the process of elimination.

The New Frontier

When John F. Kennedy was elected president in November 1960, I sensed that my life might be changed significantly. Since the ACIR office was very close to the White House, our office staff and relatives had box-office seats for the inaugural parade. Soon thereafter, I heard from Brooks Hays that Kennedy was considering him for a high office. Adlai Stevenson, a close friend of Hays, was about to be appointed Delegate to the United Nations, and he wanted Hays as his deputy. (Stevenson was disappointed not to be secretary of state, but Dean Rusk got the job after Bill Fulbright was rejected.) Kennedy overruled Stevenson's plans for Hays, and asked him to be Assistant Secretary of State for Congressional Relations. Hays then asked me to be his assistant at the State Department.

A month or two went by with no movement in the Senate on Hays's nomination. Then we found out that Speaker Rayburn had managed to put a hold on any action. It was astounding to me that Rayburn would treat Hays in this manner, just to suck up to the racists in the House, especially Hays's disgraceful successor, Dale Alford. I pled with Hays to see Rayburn and he reluctantly agreed. Rayburn equally reluctantly agreed to see Hays. In their meeting, the Speaker told Hays that he was out and Alford was in, and that's the way it was. Hays then mentioned the dozens of times he had come to the rescue of Democrats in the House—at Rayburn's request and Hays's own risk—especially when cowriting the civil rights platforms at the 1952 and 1956 Democratic conventions (along with Senator Hubert Humphrey). Rayburn finally relented and withdrew his hold. This experience caused me to lose much of my respect for Rayburn, who was prepared to put opportunism above statesmanship and morality. Hays then, of course, was easily confirmed by the Senate.

I resigned from ACIR in March of 1961 and rejoined Hays. Although I had had several security checks for prior jobs, it was necessary for Secretary of State Dean Rusk to personally allow me to start working while the security-check update was being carried out. The salary, by the way, was much higher than any I had gotten before. Hays and I hit the ground running. In hindsight, I think he should have named me his deputy, but he felt a little uneasy at the time, and decided to keep the deputy named by his Republican predecessor—a nice person but not really the right person to backstop Hays. Thus I became one of the four senior staff assisting Hays; the other three being career foreign service officers. I inherited a dedicated and intelligent assistant, Norma Maley (later Tema), who had been a Foreign Service brat. President Kennedy was anxious to move rapidly in at least three areas on foreign policy: (a) strengthening the governments in Latin America by giving them economic assistance and promoting democracy; (b) creating a disarmament administration in the State Department to push for treaties or agreements with the Soviet Union, to ease tensions and diminish threats of a world war; and (c) create a Peace Corps to employ idealistic young Americans to improve the lot of people living in Third World countries and spread international goodwill.

A number of problems arose quickly for us in the State Department. One related to the tense situation in the Middle East. The Foreign Service Officers (FSO) prepared the letters written in answer to congressional inquiries—letters that were signed by Hays. The FSOs tended to tilt toward the Arab world, with the objective of protecting the oil reserves. FSOs were also generally genteelly anti-Semitic—a result of the Harvard–Yale–Princeton dominance of the Foreign Service. (That fortunately changed over time.) Hays caught hell from former colleagues in the Congress for one letter he signed, which was severely biased pro the Arab world. He then asked me to review all Middle East letters prepared in the future, even though the area assigned to me was Latin America. I handled the task evenhandedly, but it did lead to some tensions between me and members of the Foreign Service.

The first step in Kennedy's outreach plan for strengthening Latin America was to ask Congress to make a major and immediate financial infusion to Latin American countries. This funding anticipated a future conference to promote what he would call the Alliance for Progress. As I recall, this effort would require an initial expenditure of some 500 million dollars—a measure that would have to be approved as a first step in the program by the House Appropriations Subcommittee on Foreign Aid, headed by Congressman Otto Passman of Louisiana, a friend of Hays. Hays talked to Passman in advance about the matter, because Passman was known to be skeptical of this proposal. Shortly thereafter, Hays was awakened by a call in the middle of the night from Larry O'Brien, head of the White House Office of Congressional Relations He chewed Hays out for his outreach, because O'Brien planned to end-run Passman and get the rest of the Members to vote the appropriation out of Committee. While Hays was not happy about this treatment, he complied with O'Brien's request to do nothing. Months went by and O'Brien failed to get anywhere—evidence of both his innocence of how the Congress worked and the fact that Passman was impregnable. Finally, Hays was called upon to see what he could do, and he renewed his talks with Passman, who relented, let the appropriations pass—saying that his gesture was being made because of his deep fondness for Hays. This event proved that Kennedy's judgment was right when he wanted Hays doing congressional relations rather than being at the U.N.

The next step was a major conference in Punta del Este, Uruguay, to get all of Latin America committed to economic development and political reform. My role was to determine which senators would represent the Congress in the U.S. delegation. The State Department leaned toward Senators Wayne Morse of Oregon and Bourke Hickenlooper of Iowa, but Lyndon Johnson, now vice president, was opposed. His job was really supposed to be pro forma, since Majority Leader Mansfield and the senior Democrats should have made the decision, but Johnson was adamant. After a while, I got word that Morse and Hickenlooper had been approved, and I assumed that Johnson had relented. I so notified the State Department press officer who was to announce the appointments at 4:00 p.m. that day. About 3:30 p.m., as a courtesy, I called Liz Carpenter, LBJ's press officer to let her know what would happen. (I knew her from years before, when she represented Arkansas papers as a congressional reporter.) At 3:45 p.m. the phone rang and Norma answered. The voice at the other end asked, "Is Mr. Cikins there for the vice president?" Norma responded, "The vice president of what?" LBJ roared, "This is Vice President Johnson." I got on the line, and he told me he had not approved of the appointments, but Rusk had overridden him. I told him I needed to move fast to head off the press conference, which I was able to stop about four minutes before the announcement. What a heart stopper!

Some days later I got an engraved invitation to a party sponsored by the vice president of the United States "in honor of the occasion." When I responded to the phone number listed, I got the prayer of the day. Some joker had sent out about a hundred of these invitations to anonymous key players in government who rarely got invited to anything. When I told Liz Carpenter about this, she and LBJ were furious that anyone would use the vice president's name and tried desperately to find out who it was—thereby giving the matter much more publicity than it would otherwise have had.

From Camelot to Turbulence

In 1961, I worked on the successful efforts to start the Alliance for Progress, to create the Disarmament Administration, and to establish the Peace Corps. I prepared the legally required annual report to the Congress on crucial legislation the State Department wanted. I also had several interactions with Bill Moyers who was doing key work for LBJ. Most importantly, I helped arrange what we called the Wednesday Luncheon Group. It was attended weekly by some eighty political appointees at the State Department, who needed to build alliances to offset the Foreign Service, which was often at odds with the Kennedy agenda. We worried Rusk , and he sent his top aide, Luke Battle, to monitor our behavior. Since I knew many JFK staffers from my days on Capitol Hill, I invited them to be guest speakers at the luncheons, which developed some real clout for our group.

In those days, some black diplomats had difficulties while driving from New York to Washington on official business, because of the racism in local police departments, hotels, and restaurants. I supported Pedro San Juan, the State Department's deputy protocol officer, in his efforts to mediate these problems. To be of assistance in matters of this kind, I also arranged for Stephanie Reid to come to work for Brooks Hays as his personal secretary, since she still wasn't too happy in Senator Engle's office. Hays needed expert help, which she was able to provide.

October 24, 1961 would be the 16th anniversary of the creation of the U.N. I heard that the State Department was looking for speakers to travel through the Far West to give addresses at various places during the anniversary week. I was selected to be a speaker. Once I set forth, I ended up speaking in Idaho, Arizona, Utah, Nevada, Oklahoma, and Arkansas—one or two times in each state. Not too much time had passed since China had gone Communist, and hecklers claimed that the State Department had lost China. A slogan I was confronted with often was "Get the U.S. Out of the U.N., and the U.N. Out of the U.S." The entire trip was a challenge, but I found the opportunity to address these large audiences quite exhilarating; and I generally won over a large majority of the listeners. Because one of the stops was going to be Salt Lake City, Utah, I had contacted my old friend Mark Cannon to arrange some presentations in that area. I went to Brigham Young University where Mark was chairman of the Political Science Department, and to the University of Utah. I also addressed a group of inmates at the Utah State Prison at Mark's request, and they were happy to meet a Democratic official, which was rare in Utah.

During this period, I met a Jewish graduate of Smith College, through my cousin Ida. She was wonderful person and we hit it off very well. After awhile she moved to Georgetown, where she had a Baptist roommate who knew many people Brooks Hays knew, including Baptist State Department officials. We started to go together on a pretty steady basis; but since my future was still uncertain, I was not ready to commit to anyone.

In the beginning of 1962, President Kennedy made many personnel changes in his administration. The biggest changes related to those people in the State Department who had opposed the "Bay of Pigs" invasion. Other switches also took place. JFK moved Fred Dutton out of the White House and named him to replace Brooks Hays at the State Department, while he moved Hays to the White House, with similar duties to those Dutton had had. I was delighted that my parents were visiting me when Hays was sworn in by President Kennedy in what was then called the "Fish Room" of the White House. I was able to get them invited to the ceremony, and they had a chance to chat with the president.

The situation left me still at "State." Although I had friends in the White House, they claimed that the budget wouldn't stretch for another position. But they did say that if I could get one of the governmental agencies to pay my salary (a common practice), which would make it look like the White House was being very frugal, I could come over to join Hays. Since Dutton had not cooperated very much with ACIR, I checked with Bill Colman and Frank Bane of ACIR, and they agreed to put me on their payroll for at least the next six months, detailing me to the White House.

It was quite exciting to establish myself in the Kennedy White House. As with several of the ten or so special assistants to the president, Brooks Hays had a rather wide-ranging mandate. Some of his White House outreach extended to many different religious organizations, including Jewish. I met Rabbi Dick Hirsch, who was the Washington Representative of the Reform Jewish movement, and we established a close relationship that later played a significant role in my life. Hays also gave speeches around the country to promote programs for which the president needed to gain support. Kennedy hoped that constituents would press Congress for action on his agenda, especially the renewal of reciprocal trade legislation. He appreciated Hays's invaluable powers of persuasion and also enjoyed his sense of humor. As far as direct congressional relations, Hays and Larry O'Brien had reached a more amicable arrangement on Hays's usefulness in getting recalcitrant Members of Congress to cooperate.

Hays was at his best in the field of relations between the federal, state, and local levels of government, as governors, mayors, and other local officials were very receptive to his efforts to build bridges between the levels.

Our offices were located next to those of Arthur Schlesinger, Jr., who was a key White House brain truster. He and Hays hit it off very well right away and that helped us get established in the East Wing. Since most of the key offices were in the West Wing, we got well acquainted with the East Wing administrative officers located near us who kept the organization running. That included those that assisted the First Lady and those who answered much of the mail that wasn't high-level. Among the East Wing staff were Fred Holborn, a Harvard scholar who helped the Kennedy outreach to academia, and Mary Boylan, who oversaw much of the mail operation and had been with Kennedy ever since he was a congressman. All in all, I felt very comfortable, enjoyed also meeting many Secret Service agents and White House police. It was quite easy to cross over to the West Wing, as needed, to meet with the senior staff there, including Ted Sorenson, Lee White, Ralph Dungan, Evelyn Lincoln, Larry O'Brien, and Ted Reardon.

Early in my service, I tried to honor my commitment to ACIR by getting a letter of commendation for their work from the president. Fred Dutton had been unresponsive to ACIR's several requests; and then I was also blocked by Kenny O'Donnell, who was the doorkeeper of access to JFK and seemed to resent me. But there was another door to the Oval Office that personal secretary Evelyn Lincoln controlled, and she was much more accommodating. I discovered that was the way to get all the access to Kennedy I needed. ACIR received its letter of commendation, and the leadership there was very appreciative.

Another major undertaking that I was engaged in related to improving intergovernmental relations. Mayors and governors were complaining that they were being kept out of the information loop regarding the impact of federal actions on their cities and states. Hays and I prepared a directive from the president to all federal government departments and agencies to send notification to governors and mayors when projects were being undertaken in their jurisdictions. We knew that Larry O'Brien would be upset if key Democratic congressmen didn't get a jump on press releases about these projects, so we built in a slight time lead so that Members of Congress would feel comfortable with their advance notice. With some trepidation about the political consequences of this action, I sent it to JFK through Evelyn Lincoln and he signed the directive. This certainly enhanced Hays's reputation with governors and mayors, as well as that of JFK, and the president gained significant political advantage as well.

Beginning in early 1962, I had gotten acquainted with an Arkansan in the White House Personnel Office, Dorothy Davies, who decided to have a party for White House staffers, to which she invited me. It turned out that her house wasn't big enough for the people expected to attend so she asked her brother, who worked as a senior federal government official, if she could use his house. He agreed, provided he could invite some of his colleagues. On his staff was a woman, Sara Masciocchi Friedlander, who came from Jerome, Pennsylvania, a small ex-coal-mining town near Johnstown. Her relative and friend from Atlantic City, New Jersey, Alma, was getting married the weekend of Dorothy Davies's party, and a third friend from Jerome, Sylvia Acitelli, was also in town for the wedding. And so that evening after the wedding Sara brought Sylvia to the Dorothy Davies party with the permission of her boss. It was here that I was to meet Sylvia, the woman who would become my wife. When we met, I noticed she was wearing a gold necklace that had the Hebrew letters for *chai* on it, which means "to life," but it later became clear that Sylvia did not know that meaning (the necklace had been a gift). I was impressed that when I pointed out to her all the distinguished people who were present at the party, she took it all in stride. She was more interested in dancing and, since I wasn't very good at it, taught me how to do the twist. When I found out that she worked for a private power company, I pointed out to her that I had worked for a public power company, TVA, and that didn't faze her at all either. When I asked her if she would go out on the town with me and leave the party, she said she couldn't leave the Friedlanders who had brought her. I ended up taking her and the Friedlanders to a local waffle shop before the evening ended.

By the end of April that year my relationship with my Smith College girlfriend seemed to be deteriorating, and I later learned that she had become engaged to an old boyfriend. For reasons that are hard for me to fathom now, I tried to renew our contact, but fortunately she did not respond to my overtures. It was a difficult period for me because I wasn't feeling very well, and the time on the ACIR payroll was running out. Hays was able, however, to get Bill Batt, the head of the Area Redevelopment Administration of the Department of Commerce, to get me on their payroll and detail me to the White House, which eased that pressure. I had been corresponding with Sylvia in Pennsylvania, and asked her to plan a visit to me in Washington.

At the beginning of that summer, Hays invited me to join him for a weekend at Capon Springs and Farms, a family resort in West Virginia. Lou Austen, an old friend of Hays, ran it, and the aura of the place was early New Deal. (There were many patriotic traditions, such as raising the flag at 8:00 a.m. every morning, with kids getting certificates for helping.) Just before Hays and I were to leave for West Virginia, I was stricken with a bleeding ulcer and spent the next week in the hospital. That following weekend was the very time Sylvia was to visit. Upon her arrival, she phoned me at the White House, which forwarded the call to my bedside. I apologized profusely, but still hoped she could come by to see me. The hospital then made an error, giving me the wrong blood in a transfusion and I thought I was dying. At the peak of my adverse reaction, Sylvia walked in the door. She didn't stay more than five minutes, and I thought I'd never see her again. The nurses gave me some injections that helped me recover, and days later, when I got a get well card from Sylvia, I was very grateful.

When I got out of the hospital, another challenge arose. Senator Muskie had gotten a resolution through the Senate creating the Subcommittee on Intergovernmental Relations of the Senate Government Operations Committee. Since I had gotten quite friendly with his staff, they thought I would be ideal for the job of staff director of the subcommittee. I was still weak from the ulcer experience, I worried about leaving Brooks Hays, and I wondered about my ability to do the job, in view of all the drugs I was taking to deal with my condition. But it was too great an opportunity to turn down. I went to see a special assistant to the president, Ralph Dungan, who said it would be all right for me to go on Muskie's payroll and still assist Hays at the White House, as my time permitted. That summer, I threw a big party in my apartment and the adjoining one of my friend, Dee Craven. I felt quite ill throughout the entire evening, which I see as evidence that I had bitten off more than I could chew in my work commitments.

But by the fall, I had launched the subcommittee. I worked with James Enloe Smith, who was minority counsel to Ranking Senator Karl Mundt of South Dakota. We hired Lurlene Wilbert and my neighbor Dee, who was a longtime Republican staffer. From September through January 1963, we undertook an ambitious agenda: five major hearings and reports. They included an overall examination of the status of relations among federal, state, and local governments; a review of the difficulties in disposing of Ellis Island, now that its role in processing immigrants had ended (David Brinkley of NBC News aired a television program about our hearing); an examination of the role of the federal government in metropolitan areas; and a major report on the future of intergovernmental relations. At the same time, we undertook to prepare an elaborate questionnaire to send to hundreds of state and local officials to get their opinions on some of the key intergovernmental problems confronting the country.

Since I was still assisting Hays at the White House, I had the fun of sending a letter I prepared for Muskie to the White House raising questions about the Kennedy administration's policies on intergovernmental relations. Kennedy referred the letter to me to draft an answer, which I promptly did. The letter was then signed by Kennedy and returned to Muskie. I obviously enjoyed this opportunity to correspond with myself.

Unfortunately, I had another attack of bleeding ulcers, and by the end of the year I was totally drained. Professor Carl Friedrich invited me to give a lecture on intergovernmental relations to his class at Harvard, but I kept postponing the trip, and finally sent my regrets—pretty much ending my relationship with him. I guess that with my health becoming more questionable, I confronted a midlife crisis when I was only thirty-two. Despite a great future facing me in working for Senator Muskie, I considered resigning my position.. Muskie agreed to my making a two-week trip to England and France to try to get my act together. In Paris I met with Count Rene de Chambrun, who treated me to dinner at Maxim's. The meeting was set up by his law partner, Dumond Peck Hill, a former staffer of the House Foreign Affairs Committee. Whitney Dyke of Arkansas went with me, and we were both fascinated to learn that de Chambrun was related to Lafayette. After returning to Washington, I finally announced my resignation from my position as staff director of the Senate Subcommittee on Intergovernmental Relations.

Chapter 4

A Remarkable Decade for Civil Rights

It was Brooks Hays who came to my rescue once more by arranging for me to continue to stay at the White House, with my salary again paid by the Department of Commerce and later by the Post Office Department, in an arrangement similar to others that I have earlier mentioned. Sometime that spring I had a third bleeding ulcer attack. I arranged for a full checkup at the Lahey Clinic in Boston, which revealed very little that was causing my condition. (A number of people who worked at the White House developed physical ailments because of the pressures of the work.) The Lahey report did relieve some of my anxieties, and I did not have another ulcer attack.

Hays and I threw ourselves into the drive to get a major civil rights proposal through Congress. Hays talked to Attorney General Nicholas Katzenbach and Assistant Attorney General for Civil Rights John Doar about how we could help, and they had us work with a senior staffer at the Department of Justice, Jerry Heilbron. We also worked with Roger Wilkins who would later become head of the Community Relations Service created by the 1964 Civil Rights Act. (Hays would serve as his deputy, while still based at the White House). And I developed a close relationship with Marvin Caplan, on the staff of the United Auto Workers of the AFL-CIO, who was detailed to direct the Leadership Conference on Civil Rights—a group of about one hundred entities who gathered together to promote racial justice. This conference became a major force for the legislation. Hays and I also reached out to the U.S. Commission on Civil Rights and its director, Berl Bernhard, to develop a cooperative effort in promoting the legislation. One of the great architects of the Civil Rights Act of 1964 was NAACP lobbyist Clarence Mitchell, who, after some doubts about Hays's commitment, became his greatest admirer. I watched Mitchell do wonders in lining up support for 1964 act, as he later did for the 1965 Voting Rights Act and the 1968 Fair Housing Act. I was privileged to participate in strategy meetings on all of these legislative proposals and believe that Mitchell's performance was superb in bolstering the spirits of those who were fainthearted. We were not too pleased that the draft legislation of the 1963 version of the Civil Rights Act did not have enough teeth in it, but understood that JFK was concerned about the reaction of his southern supporters, with an election coming up in 1964.

During this time, Sylvia and I were getting better acquainted. We made several trips to each other's houses, and I found myself quite smitten. I enjoyed getting to know her parents, who were well informed, and I was very impressed by their outlook and integrity. Sylvia's father, Dominic, was born Italian Catholic; but had become quite agnostic if not somewhat anarchist, and very admiring of Sacco and Vanzetti, unjustly treated by Harvard's President Lowell. Sylvia's mother, Mary, was Russian Orthodox, but didn't seem to be too caught up in her background. She was very kind and supportive of me which I appreciated. She prepared great Italian dishes that she learned from her mother-in-law who lived in the same house. Sylvia had been attending a Lutheran church and sang in its choir. I met her minister, and he was definitely an enlightened religious leader, possibly too progressive for his community. Sylvia told me she had visited a Reform Jewish temple in Johnstown to see what the services were like. By late spring we were clearly on the track to becoming engaged.

Sylvia agreed to take some instruction on converting to Judaism. Since I attended an Orthodox synagogue, she met first with Rabbi Philip Rabinowitz, who—in order to test Sylvia's commitment, tried to discourage her, as is the Jewish custom. I also asked Rabbi Dick Hirsch, the Reform rabbi I knew in Washington, to help out. He decided not to get personally involved in the conversion, but recommended Rabbi Laszlo Berkowits, who was starting a new temple in Virginia. So Sylvia was getting instruction in ritual and Hebrew language from Rabinowitz and in philosophy from Berkowits. In the summer of 1963 she moved to the Washington, D.C., area, where she found an apartment in Virginia. My former assistant at the State Department, Norma Maley, had left her latest job with a lobbying group, the American Maritime Association—to join Hays and me at the White House after Stephanie Floyd left. Sylvia was hired to replace Norma, but soon my friend Gerry Grinstein arranged for her to work for the Senate Committee on Commerce, Science & Transportation. It had been earlier known as Senate Committee on Commerce, which is still what people generally called it.

Hays and I both began thinking of moving out of the White House before the 1964 election. Rutgers University had approached Hays about accepting the Arthur Vanderbilt Distinguished Chair for Visiting Scholars. I started negotiations with Berl Bernhard about joining the Civil Rights Commission.

Meanwhile, a White House policeman, Officer Giordano (whose first name I regret I cannot remember), had become acquainted with Sylvia as she came to visit me at my office and he kept saying to me that I would be crazy not to marry her. (Several years later he met me on the street and asked how many *bambini* we had.) On one of Sylvia's visits to the White House, when President Kennedy was away, another officer, Willy Brandt (whose first name I remember only because it's the same as that of a German prime minister!), was able to show her the Oval Office and let her sit in the president's chair. In the midst of all the atmosphere of Camelot, the idyll was ended by President Kennedy's assassination of November 22, 1963.

I remember being at lunch with a prominent Arkansas attorney, Marcus Hollabaugh, at the Democratic Club, in the Sheraton Carlton Hotel (opposite the Statler Hilton), when, at about 2:00 p.m., a group of people in the dining room rushed to watch television. I asked the waitress what had happened, and she said she thought the President had been shot. I then hurried back to the White House and soon found that Kennedy was dead. Everyone was in a state of shock. People wandered about the halls not knowing what to do.

Later that day or the next, I can't remember which, Mary Ferro, a very dedicated employee of AID who had been detailed to our office, asked me what she could do to help. Mary tended to be overly solicitous in her dealings with other people, a behavior that often was not well received. She was also, however, often able to do incredibly kind deeds. I suggested that she go over to the travel office down the hall, which was in a state of chaos because phones were ringing off the wall from senior officials from countries all over the world. Apparently, Mary must have rubbed the handful of staff there the wrong way. I guess I was not surprised when she soon returned to our office (and I was as amused as one could be in such tragic circumstances) when she said "Oh, that Homer Gruenther (head of the travel office), he goes to pieces in a crisis." But Mary was also capable of doing great things in times of crisis. On her own initiative, when the White House mess was shut down and many staff were still on duty and hungry, she went down to a small pharmacy located on K Street, N.W., about 15th or 16th Street, a store that had a food counter, and persuaded the proprietor to prepare dozens of sandwiches (possibly a hundred), which Mary brought back to feed our White House colleagues. No one else on the staff was as thoughtful in that way on that horrendous evening.

After Kennedy's body arrived back at the White House, it was placed in the East Room, where staff members could pay their respects.

I remember Larry O'Brien and Kenny O'Donnell sitting on a bench in a state of grief and disbelief. I did attend some of the funeral ceremonies, which are all quite a blur to me to this day. One evening, when the president's body lay in state in the Capitol, I think I actually walked all the way to my apartment on the Hill, because driving a car to my home would have been impossible. Another time, I decided to just stay at the White House and sleep on a sofa, with an old Army coat as a blanket.

Thinking of the old Army coat brings back memories of one of the most poignant events that took place not long after President Kennedy's death. Ted Reardon, who had been with Kennedy the longest of all his staff (along with Mary Boylan), was so crushed by events that he left the White House employ immediately to work at some federal government agency. Early in January of 1964 there was an unseasonably warm day during which it also rained. Mary Boylan came into my office for help, since she needed to go to a nearby store to get medicines, and she did not have a raincoat. I showed her my old Army coat, which was all I had, and even though it was a sorry sight and came down to her ankles, she decided to wear it to rush over to the store and back, hoping that no one would see her. As fate would have it, on her way back, she bumped into Ted Reardon. Ted looked at Mary up and down, with her being so bedraggled and wet, and said, "Oh, Mary, to think it should have come to this!"

Lyndon Johnson, of course, became the president, and he gradually took over the reins of power. Although as vice president, he had been ignored by many of Kennedy's staff, he was very gracious to all and placed many people in good jobs elsewhere. Bill Moyers took on many responsibilities and was very kind to Hays and me, and I wondered if I might have an opportunity to be of greater service. Some of the old Kennedy staffers, who had ignored me in the past as not being one of the "in group," became much friendlier. Bill Moyers showing his friendship for me did not hurt. Ultimately Hays worked out the arrangement where he went to Rutgers and I went to the

Commission on Civil Rights, but we were able to keep our White House East Wing office and spent at least half of our time there. For me, that meant putting in many a hundred-hour week. I did not ask Moyers for more responsibilities because I was still recovering from my bleeding-ulcer attacks and didn't think I could cope with greater duties. Many months later, LBJ was wandering the White House and came by our office. He asked where Hays and I were. When he was told that we were both away for the day, he took immediate action. He had another staffer in mind to use the space. The next day, when I arrived for work, I found that all of Hays's and my desk items and file materials had been moved to Room One of what was then called the Old Executive Office Building (OEOB),adjacent to the White House and considered an integral part of it. LBJ's housecleaning was something of a surprise, but the new location actually worked out better for me. The new office was not only a beautiful one but a very large one, and the OEOB was right across the street from the building where the Civil Rights Commission was located.

By the beginning of 1964, I was officially "Special Assistant to the CCR Director," Berl Bernhard, but he soon resigned to go into private law practice. Deputy Director, Howard Rogerson, became the acting director. We became good friends, and he asked me to move into the deputy director's office. In our close relationship over the next nearly two years, we worked to promote the adoption and implementation of the Civil Rights Act of 1964. Bill Taylor, general counsel of the commission, in addition to focusing on concerns pertaining to the act, worked hard to get legislation enacted to guarantee voting rights for minorities. We made efforts to strengthen the work of state civil rights commissions to get closer state cooperation on all civil rights matters. The commission leaders were people of outstanding stature and commitment. As a six member commission, they included John Hannah, (the president of Michigan State University), Chairman; Father Ted Hesburgh, (the president of Notre Dame University), Vice Chairman; Erwin Griswold (the dean of Harvard Law

School), and three other distinguished people in the field of civil rights.

One of the more exciting actions we took was to hold a hearing on the denial of voting rights to blacks in Jackson, Mississippi. The police there offered no guarantees of our personal safety, and integrating the hotel we stayed at was not supported by law, since the Civil Rights Act of 1964 was not yet enacted. Among the witnesses at the hearing were white election officials, who were semi-literate, and black college professors—who had been denied the right to vote on the grounds that they were illiterate. All in all it was quite a show, and we all managed to survive it. It led, as I earlier mentioned, to the enactment of the Voting Rights Act of 1965.

They Said It Couldn't Be Done

Sylvia was completing conversion lessons with Rabbi Berkowits, and we set a marriage date of October 24, 1964. (Friends on Capitol Hill thought I was a confirmed bachelor.) My health was making steady improvement. Our friend Zel Lipsen recommended a jeweler named Zuckerman, who provided Sylvia with a beautiful engagement ring. Our caterer recommended a conservative (bordering on Orthodox) synagogue in Washington for the ceremony and the dinner-dance to follow. While Rabbi Berkowits was Reform, he was brought up Orthodox (in Hungary and was a concentration camp survivor) and would be able to conduct a ceremony along Orthodox lines. We made sure to plan for a kosher meal to please my parents (and me), and Sylvia was wonderful about agreeing to these arrangements.

It was during the time that Sylvia and I were engaged that the Civil Rights Act of 1964 was enacted by Congress. I was present when my old boss Senator Engle, who was dying of a brain tumor, was wheeled into the Senate floor so that he could vote to break the Southern filibuster. He pointed to his eye when his name was called on the roll, since he couldn't speak. I was also present when LBJ signed the legislation in the East Room of the White House on July 2nd.

There were several hundred people present for this historic event, and I nearly knocked over a dozen of them in my dash to get one of the very few pens that LBJ used to sign the act into law. It is now one of my prized possessions.

That summer Sylvia and I flew to Boston so that she could meet my parents for the first time. I told my dad that I would rent a car, but he insisted on meeting us at the airport. Since he was a typical Boston driver, it was quite a harrowing ride to my family's home, but Sylvia survived it. She got along very well with my folks, and there were no problems. Rabbi Berkowits formally completed the conversion and assured my parents that Sylvia was a worthy partner for their son. I was amused when my dad felt the need to assure the rabbi that I was worthy, too.

About a hundred guests attended our wedding in the fall. The ceremony was especially beautiful because the rabbi had an outstanding singing voice (his seminary threatened to flunk him to keep him around to conduct the school's services), and he did a marvelous job of putting us and all the invitees at ease. It was a sublime moment for me, because I had begun to wonder if that moment would ever come. We told everyone we were going to Hawaii, which wasn't true, but we spent the night at a nearby hotel with a Hawaiian motif. The next day we miraculously appeared at Cousin Ida's house for a reception for all the attendees from outside of Washington. My Aunt Flo (my godmother) had hosted a pre-nuptial party for all the relatives attending, the night before the wedding. I was delighted that three of my dearest friends from age twelve on, Joe Rosen, Dave Bloom and Ed Shore, were able to attend with their spouses.

Sylvia moved out of her apartment and crammed her possessions into my small place. We planned to move after we returned from our honeymoon. But we decided to wait until the presidential election was held a couple of weeks later before we took that trip. LBJ won a great victory over Barry Goldwater and we could relax. We planned an ecumenical honeymoon to Israel and Italy, meeting the Israeli grand rabbi in Jerusalem and the Pope in Rome. Since I still wore a White House "hat," I was able to arrange for some preferential treatment on our trip.

We arrived in Israel at the Tel Aviv airport on a Friday afternoon and made a mad dash by cab to Jerusalem to get there before the arrival of the Sabbath at sunset, when much transportation stops. Being in Jerusalem was a very emotional experience for me, since I had been inculcated with the deep significance of the city to the Jewish experience. I have always felt my strongest loyalty to the United States as a citizen, but I also recognized some strong identification with the Holy Land. What was reinforced on this visit was the fact that I was profoundly concerned with the fate of Jewish brethren in Israel, but I would not want to live there.

Immediately after checking into the Eden Hotel, we decided to walk about the city. Near the hotel was a somewhat lower-middleclass neighborhood and we noticed young men wearing black leather jackets loitering around. It was astonishing to me to hear them chatting in Hebrew, since my whole experience involved Hebrew as the sacred language in my Bible, and used only in synagogue prayer. The next morning, we decided to synagogue-hop and the desk clerk, who had come from India, helped us choose our itinerary. The first stop was an Orthodox synagogue, attended mostly by Italians, in the middle of a very elaborate building; and Sylvia was sent upstairs to sit in the women's section, where she was the only woman present. I joined about twenty men, and I found the prayers very familiar, except that they were sung with an Italian lilt. We then moved on to several other synagogues and ended at a Reform temple, where we were familiar with only about one-third of the prayers. The service was conducted almost entirely in vernacular Hebrew, accompanied by flute and cello. We sat next to two men, who surprisingly said they were Orthodox, but enjoyed participating in a musical service.

We saw many Jerusalem sites, which were awesome indeed. We went to the Mandelbaum Gate, which divided Israeli Jerusalem from

Jordanian Jerusalem. It was impossible to visit the "Wailing Wall," because it was still in Jordanian hands. We could also not visit some of the university facilities, isolated on an island-like piece of land, surrounded by Jordanian territory. The Israeli government provided us with a guide for much of our time in Jerusalem—Meir Padan of the foreign ministry. He took us to Yad Vashem (the Holocaust museum and memorial of the Nazi horror), the cemetery where the founder of modern Zionism, Theodore Herzl, and other key figures were buried, and a splendid Italian restaurant, La Gondola. We spent the rest of the two weeks traveling all of Israel, from the Sea of Galilee to Eilat (where I rode a camel) to the major cities of Tel Aviv and Haifa and a number of smaller ones, including Jaffa (where we saw the Hebrew version of *My Fair Lady*). For much of these visits, our guide was a man named Gedaliah (once again, an Israeli government official), who took us to Beersheba, a historic commercial city on the edge of the Negev desert. In a restaurant called Gingi's, I had the best kreplach since my childhood, back when my grandmother had made this stuffed-dumpling delicacy. We also had a chance to visit a kibbutz outside of Jerusalem and meet the sister of our Washington jeweler. The kibbutz was very communal, and this woman was bitter over the suppression of her individuality. The kibbutz leadership always turned down her request for funding a trip to the U.S. to visit her brother, whom she had not seen in thirty years. While it was a very tidy and well-run kibbutz, I certainly did not relate to the lifestyle. Before we left Israel, we had a visit to the Knesset arranged by my Israeli contacts, and we had several informal discussions with a number of officials about the legislative body's operations.

Next we went off to Italy, where we landed at the Rome airport at virtually the same time a TWA plane crashed on take off, killing about fifty people. This tragedy quite understandably limited the time American Embassy people could spend with us, but we still managed to have a wonderful visit, seeing all the stops a tourist would want to see. The embassy did arrange for us to go to the Vatican to attend an audience with the Pope, along with about three hundred other people. The Pope addressed the group in perhaps six languages. On the last day, we visited Sylvia's relatives in Rome. The lady of the house made a delicious meal, and we had a wonderful visit with cousins Rosa and Albo and their two teenage boys. I used my high school German to converse, since none of them knew English and we knew no Italian; but Albo knew some German (having been forced to work in a German work camp during the war). All in all, this honeymoon was a wonderful beginning to a beautiful marriage.

Starting Life in Virginia

Since I was already thinking about the possibility of a political career and running for elective office, we soon moved to a most enjoyable apartment for newlyweds in Arlington County, Virginia. Our lifestyle was enhanced by the fact when we looked out our window we saw planes landing and taking off from National Airport, a feature that friends enjoyed when they visited. Marriage itself made a significant contribution to my health as well as the ministrations of Sylvia. Unfortunately, about the same time, Howard Rogerson, who had done a great job leading the Civil Rights Commission, died of cancer.

Shortly thereafter, LBJ appointed Bill Taylor to the Civil Rights Commission directorship. Bill wanted another official of the commission, Peter Libassi, to be deputy director, so I moved back to the special assistant office. Bill and Peter had a very different idea of how to run the commission than Howard and I had had. It wasn't very long before I felt uneasy about my position. My style was always one of outreach: I believed in bipartisanship, bridge-building, compromise, and civility. Confrontational approaches were an anathema to me. As Brooks Hays had taught me, "Half of something is better than all of nothing." That belief did not mean compromising on principle, but recognizing that other honorable people might have equally strong convictions that needed to be considered. In a meeting one time, when a person was so vehement about the righteousness of his views, I remember blurting out, "I wish I was as certain of anything as you are of everything."

It was obvious that I needed to make overtures for another job outside the commission. Soon I had an offer to be director of Congressional Relations for the National Institutes of Health (NIH), an impressive organization indeed. Its director was Jim Shannon, who was already a legendary figure. Not only was this an appealing, well-paid and challenging job, it would lead me back to Capitol Hill, which was my first love. But there was one significant complication. My dear friend Del Goldberg was the congressional staff member who kept watch on NIH for a subcommittee of the House Government Operations Committee. Del was a fearless, albeit gentle, investigator of the activities of NIH. Shannon was aware of my friendship with Del, and I was concerned that he might want or expect me to mute Del's challenges. One could also have said that I might bring the Congress and the NIH closer together in an honorable fashion, but I wondered if I would put Del in a difficult position. (In fact, he wasn't concerned.)

While I was deliberating this matter, another good friend of mine in the civil rights world, Bob Cole, was leaving his position as special assistant to the administrator of the Agency for International Development (AID), then a part of the State Department, and he was prepared to recommend me for that position. The administrator, David Bell, was a most distinguished public servant, who had been director of the Bureau of the Budget. JFK sent him to AID to make it more responsive to world needs. A measure of his integrity was his reputation for not submitting inflated budgets to Congress, even though Congress would often automatically cut some government-agency budgets by 10 percent. Bell was ready to hire me after he was assured that I was not one of those Kennedy-era White House staffers who made up for incompetence by being "tough."

I made the decision to go with AID, because I thought I could make the greatest difference there. The issues of civil rights were so fundamental to making the U.S. a better country that I felt the continued pull in that direction. In hindsight, I believe the 1960s was the greatest decade of advancement in human rights in the history of our country. It was very difficult for me to give up the NIH opportunity to become involved in the great work of improving the health of Americans, but I hoped to make a contribution in that direction in the future (and I did).

Returning to the State Department after only four years was a pleasant surprise. David Bell was a delight to work for. He was demanding, but no more than he demanded of himself. To make my job more significant, he offered many "perks," including use of the eighth-floor dining room, to help me impress key people I had to deal with. Since my job involved attracting highly qualified minorities to work for AID, inviting them, or possibly their mentors, to have lunch in a room that might have the secretary of state, undersecretaries, and other high officials, was a great selling device. I do remember, however, one African-American university president, who had been an ambassador, denouncing me for asking him to help recruit African-American economists, because he did not want me to consider his race a relevant factor. I was quite shocked by his attitude, but later got the satisfaction of noting in the press that he had made a dramatic change in his so-called color blindness, to appease President Johnson.

Among the many memories I have of my experience at AID, two stand out. Bell was invited to speak at Tuskegee University in Alabama, and I went along with him. He asked me to prepare some draft remarks, which I did, utilizing the biblical reference to the "repairer of the breach" from the book of Isaiah. Bell read it and said nothing. When he made his speech later, it was entirely different. Not surprisingly, he never said a word to me about it beforehand. I remember that we flew into Columbus, Georgia, where a black driver was waiting to take us to the university. Bell got into the front seat with the driver and I sat in the back. I was a little nervous about that arrangement (which was a biracial no-no in the south at that time), and I got even more troubled when we seemed to be followed several times by rednecks in trucks that could have caused trouble, but we arrived safely.

The other special memory is related to the plan of action for affirmative hiring that I was expected to generate. I worked carefully to prepare a document similar to ones I had prepared before. When I showed it to Bell, however, he found it quite unacceptable and sent me back to the drawing boards to elaborate on the content in a more meaningful and productive way. When I then produced an exceptional document that was later copied by other federal agencies, he was satisfied. Based on what was in that plan, I named every AID division head a deputy "equal employment opportunity" (EEO) officer—responsible to me—even though they outranked me. Bell made it clear I spoke for him.

Based on the EEO document, I prepared monthly charts that were put up on the bulletin boards all over the agency. They reflected how each division was doing in minority hiring, and the numbers were broken down to reflect grades and salaries, emphasizing the need to do hiring at the higher grades. This device embarrassed some division heads and made my job helping them take corrective action easier.

Bell also agreed to start the process of making my position a career civil-service position, rather than political Schedule C, to give me some security. He did seem satisfied with my performance, and I gained stature with my peers. Because I opposed any double standard and demanded the same quality performance from minorities as anyone else, I won the respect of the agency's white officials. One frustration was that as my reputation grew at AID, other agencies raided AID to entice those I had recruited to go to their agencies at better salaries. It seemed "the harder I ran the slower the gain." One satisfaction was that I knew I was peopling the whole federal government with qualified minority employees.

While I was happy at AID, I began to wonder whether this position was one that I should continue to occupy for the long run. I was slowly becoming accepted into the inner circle, which meant that I might be asked to go abroad as an AID mission director. That possibility certainly made me feel conflicted. Meanwhile I had become friendly with Eddie Williams, the African-American head of the Department of State's overall EEO program. Through his efforts, the Ford Foundation had made a sizeable grant to Howard University to help young African-Americans pass the Foreign Service exams, which very few had been doing. Eddie and I and others essentially implemented the Ford grant. We had a board of predominantly black college presidents to assist us. The concept was to identify about forty students per year from a hundred predominantly black colleges for this program, chosen on visits to various black colleges by members of our team, including me. We would then use the summer and one year at a fine graduate school to prepare them for the exam. The entire program was designed to last four years. I urged the board to support an effort to teach these students the techniques of "cracking open" exams, techniques that had been refined by social psychologists. As a somewhat basically lazy person, over the years I had taught myself many techniques for getting the highest grades with the least effort, such as tearing through exams to get done first what I knew and then struggle with the rest as best I could. I also memorized whole passages of relevant data and plugged it where it could do the most good. I could go on and on regarding my own self-taught techniques; the main point is that I knew they worked.

The first time I described this approach to learning, the board recoiled in horror. How unacademic this appeared! They refused. Underneath it all, the college presidents must have realized that oftentimes minority students are examination-phobic no matter how much they know. But the board felt the need to uphold academic standards and refused to accept my approach. When none of the first forty made it into the Foreign Service after the first year, the board reconsidered. We were worried about the counterproductive results that might accrue if we raised expectations that could not be realized. Thus we added my approach the second year and slowly began to get more minorities into the Foreign Service. Some people had pushed to have the standards of the exam lowered, but I was firmly opposed, because such a move could give aid and comfort to those who wanted to prove that minorities were inferior. I wanted to rub the noses of the racists in the success we could achieve by playing according to society's traditional rules, and we did. I later wrote up my experience in this effort, and related efforts, in the *Public Administration Review*, the journal of my profession; and my article came in second in the award for best article of the year.

This was a blissful period in our marriage, since we had furnished a beautiful apartment, we had a very loving personal relationship (as it continues today), and my health had stabilized. Sylvia and I both had good jobs which brought satisfaction. While we expected to have children, we were not ready yet. With regard to my religious convictions, I was living on a two-track theological road. My devotion to Orthodoxy remained, and I attended Kesher Israel faithfully on Saturday mornings. Sylvia did not accompany me. On Friday night, however, we went together to the Reform temple, Rodef Shalom, listened to the beautiful services sung by Rabbi Berkowits, and got to know many of the early members. I was on the board of directors for a number of years and was chairman of the Social Action Committee. Sylvia sang in the choir and thereby learned the prayers. Kesher Israel fed my need for participation in the rituals of Judaism, and Rodef Shalom fed my need for intellectual stimulation and learning. At the same time I became active in the Washington chapter of the American Jewish Committee (AJC) and was soon chosen as its secretary. The AJC developed into a significant player in the Washington intellectual and political scene. My service to AJC lasted for about twenty years. I also volunteered at the Rodef Shalom Sunday school, teaching young members the rudiments of Hebrew.

During 1966, in addition to my AID job, I still had an office in the OEOB with Brooks Hays and still carried out some White House research on civil rights. It seems I had developed a lifestyle of wearing many hats, a pattern that lasted my whole working career. It still meant only one federal salary, at the highest level for civil servants, and also a very meager remuneration for my college teaching, which I continued for some fifty years. I loved the opportunity to share what I had learned in government with bright young students and to try to motivate them to come into the public service. In that regard, the Civil Service Commission (later the Office of Personnel Management) often invited me to speak to its classes to teach how change could be effectuated by taking initiatives that were still within the organizational mandates. I believe that I spoke on more different topics than anyone else ever did—a reflection of the many areas in which I had held significant positions. All of these lectures also contributed to my keeping my mind alert and my knowledge current, since I was compelled to do significant research to prepare my remarks—much more preparation than the students had to do.

My uncertainty about continuing at AID increased when David Bell left to become deputy head of the Ford Foundation. He was replaced by Bill Gaud, who was a splendid person and a good leader, but I felt he did not have the same priority concern about equal employment opportunity as had Bell. Our working relationship was fine, and I did not have any reservations about bringing problem areas to his attention. At the same time, Steve Shulman had become chairman of the Equal Employment Opportunity Commission (EEOC), set up under Title VII of the Civil Rights Act of 1964. He reached out to me and urged me to join the EEOC as legislative director, saying that he was building a topflight team of senior officials. We would be working to make a real difference in ensuring fair hiring treatment and fair conditions of employment for minorities and women. When I pointed out that I was anxious to maintain a civil service status, he promised to make my position a career one, even though it was now political, or Schedule C.

While I was mulling over this situation, Brooks Hays informed me that he was going to run for governor of Arkansas, since Orval Faubus, after twelve years in office, had decided not to run for re-election. Hays still wanted to fulfill his lifetime dream of being governor, dashed in 1928 and 1930, when the power structure had stolen the elections from him. Here he was, running again four decades later. He met with Orval Faubus, who gave him every reason to believe that he would give Hays his support to at least partially offset the way he had treated him in the 1958 congressional election. Among those rallying around Hays was Bruce Lindsey, who later cited Hays as the person who gave him his commitment to public service. In the 1990s, Lindsey would become special counsel and alter ego to his old friend, President Bill Clinton.

Just before the filing date closed, Frank Holt, who had been attorney general in Faubus's administration, announced his candidacy for governor. Although he was somewhat of a moderate, it was clear that Holt was Faubus's candidate, and the Establishment in Arkansas that had always opposed Hays, and was generally racist, lined up behind Holt. One of the people on that team was young Bill Clinton. While Clinton has always said that he opposed what Faubus had done at Central High, I find it interesting that as a young man he supported the Faubus candidate for governor.

The biographers of Clinton that report that he was always an opponent of racism may have seemed to overlook his actions which might be considered opportunist to further his budding political career. If he tries to argue that he didn't think Hays was a strong enough candidate, isn't it interesting that his friend Lindsey didn't think so, as well as the great liberal political moviemaker Charlie Guggenheim who came to Arkansas to help Hays by filming him in action during the campaign. The David Maraniss book on Clinton, *First in His Class*, gives him the benefit of the doubt, but others of the liberal persuasion do not. When I wrote to Maraniss asking him to meet with me to discuss this history, he managed to avoid such a meeting even though he wrote me back saying he would welcome such an exchange.

A fanatical racist, Jim Johnson, an elected justice of the Arkansas Supreme Court, also entered the Democratic primary. Winthrop Rockefeller, a transplanted scion of the ultrawealthy New York family, had announced on the Republican ticket. While Rockefeller was spending a lot of money to run what was a very high-tech race for that time, no one thought he had much chance. He was presumed to be unsophisticated as a candidate, despite his election team's use of high-tech methods. It looked like this race would be one of the more interesting races in the history of Arkansas.

Friends of Brooks Hays in Washington opened an office to raise money to help Hays compete on an even basis. I wanted to help, but the restrictions of the Hatch Act for Federal Employees limited my opportunities. I would sometimes go by the Hays office after work to call the many friends I knew Hays had in Washington to ask for contributions. While many responded with significant contributions, making these requests was a learning experience for me. Some of Hays's closest "friends" begged off for a variety of reasons. I think we still managed to raise at least $60,000, which was a considerable sum at that time. Unfortunately Hays came in third in the primary, not far behind Holt. In the run-off Jim Johnson beat Holt, showing that extreme racism was still a strong force in much of Arkansas. And then, because every decent person in the state—Democrat or Republican—voted Republican that November, Winthrop Rockefeller was elected governor of Arkansas. (He was the first Republican governor of Arkansas either since Reconstruction or forever, I'm not sure which.) I've got to believe that if Faubus hadn't betrayed Hays one more time, Hays would have achieved his lifetime goal of being governor. He would have been a much better bet to beat Jim Johnson in the primary, one on one, if Holt had not been involved and Hays had at least lukewarm Faubus support. Being the Democratic nominee, he certainly would have defeated Rockefeller, who won only because a majority of the Arkansas voters would have been terrified to have Johnson as Governor. The experience of this election ended Hays' political involvement in Arkansas.

When Hays returned to Washington, he and I consulted about the future. He seemed supportive of a move by me to EEOC. As I recall, he had been offered yet another visiting distinguished professorship. We still had the office in the OEOB; but we were getting disillusioned about the chance for success in the War on Poverty, since LBJ had become obsessed with the Vietnam War. LBJ demanded 100-percent loyalty on this issue of those who worked for him, which I suppose he was entitled to. Hays and I hoped that he would work harder to extricate the U.S. from the quagmire. Very reluctantly, Hays and I resigned from our part-time positions. LBJ was very gracious, but he was determined to see the war through. When I left the White House, I was allowed to keep my pass, which I have still kept as a memento.

Since I was in the mood to make changes, I decided to also resign from AID, which ended up being a mistake. I accepted the offer to move to the EEOC. The ambiance was excellent, and I inherited a fine assistant, Cathy Carroll. The agency seemed to be in some disarray, but I thought it would be sorted out soon by the Shulman team. That never proved to be the case, and I gradually took on all the authority I needed to do my job alone, building a wall around my operation to avoid being crippled. I was in excellent physical condition because I walked about five or six miles a day around Capitol Hill, touching all the relevant bases I needed to do my job. My first assignment was to try to get legislation adopted that would enable EEOC to take cases to court itself, rather than relying on the Department of Justice. There were numerous other issues that involved several committees of Congress. In my outreach, I also got to know key players on the judiciary committees and the health and human services committees of both the House and the Senate, such as Gene Mittelman and Roy Millenson on the staff of Senator Javits's committee. And I was worried that the amount that would be appropriated for the agency would be much too small to deal with its workload. The statute called for the agency to act in ninety days, and it was already thousands of cases behind. I gained some comfort from knowing Luther Holcomb, a Baptist minister from Texas, who was a commissioner (and a friend of Hays) and getting to know Commissioners Bill Brown and Sam Jackson.

One of the more adventuresome efforts I undertook involved the agency's appropriation. The House Appropriations Committee had voted out a $2 million appropriation, which I thought was an insult. Traditionally, the agency budget office would deal with this matter, not legislative affairs, but I doubted that the budget office would act. In this era, the House did not have roll-call votes on the amendments to the appropriations bill, but simply had Members walk down the center aisle to indicate yeas and nays. The party whips were supposed to ensure that an adequate number of Members were on the floor at the time of the amendment votes, but often these votes would be quite small, something like 90 to 70, even though the House had 435 members. So I organized my own informal whip system, in which our group called all of the friends of EEOC to be on the floor for the key equal employment vote. Civil rights–oriented Members had organized and had chosen one Member to offer the substitute provision to raise the money to about $45 million. The substitute motion passed handily. I had helped the civil rights community beat the House Appropriations Committee, which was a rare event indeed. If I had been discovered being involved in this effort, I probably would have been fired; but I couldn't abide the Congress starving the EEOC, making a mockery of its commitment to end job discrimination.

I had only been with EEOC a few months when Shulman suddenly resigned to enter private law practice. I felt left in the lurch, especially since my civil service status had not yet been finalized. Clifford Alexander had worked for LBJ in the White House and was named EEOC chairman. He had quite a different approach to EEOC matters than I had, and we never really developed good chemistry. The rest of the commissioners assumed that I felt comfortable in my position, but to me, it was a Bill Taylor situation all over again. I watched my actions very carefully so that I did not leave myself open to criticism. I had managed to get tickets to see *Fiddler On The Roof* on Broadway—tickets which were extremely hard to get at that time—but the timing appeared to be in possible conflict with some EEOC-relevant congressional action. Fearing retribution if I left town, I turned in the tickets. They would have been wonderful seats. Sylvia and I did go at a quieter time, but could get only one fairly good seat for her and standing room for me,—pretty much ruining the experience. Nothing happened in the Congress anyway.

In 1964, an archconservative, Congressman Howard Smith of Virginia, offered an amendment to add the word "sex" to the "race, creed, and national origin" language that was in the Civil Rights bill. He thought that would help defeat the bill. His joke ultimately backfired when a handful of congresswomen, led by Martha Griffiths of Michigan, succeeded in retaining the word "sex" and getting the bill passed. At the EEOC, we were receiving a great many complaints of job discrimination from women, about one-third of the total, much to our surprise. The work of Congresswoman Martha Griffiths in getting Congressman Smith's joke of an amendment included the Civil Rights Act was really paying off. It was an incredible eye-opener for me. While I thought of myself as pretty liberal on women's rights, I discovered that I wasn't too far from the image of a MCP (male chauvinist pig) that dominated the American scene. The EEOC experience changed me forever. I became an unabashed supporter of full equal rights for women. It became a high priority for me to fight for those rights, as I had already done for African-Americans. When the *Roe v. Wade* Supreme Court decision granting women the freedom of choice in having children was handed down a few years later, I was a full supporter. At the same time, I still tried to respect the view of others who felt differently, especially some very close Catholic friends of mine.

Becoming a Father and a Homeowner

Ever since I had moved into college housing in 1948, I had always lived in rented accommodations. But now, almost twenty years later, Sylvia and I agreed the time had come to buy a house. This was influenced, of course, by our decision to start having children, leading to Sylvia soon becoming pregnant. We did what many others usually do; we looked at numerous houses with the aid of real estate agents and almost committed several times, only to back off at the last minute. We finally did buy one in a new section of Fairfax County, Virginia, called Collingwood Springs—a nice, brick, four-bedroom, split-foyer, corner house abutting what was then the Fort Hunt High School football field. As I recall, the price was about $32,000, which was a significant sum at that time. Before we committed, we rang the doorbells of our two neighbors-to-be. They were both Army colonels, married, with small children, who seemed to be extremely nice families—the Dierksmeiers and the Schuesslers—and that was reassuring. A house purchase was an awesome step for me, this product of the 1930s Depression, to be taking.

My sense of assurance was shaken when we were in the process of moving. In the days before the moving van arrived, we made several trips from the apartment to the new house to bring special valuables. On one of those trips Sylvia was ahead of me in her car and stopped at a local bank (in the Hollin Hall Shopping Center) to set up a new account. She was about eight months pregnant. While she was dealing with an account manager, that person said quietly that she should lie down on the floor. That seemed like a strange request until Sylvia realized the bank had grown quiet and it was being held up. After the holdup, everyone was very solicitous of Sylvia, fearing that she might have a premature delivery. We later teased our son that he might become a bank robber because of the prenatal influence. One consequence of this event was that the bank didn't handle the account properly, and the checks written by Sylvia bounced. The bank quickly wrote letters of apology to the recipients. To compound the process, on another such trip from apartment to house, Sylvia was followed by a car driven by a creepy man who came right up to her in the driveway of the house. She told him to get lost in the toughest way she could, and he complied, just before I arrived to join her. What a way to move into a new neighborhood!

After a very long labor for Sylvia, our son was born at Sibley Hospital in Washington, on January 27, 1967. We named him Dean Franklin, with the Franklin for President Franklin Roosevelt, whose birthday was January 30. He was a wonderful blessing, and we brought him home to our new house, which we had just moved into. We were about to have the awesome experiences of raising a son (the first of two) and maintaining a house, about both of which I knew nothing.

We had two special ceremonies at this house. Rabbi Berkowits nailed a *mezuzah* to our front doorpost, a decorative tube with verses from the Torah inside, to mark this as a Jewish home. And with a significant gathering of loved ones, including my parents, Sylvia's mother, and the Hayses, we had the circumcision ceremony or *bris,* which is traditionally held on a boy's eighth day of life. A mohel—a person trained in ritual circumcision—performed the surgery, while Brooks Hays held the baby in the role of godfather. It was a great moment in the history of religious ecumenicity to have a president of the Southern Baptist Convention act in this capacity.

I had explained to Hays that I would have named the child for him, except for the Jewish tradition of naming children after the departed. Hays replied, "I would have loved to have that lad carry my name, but I am not prepared to make the supreme sacrifice." He was courageous in his godfatherly role, while Sylvia, her mother, and my mother fled to the nearest bedroom. Jerry Heilbron, the Arkansas lawyer who had worked with us on the 1964 Civil Rights Act, laughingly threatened to file suit on behalf of Dean because we performed the surgery without his permission.

Still on the White House Watch

As part of my weekly work schedule, , I attended a meeting in the Fish Room of the White House every Monday with representatives from the offices of congressional relations for each of the major government agencies. We were briefed by LBJ's political and legal advisor, Barefoot Sanders, who was the head of the White House Office of Congressional Relations, and often by LBJ himself. If LBJ was there, he usually pled with us to stick with him on the Vietnam War, even as national opposition grew. We then turned to the topic of the week, which was always a proposal LBJ wanted passed by Congress. Each of us was responsible for fifteen members of Congress on a regular basis, and we were to meet with them that week to gain their support. It was assumed we could get enough information on this topic to answer any questions, a very dubious assumption indeed. Most of my assigned Members had become friends, since they were generally on committees I dealt with in my regular work. I found, however, that they often resented my attempting to win their support on issues that were not in my domain, no matter how well informed I was. Overall, I think LBJ's system was often counterproductive. The LBJ magic of 1964–65 was fast wearing thin.

My sense of unease working at the EEOC was reinforced as the unrest over the Vietnam War grew. LBJ was obviously completely committed to seeing the war through and would brook no challenge. Even though I was no longer at the White House, I was still part of the LBJ team. I started to consider other career options that might be available to me. I was interviewed by representatives of management consultant companies, but I wasn't too happy with the requirement of much travel. None of my congressional friends had any openings, except John Brademas of Indiana, who was moving up the House leadership ladder, but could only offer a minor position. I probably should have accepted it, since I would surely have risen rapidly, but I wasn't willing to gamble. Hays was now a professor at Rutgers, and the head of the Urban Affairs Department there offered me a part-time position that paid almost as much as my salary. It would have been a three-way arrangement: doing some teaching and consulting in Washington, going to Rutgers twice a week to lecture, and maintaining an office back at the Advisory Commission on Intergovernmental Relations, which ACIR had graciously offered me as a place to work on completing my Ph.D. (my thesis was to be on a study that would have been valuable to that commission). All the appropriate parties were agreeable, but I could not bring myself to take this step.

In early 1968, I became familiar with the National Conference on Citizenship (NCC). Congress had chartered this organization in 1946 to assist in the development of procedures for making citizenship more effective and citizens more enlightened and conscientious. It had a distinguished board of directors, chaired by Justice Tom Clark. There were a number of outstanding young people involved in the organization, including Bob Sailor, with whom I became quite close. The director was a retired judge, Judge Hyatt (I don't recall his first name), a delightful public servant, who ran the operation from offices in nearby Rockville, Maryland. Brooks Hays was also associated with NCC, and it looked like the organization held some promise for me, even though it had seen better days and its finances were limited. But the country was concerned about youth unrest, and legislation was being considered to help reduce crime, which might include dealing with some of the root causes of antisocial behavior. For the rest of 1968, I worked with Hyatt and Sailor and others to fashion a major grant dealing with improving the situation on college campuses, a contribution that might make the NCC a viable organization. I did this pro bono.

At the same time, I worried about the chance that Richard Nixon might be elected president. Again, because of the Hatch Act, I couldn't get directly involved in politics. Through friends, however, on my own time, I provided some major research on significant issues that could be made available to people competing for the Democratic nomination for president. LBJ shocked us all by withdrawing from consideration early in 1968, and the rest of the time was spent with the party choosing among Hubert Humphrey, Eugene McCarthy, and Bobby Kennedy, who was tragically assassinated in the midst of this struggle. The assassination of Martin Luther King was another horrible development during this period. I remained heavily involved in my work at the EEOC, of course, but Congress resisted any legislation to strengthen the commission. It seemed that the nation was not too concerned about solving the job discrimination problems with any speed, if at all.

After Richard Nixon was elected, I was still at the EEOC, but worried about the future. Clifford Alexander was replaced as chairman by Bill Brown, with whom I had a much more cordial relationship. Nixon did not put me on his "enemies list" because of his admiration for Brooks Hays. But Shulman had left EEOC before my civil service status could be ratified, so my job was still classified as political, and I was very vulnerable. To make matters even more complicated, as we moved into 1969, the Republican leadership asked me to help clear the credentials of a number of potential appointees to the Nixon Administration. I carried out that assignment faithfully, calling many Republican leaders around the nation to learn their opinions of the candidates. Getting more deeply involved in Republican matters, I accompanied Brown to White House strategy sessions on civil rights, conducted by Deputy Attorney General Richard Kleindienst.

In 1968, Congress passed the Law Enforcement Assistance Act (LEAA), to get tougher on crime. Ramsey Clark was slated to be attorney general, and Justice Tom Clark did not want his son denied the job because of conflict-of-interest considerations, so he resigned from the Supreme Court. He was then available to give greater attention both to the NCC and to the operation of a new judicial agency, whose creation he had championed. It was called the Federal Judicial Center (FJC), an education and research center for and about the federal courts. Clark had always been very interested in the administration of justice, and he was happy to be named the first director of FJC.

When Congress realized that Ramsey Clark would be the attorney general, those who distrusted him managed to have the LEAA legislation provide that a troika, three people of senior status, approve of each of the LEAA's grants. The first director of the LEAA was Pat Murphy, a distinguished police chief who had been chief in New York City and Washington, among other places. He was still in charge by the middle of 1969, when I felt I was ready to submit my proposal to help calm the national troubled waters. I was considering resigning from the EEOC in order to move over to the NCC. I did so after the grant to NCC by LEAA was made in the fall. Being in a relatively newly-purchased house, having a new baby and a wife who had resigned from her job to raise our children, I would be taking a big chance.

At the same, Don Tacheron, who was head of the Congressional Research Service (CRS) at the Library of Congress, came to see me and said that CRS had a vacancy for the head of its Government Division. That division had been headed by Jim Carroll, who was returning to a job in academia. After some negotiation, he offered me the job. In hindsight, I should have grabbed it immediately. Instead I asked that my starting date be deferred until January. I felt deeply committed to seeing through the start of the LEAA grant, to enable Brooks Hays and an old friend who had joined us, Dean Determan, carry out the mission we had established.

We undertook a massive first conference at the Mayflower Hotel in Washington. Our grand design was to prepare an agenda involving a wide range of elements in American society to find middle ground. These elements ranged from the Daughters of the American

Revolution, whose members can trace their descent back to the start of the country, to the Blackstone Rangers, a Chicago street gang. While we had a lively and successful exchange between the disparate groups, the event had some serious shortcomings. Although the hotel staff was instructed not to allow participants to make long distance calls from their rooms, they were too intimidated to comply. The ultimate bill was beyond our budget by several thousand dollars, which the hotel and our organization ultimately split. Many personal confrontations took place, but not enough to totally disrupt the proceedings. The end result of the conference was the generation of evidence that many factions could be drawn together, even under the most difficult of circumstances. It was not my finest hour, however, since I worried so much about possible disruptions that I seriously delayed the start of the major finale dinner. Brooks Hays was able to take charge and save the day.

One great event and three disasters hit me shortly after the conference. The great event was the birth of our second son Neil Winston on December 7, 1969. The choice of his middle name was to honor Winston Churchill, born on a nearby date, November 30. Maybe December 7 was an omen, being the twenty-eighth anniversary of the Japanese attack on Pearl Harbor. I had already resigned from the EEOC and was looking forward to starting at the CRS. I was proud of the fact that the Republican chairman of EEOC and the past Democratic chairman both came to my farewell party, even though they were feuding with each other. But then Don Tacheron came to tell me that CRS had withdrawn the offer to hire me because they preferred an old friend of mine from ACIR, Norm Beckman. I was devastated. The opportunity to work for the Library of Congress was lost and never to be regained.

In the meantime, I had let a dear friend talk me into investing some $20,000 (a huge sum to me at that time), which involved borrowing about $7,000 on my insurance, for what I was told was a "sure thing" in Fort Myers, Florida. The sure thing turned out to be a total dud, and I was now out all that money. My friend's partners paid me back a small part of the investment; I sued another partner for another part of the investment; and declaring the loss on my income tax helped. Over the next two years, I did recoup about $14,000 of the $20,000; nonetheless, it was a grave lesson in stupid investments that I learned at the worst possible time in my life.

The final blow was the word that the Department of Justice had withdrawn the grant to the NCC. Tom Clark and Brooks Hays were furious. The LEAA troika of Henry Ruth, Pete Velde (with whom I later became quite friendly), and Charles Rogovin, pulled the rug out from under us on the guise that they were not interested in preventing disorder on college campuses, but simply in fighting crime. This LEAA action came at just about the same time as the horrendous murders by National Guardsmen at Kent State University. I convinced Clark and Hays not to challenge the LEAA action with calls to the White House, because I knew Nixon planned to campaign for law and order in 1970 against disorderly university students and attempt to capture control of the House and Senate in that nonpresidential election year. Instead, I negotiated a scaled-down amount from LEAA to help us complete the work we had already planned. In a further setback, the LEAA welshed even on this compromise and paid not a penny more.

Chapter 5

From Career Crisis to the Challenge of New Worlds

So there I was in the beginning of the 1970s with a wife staying home with two small children, no real job, most of my rainy-day fund squandered in a stupid investment, and a house purchased just three years earlier. And the Republicans were in power, making government job possibilities for me remote. The only income I could rely on was the low-paying, part-time professional jobs I had at GW and the American University. But I had my health, having overcome the impact of three bleeding-ulcer episodes a few years earlier, and a very optimistic attitude.

Then all the good people I had been associated with came to my rescue. Brooks Hays and his great friend and colleague, retired Congressman Walter Judd, created the United States Association of Former Members of Congress (USAFMC), and I became its first Executive Director, with a small measure of monetary compensation. Hays put me in touch with Congressman Porter Hardy of Norfolk, Virginia, who was heading up a group creating a new institution, the Eastern Virginia Medical School. I was hired as a consultant to help him make fund-raising contacts. Hays also put me in touch with James Mitchell, head of the educational division of the prestigious think tank, The Brookings Institution. This connection ultimately led to a major career shift for me in 1975.

My older brother Milton had college roommates named Danny Yankelovich and Arthur White, who became very successful on Madison Avenue. They had clients among the super-rich. The Rockefeller Brothers Fund (RBF) had an interest in dealing with college unrest because of the Vietnam War, and Arthur White brought that interest to my attention. My pursuit of this connection produced a grant from RBF to NCC that helped keep us functioning. Our proposal involved reaching out to fifty major colleges around the country. We had the college presidents nominate two of their best student leaders to attend our seminar on how to get involved in winning elections. The theory was that students would be less confrontational if they felt they could change society from within. The only obligation they had was to go back to their colleges and tell others what they learned. We held sessions conducted by leading figures in Washington on overall structuring of campaigns, fundraising, TV advertising and other promotional methods, speech preparation, door-to-door campaigning, proper use of signage and mailings, and getting out the vote on election day. These sessions were a great hit indeed. The one hundred participants were a wonderful cross section of the youth of America and they responded to the classes beautifully.

My dear former roommate, Mark Cannon, was now the administrative assistant to Chief Justice Warren Burger, and arranged a consultancy for me with the Supreme Court (I worked principally on the issue of minority hiring) and one with the Federal Judicial Center, as well. An old friend in the civil rights world, Bob Cole, enabled me to meet Dr. Jack Durell, the director of the Washington Psychiatric Institute, and he hired me as a consultant on matters of equal employment opportunity. A former student of mine, John Parker, whom I had taught when he was a Marine captain at Quantico Marine Base, and who went on to have a very distinguished career as a senior public servant and university professor, provided entree to the Sperry Rand Corporation (the IBM or Microsoft of that era, now called Unisys); and they hired me to be a part of their Washington representation team. They were anxious to promote innovative uses of technology with the federal government and believed that my friendships in the legislative, executive, and judicial branches would be of value in that regard. (I quickly called my dad to tell him that I was now an engineer at last, since Sperry Rand identified me in their personnel listings as a "urban science engineer.") I was also hired as consultant on transportation planning at the Advisory Commission on Intergovernmental Relations, and also as a consultant on economy and efficiency in local government for the District of Columbia Commission on Home Rule, chaired by Congressman Ancher Nelsen of Minnesota. Once I hit my stride, other assignments came, enabling me to maintain a most satisfactory annual income from 1969 to 1975.

Another fascinating assignment I obtained was with the U.S. Office of Education, working on a program (Title III, Higher Education Act) to determine which minority universities and colleges would be the best for the federal government to assist to enable them to remain viable institutions. On a different note, I had a weekly radio program on the international Voice of America explaining how the U.S. government works in answer to questions written to "the Voice" by people all over the world. The Voice commended me especially for providing an impressive response to a letter written by a citizen of the Soviet Union challenging the integrity of our Founding Fathers.

Later I got a grant from the Smith Richardson Foundation to tape the oral histories of former North Carolina Members of Congress. They were all quite interesting, but two were especially outstanding. One was my interview with the great Senator Frank Graham, who had championed human rights and lost his seat to a racist demagogue, in a manner similar to the experience of Brooks Hays. He was also the United Nations mediator in the dispute over Kashmir and tried mightily, if not successfully, to get India and Pakistan to agree. The other particularly memorable meeting was with Congressman Carl Durham, who had twice been chairman of the Joint Committee on Atomic Energy and led the successful fight for civilian oversight of atomic-energy usage.

While there are those that might think that my recitation of these assignments is what we called in Arkansas "over-eggin' your puddin'" one would have to understand how distraught I originally was.

Exploring Virginia Politics

Still considering some involvement in politics, I was pleased that Sylvia joined the Mount Vernon Democratic Committee, since that enabled me to get acquainted with many local Democrats. It was a wonderful committee and Sylvia enjoyed the activities. Life for us was pleasant, because my management-consultant lifestyle alternated between feverish activity and times of quiet. I thus was able to spend more time at home watching the boys grow up. Our finances improved enough to enable us to buy two new cars, as well as make a vacation trip to Puerto Rico. Sylvia's mother, Mary Acitelli, was kind enough to come to our home from Pennsylvania to look after Dean and Neil. It was a bit of a trying experience for her, since Neil put his head through the front storm door, the garbage disposal got jammed, and the storage room shelving collapsed, raining all the materials on the floor. I felt blessed to have such an understanding mother-in-law. The Puerto Rico experience was arranged through the office of the Puerto Rican delegate in the Capitol. He made it possible for us to attend a reception at the historic Governor's Palace, also known as La Fortaleza. All in all, the trip was a wonderful respite.

For closer-to-home relaxation, we visited Annapolis, Maryland, frequently, giving thought to buying a condo with a slip for a sailboat. (That might have guaranteed frequent visits from our sons when they grew up!). We enjoyed eating at a famous restaurant, Chick and Ruth's, where I could get a good corned beef sandwich. During one of our meals, a young reporter Mike Isikoff (now with *Newsweek* magazine) came in and asked what we thought of Governor Marvin Mandel, who was having a well-publicized legal problem. We were sitting in the "Governor's Booth" (created just for Mandel, when he came in for a meal, but one we were allowed to use in his absence). We praised Mandel for being so accessible to the citizenry, unlike Virginia's governor. That interview made the front page of the newspaper the next day.

During this same five-year period, when I was operating what might be called my own management-consultant organization, I really learned who my friends were. Certain people who had sucked up to me when I was in the White House were difficult to reach. Others, who had behaved only in an appropriate professional manner during that same time, became fast friends. In 1970, as part of my long-range plan, I gave serious consideration to running for Congress, since the incumbent congressman, Republican Bill Scott, was not an impressive person. When some professional group reported that he was the least competent Member of Congress, he foolishly held a press conference to deny it! The heir apparent to the Democratic nomination was Virginia State Delegate Dorothy McDiarmid, a very fine person, but someone I believed could be beaten in a Democratic primary. Sylvia and I had made some political friends who would support me, and I had found an outstanding campaign manager. While I had not yet raised much money, I believed I could succeed in reaching out to many prominent national Democrats. Brooks Hays, of course, was very supportive.

The night before we were to launch our all-out effort, my campaign manager slept at our house, so we could get started very early the next morning. Two things happened that derailed my start. First, my sister-in-law Marnie called to say my oldest brother, who worked for the Social Security Administration and lived in nearby Maryland, had come down with life-threatening pancreatitis. To compound the situation, it rained furiously that night, and since we forgot to clear leaves from the important drain alongside the house, the lower level of the house flooded somewhat—something that never happened before or ever again. I turned to my campaign manager and said the Almighty was telling me that this was not the right time for me to act. He accepted my judgment. Soon thereafter, the house righted itself and my brother recovered. Darrell Stearns, a local government official, took over my campaign team and won the nomination, but was badly beaten by Scott.

It was a couple of years after this, in 1972, that Brooks Hays ran for Congress in North Carolina. I am proud to say that I visited North Carolina during that time to help his campaign. I am also delighted that as a Jew, I served as a consultant to Hays's ecumenical institute, a part of a Southern Baptist University, Wake Forest.

In the meantime, I had stepped up my activities at Temple Rodef Shalom. As a member of the board and chairman of the Social Action Committee, I worked to get the temple involved in many regional activities that promoted civil rights and civil liberties. Rabbi Berkowits was very supportive and in return I was very supportive of him. We were in the process of building a new $500,000 facility, considered a lot of money at that time, and our temple membership was somewhat uneasy and in need of reassurance.

By 1972, participation in the Former Members of Congress continued to grow and had reached about eight hundred members. Dean Determan and I had pushed successfully for the creation of Alumni Day—a day on the House floor each spring, when current members (along with some senators) would extend a welcome to their old colleagues. It was the only time that non-Members of Congress were allowed to address their former colleagues on the House floor.

Senate Majority Leader Mike Mansfield of Montana was unfortunately never very supportive of this effort. I remember his treating a former senator from California, Thomas Kuchel, rather rudely when a delegation from USAFMC (including me) went to see Mansfield, He kept us waiting for quite a long time and gave no sign of having any interest in our agenda. It appeared that he feared

USAFMC would become a lobby group, which it never did, but rather worked to help build public support for the institution of the Congress. Other countries were so impressed by our organization that they created similar legislative alumni bodies in their countries, but Mansfield remained unimpressed.

One person who was impressed, surprisingly, was President Nixon. Since he was eligible to become a member of USAFMC, we approached him in that regard and he responded warmly. He invited the whole group to the White House, where a reception was held in the East Room. Sylvia was not too eager to go, since she did not like Nixon, but she reluctantly came at my request, and reluctantly shook Nixon's hand. I was pleased to conduct the ceremony where the President was sworn in by a member of the FMC. He handed me a check for his dues and told me to be sure to cash it. I assured him I would, after making a copy, of course, which showed it was drawn on the Key Biscayne, Florida, bank of his friend Bebe Rebozo, and had his wife Pat's name on it also, showing them to be pretty regular people in this circle.

In my service to Sperry Rand, I made numerous trips to Florida with my colleague Tom Garrigan, especially to Tampa, but also to many other locations. We devised a detailed plan for Governor Reuben Askew to provide for rational land use in the state, but, because of the legislature's reluctance to act, we barely dented the runaway construction of housing. A wonderful corollary trip took place for my family one year when, on the very June day school concluded, Sylvia, the boys, and I flew to Tampa. We stayed in a terrific motel—which we later found out was owned by the Mafia. I had several days of work to carry out, but each day Sylvia drove the boys over to Disney World where they had a grand time. As soon as I finished my work on Friday, I joined them, and we had the best weekend as a family that I can remember. It was such a magic moment that I turned down opportunities to return, because I did not want to dilute the memory.

Garrigan and I made some other significant contributions to Sperry Rand. One was a survey for the National Science Foundation made prior to the time of the OPEC energy crisis, We explored the potential for using geothermal energy to reduce dependence on oil, along with a review of solar, shale, clean coal, and numerous other options, to reduce dependence on oil, and evaluated the economic feasibilities; but the country, even today, still doesn't want to face up to the impending dangers of not having enough alternative-energy sources to function. Another report we made was on metropolitan-transportation planning for the Advisory Commission on Intergovernmental Relations, where we explored alternative trans-portation options for a balanced national system.

When Sperry Rand decided not to continue its sponsorship of my efforts, I created a separate entity called the Urban Science Cen-ter. John Parker was the head of an organization called Public Technology, Inc. (PTI), which was funded by many state and local organizations. He suggested that we team up on an intergovernmen-tal relations project. We put together several reports on the possibility of local governments benefiting from recent developments in science and technology, such as new types of hoses developed by NASA that could be used by local fire departments.

One of my major solo undertakings was assisting the Washing-ton Psychiatric Institute prepare its EEO (equal employment opportunity) plan of action. Dr. Jack Durell, the institute director, seemed genuinely interested in developing a fully integrated staff to meet some major interracial issues the institute was confronting. He was, of course, anxious to meet, in a full and complete way, what-ever legal obligations were required, so that he could not only justify receiving black patients, but also be fully able to treat them success-fully. However, he had the problem of convincing his colleagues that what he was doing made medical sense. I remember meeting with about thirty-five psychiatrists, all white, who constituted the gov-erning body of the institute, to explain what I intended to do. I recognized that developing an EEO program for such a group required having some fundamental understanding of the discipline, so I had given myself a crash course in psychiatry by reading a number of relevant books by leading psychiatrists, including Freud and Adler. Addressing such a group was a somewhat unnerving experience, but I believe I made a good impression on most of them. The rest went along anyway, albeit reluctantly, because some kind of EEO program was required by federal law, for the institute to receive minority patients.

One interesting discovery I made was that all the nurses were white, but a category called "psychiatric aides" had been created, and all the aides were black. These men were mostly returnees from the Vietnam War, where they had been medics. There were clashes between the two groups occasionally, because of their different status. But there also were some biracial romances, as well. All in all, having a biracial staff did cause some complications in the treatment of the patients. In another consideration, I pushed hard for the employment of at least one black psychiatrist, since many of the black patients had doubts that a white psychiatrist could really understand their problems. I was originally told there were practically no black psychiatrists, but then I discovered an organization of about five hundred of them. I met a black psychiatrist, named Prudhomme, as I recall, and he and I had some very helpful conversations. While I made some significant changes in how the institute operated, I was never successful in getting a black psychiatrist hired.

In October 1973, Sylvia and I thought it would be fun to build a *sukkah* for *Sukkot*, which is a festival to celebrate the harvest and commemorate the temporary shelters used by the Jews during their wandering in the wilderness. While we may not have met all the technical requirements, we did set up such an edifice. We then invited a number of friends to a party to celebrate the holiday. A day or two before the event, however, Sylvia's dad died. He had owned and operated a garage, which exposed him to many fumes, and he also smoked. Throat cancer took its toll. I was very fond of him, since he was a man of great self-taught learnedness and wisdom. He had been a recreational pilot for many years and encouraged Sylvia to take flying lessons and make her first solo. He loved to gain the solace of soaring in the sky doing this for more than forty years. We naturally canceled the party and mourned his loss. Every year, our temple honors Dominic Acitelli on the anniversary of his death.

Some New Opportunities

In the early fall of 1974, friends recommended me as a consultant to Congressman John Conyers of Michigan, a man I already knew because he was one the fifteen Members of Congress I was responsible for in Lyndon Johnson's outreach program. I thought this could be a splendid opportunity to utilize my wide range of contacts to help Conyers become an even more major player, but he had different ideas. He wanted me to review his office operations and make recommendations for improvement. While I did find many ways that he could use his staff more efficiently, in the process I found that we did not establish the kind of chemistry that I had usually achieved with other clients. I assume that after I filed my report, it ended up in the waste paper basket.

During this same period, Brooks Hays arranged for me to meet Jim Mitchell, who headed the educational division of The Brookings Institution and was a fellow member with Hays of the George Washington University board. Both of them were quite concerned about the state of civility and ethics in governmental affairs, and Hays, Mitchell, and I began to amass a considerable amount of materials in anticipation of setting up a Brookings Center on Public Ethics, which I would direct. By the time I firmly established a relationship with Brookings, Jim Mitchell had retired, and his successor Walter Held was much more interested in my background in congressional and judicial matters, rather than in pursuing the ethics issues.

In November 1974, there was a major election backlash, in light

of Richard Nixon's possible impeachment. A large number of Democrats were newly elected to the House, including Herb Harris,
Supervisor of the Mount Vernon Magisterial District of Fairfax
County, Virginia. Not long after the election, a group of members of
the Mount Vernon Democratic Committee urged me to run in a special election to succeed Harris as supervisor. They included Alice and
Bob McNeil, Ginny Lehner, Kelly Hedgepeth, Peg Kelleher, Emily
Myatt, Ferne Walther, Sandy Hoffman, and a number of other splendid people. I wasn't too enthusiastic at the time. I suggested they
approach Ray Colley, who was deputy clerk of the House of Representatives. They did, but he declined. By then, it was coming close
to Thanksgiving, when we were planning to go visit Sylvia's parents
in western Pennsylvania to celebrate the holiday. I told the group I
would decide whether I would run by the time we returned. We had
recently bought a new Dodge Dart, in which the family set off
Thanksgiving morning. As we entered Maryland, the car started to
act up and nearly broke down. We limped to the home of my cousin
Ida in Kensington, Maryland, who graciously offered one of her cars
for our trip.

When we got back to Mount Vernon several days later and managed to get the Dart to the dealer, we found out that practically the
whole engine would have to be reconstructed. (It was, fortunately,
under full warranty.) I decided that this time, unlike my aborted bid
for Congress, I would look upon this "sign" as the kind of challenge
that I must meet by running for office, and I announced my candidacy for the special election to be held at the end of January 1975.
My major Democratic opposition was Sandy Duckworth, who had
been active in local community affairs. Another candidate was Gerry
Hyland, who had run unsuccessfully for state legislator. There were
three other candidates, making six in all. The opponent on the ballot with the Republican Party endorsement would be Howard Futch,
a popular member of the Fairfax County School Board.

This might be a good place for me to describe the governmental structure of Virginia, which is quite a simple one. This is one of the commonwealth's good features, unlike the morass of such states as Pennsylvania. (To be fair, I once teased about Virginia's backwardness by saying that a movie was being made about Virginia by Eighteenth Century Fox.) Thus Virginia is divided into a fixed number of cities and counties, and there are no cities within counties and vice-versa. Fairfax County, I believe, is the most populated of the counties and has about a million people. It provides all the necessary services for its citizens. It has a board of supervisors of ten persons, nine from separate, defined geographical districts (called magisterial districts) and an at-large chairman (there were only eight districts plus a chairman when I served). Mount Vernon is one of those magisterial districts.

Fairfax County is quite an affluent county, one of the top two or three in the country. In the Mount Vernon District, however, the major highway Route 1 (which we refer to as the Richmond Highway Corridor) has a number of pockets of economic difficulty surrounding it. County boards in Virginia deliver just about all the services that government provides to the people, with two partial exceptions: schools, which are funded by the board of supervisors but run by an elected school board; and roads, responsibility for which is divided between the state and the board of supervisors. The overall annual budget for Fairfax County when I served was about one to two billion dollars per year, but is now more like three to four billion dollars. These figures are probably greater than those of about a half-dozen states.

Once I made the commitment, I threw myself fully into the campaign. We had only a month to prepare for the mass meeting to be held between Christmas and New Year's at a nearby school. The mass meeting was the technique chosen to determine the Democratic candidate. It was hard to know how many people would participate. Sandy Hoffman had agreed to be my campaign manager, and she was relentless about both pushing me to raise money and driving me to get out and knock on doors. A dear friend and neighbor, Ed Aileo, a retired Army colonel, agreed to be the campaign treasurer, and he was also a dynamo. The many chores that had to be carried out were parceled out among other supporters, mostly Democratic Committee members.When I walked into the school cafeteria, I was amazed that about six hundred citizens had turned out to participate in the vote. I had not attempted to provide any organized orchestration of the vote, other that preparing my remarks and having several people put my name in nomination. (I noted that Sandy Duckworth was very well organized, with her followers wearing black matching armbands to help them coordinate their efforts, which, frankly, reminded me of the Gestapo.) Pat Berg, among the original founders of United Community Ministries, did a splendid job of telling the group why she was supporting my candidacy. She pointed out she was not of my sex, not of my religion, not of my region of origin, and not of a similar social-and-economic background, but I was simply the most qualified candidate. I felt I did a reasonably good job of presenting my own case. It was clear that much of what I had achieved to date would be of little interest to the people who would really want to know what I could do for them as supervisor. After a series of votes, we came down to Duckworth, 190; Cikins, 190; and Hyland, about 120 votes. The other one hundred or so voters had already left, since the hour was now late. Gerry Hyland had let it be known that he was giving his support to Sandy (saying that he "related" to her), so I thought she would win the runoff. I was sitting in the audience, watching with fascination as the democratic process played itself out, because at that point, the political scientist in me was dominating the candidate. Suddenly, the man sitting next to me prodded me in the ribs and urged me to get busy asking people for their vote, since he thought I could win. I put aside the concession speech I was prepared to make and did as he suggested. When the final vote was announced, I had won by about twenty-five votes! Sandy Duckworth was so shocked that she immediately left the school without saying anything, which was understandable, considering her level of confidence. She did later endorse my candidacy.

The election was scheduled for the end of January 1975, and that month was a whirlwind of making speeches at civic associations, raising money, knocking on doors, and generally keeping the team focused. Sandy Hoffman was great on organization, but she did have some personal-relations problems with the rest of the organization that I was happy to mediate. And then the day was nearly upon us, when we would find out if Howard Futch or I was the winner. I remember spending the evening before calling all the campaign workers to thank them for their efforts, win or lose. Voter turnout would be a significant issue, because this was a special election, and the office of county supervisor was the only spot on the ballot. We woke up on the day of the election to a very serious snowstorm. Several precincts where I was politically strong were snowed in, and I spent a lot of time calling the Virginia Department of Transportation requesting that they plow the roads, with limited success. Despite the weather setback, about 20 percent of the registered voters came out, as compared to a usual 10–15 percent in a special election.

Sylvia was the Democratic precinct captain for our home precinct, Stratford. It was usually a toss-up precinct, but Sylvia had worked hard to win support for me. I waited with her that evening until the vote for the precinct was tallied and found I had won that precinct by 120 votes. I was feeling good as we headed to a nearby fire station where the party faithful had gathered. What I didn't know was that I was losing by some 500 votes with all the precincts reporting except Kirkside, which was strongly Democratic. Sandy Hoffman had pushed me hard to knock on doors in Kirkside day and night, and we would find out if my efforts had paid off. When we walked into the fire station meeting room, there was a hushed silence as Kirkside's vote was reported, and then the room erupted as I had carried Kirkside by almost 600 votes. I was the winner of the election by less than 100 votes! Sandy Hoffman was deliriously happy, and I lavishly thanked her and the rest of the team. Shortly thereafter Howard Futch called and generously conceded, saying he would not challenge the closeness of the result.

There are many additional people who helped me get this opportunity to serve, and I can only cite a few examples. Congressman Jim O'Hara, whom I mentioned earlier as helping me when Senator Engle was injured, lived in the magisterial district and he had many children who helped get my message out to the people. On the Democratic Committee, our researcher Sylvia Broida provided valuable data on the backgrounds and views of constituents, which enabled me to make meaningful connections as I went door to door, escorted by members and spouses of the committee. The professional firefighters were a tremendous asset, led by Harold Schaitberger, who has now risen to be international president of the union. I was honored that he offered to help and even more honored when years later he paid tribute to me as the person who got him involved in public affairs. In the black community of Gum Springs, Cal Ferguson and Kay Holland were leaders of that community whose early support was invaluable, as was that of Judy Burton later on.

I was elected on a Tuesday and sworn in at a special county board meeting that Thursday evening. Brooks Hays honored me by attending. The other seven Democrats on the board congratulated me, while Jack Herrity, the lone Republican, with whom I later became very friendly, teased me by saying how disappointed he was not to have another Republican with him. I'm sure my dad had something to do with the fact that I got a congratulatory telegram from Kevin White, the mayor of Boston, saying that Bostonians excelled wherever they were.

I asked Cindi Hollomon, who had worked for my predecessor, Herb Harris, to stay on as office manager, and she agreed. Barbara Rosenfeld, a very able researcher, joined my staff. And, quite remarkably, Addy Krizek, who had worked with me in Senator Engle's office, surfaced during the campaign and had been of great help. She (on human affairs) and Ed Aileo (on physical affairs, such as roads and land-use planning) rounded out my staff, with various additions as time went by. It was a tremendous group and served me very well indeed.

My first year as supervisor was spent learning the job as thoroughly as I could. While I had easily raised the $25,000 to $30,000 necessary to pay campaign expenses, I now faced dealing with a salary of $10,000 a year for about a fifty-hour week (when my usual annual income was $40,000 at that time). My total income in 1975 took a nosedive, since my consultant clients did not get a whole lot of my time. At the beginning, I was spending about seventy hours per week on county matters, because the county was in the midst of a major planning process known as the PLUS Plan, and my predecessor had understandably not gotten too far on the Mount Vernon part of the process, since he had been running for Congress. The board of supervisors was often meeting two or three times a week in addition to the usual Monday meeting, and much preparation was needed. County staff, in addition to a local citizens committee I assembled, were helpful but the major burden fell on my shoulders. Having majored in the planning process at Harvard Graduate School was of considerable assistance.

At the same time, I followed up on a campaign promise and assembled several key people to consider creating what we came to call the Route One Task Force for Human Services Delivery. Anne Andrews agreed to become what she called "convener" of the task force and now, some twenty-nine years later, she continues to lead. All the organizations on the corridor, both public and private, cooperate with the coalition in what might be called a major clearinghouse for keeping track of all activities relevant to the disadvantaged and for recommending actions that would be of assistance. Eleanor Kennedy, Director of the United Community Ministries (UCM), the successor to Pat Berg, came to me for help on several occasions to ensure that her organization could continue its remarkable efforts. UCM needed that help to get greater county support for crucial services, such as providing food, clothing ,and shelter to the disadvantaged. In addition, I agreed to serve as the board representative on the Public Safety Committee of the Council of Governments, made up of elected officials of the entire Washington metropolitan area, since I had some background in criminal justice and had the District of Columbia Lorton Reformatory located in my magisterial district. At my first meeting, Marion Barry, then a Washington, D.C., city council member (later the mayor of that same city and now once again a D.C. council member), accused me of being a typical Virginia racist, a category he assumed all Virginia officials represented.

I was also appointed to the board of the Northern Virginia Planning District Commission, the regional Health Systems Agency, and the board of the Fairfax Hospital Association (now known as Inova)—a not-surprising assignment since a hospital was being built in Mount Vernon,. The Fairfax Board of Supervisors was heavily involved in transportation matters, with members such as Joe Alexander having great expertise. And although I myself had a significant background in that area, I decided to defer to them. It seemed more appropriate for me to concentrate on crime matters and health-care matters, since they fit my work as consultant and were not as carefully overseen by my colleagues as was transportation. Other activities I became engaged in included planning for seven or eight task forces on youth and keeping pressure on the Fairfax County Park Authority to consider building what became known as the Mount Vernon Recreation Center—with ice skating, exercise, and swimming facilities. Recognizing how dependent the board was on the information provided by the county executive, in this case Bob Wilson, I called for the creation of a baby General Accounting (now called Accountability) Office (GAO). This would provide the board with an independent source of information, as well as a system for reviewing the activities of the county staff. We had a full discussion at the board about this idea, but the vote was 8–1 against me. (To this day, the board continues to consider this idea but does not act.) The only result of my effort was that it got Wilson angry at me. He said that a GAO wasn't needed and the board agreed.

I very soon learned another lesson about being a supervisor, when two doctors, Titus and Lieberman, proposed a zoning change to create a major clinic in Mount Vernon. I thought it a splendid idea and supported their recommendation when it came before the board. One person opposed the clinic, which would be located near her house, on the grounds that it would be the "nose under the tent," leading to commercial encroachment on a residential street. She also feared greater traffic, and got quite emotional about the matter. I thought her arguments were without merit and pushed ahead. Supervisor Alexander urged me to defer the matter to let the situation cool. I did not listen, and when the vote was taken to my amazement the proposal was turned down by a majority of the board. I never forgot this experience, and it was the only similar setback I ever suffered in my five years as supervisor. I also learned to listen to advice from Joe Alexander.

What little consultant or teaching income I earned that year came from only four or five sources. I continued to teach a course at American University and became familiar with a school in Ft. Lauderdale, Florida, Nova University (today merged with another institution as Nova Southeastern University), which wanted to have a satellite in Washington, D.C. I became involved in planning for that center and helped it get accreditation in the Washington area by making a videotape extolling what was then a unique orientation. In a program to grant doctorates in public administration, the center would reach out to people who already had master's degrees and generally worked full-time. Once accepted, the students started this program by spending a week in Washington, meeting with a range of government officials as well as getting their course agendas put together. They would then meet monthly for an entire weekend, having prepared a seminar paper on a designated topic that was sent ahead to the professor for review. As Nova strengthened its operations, I started teaching for them in 1976. Incidentally, I had become aware that senior staff of The Brookings Institution had played a significant role in the creation of this program, such people as Jim Carroll and John Clarke, whom I became colleagues with at a later time.

My work with Porter Hardy, in helping to get some backing for the Eastern Virginia Medical School, continued. Brooks Hays was once again of assistance, because he had served at the U.N. with former Governor Colgate Darden, the most influential statesman in the Virginia, who was not too supportive of a third medical school in the commonwealth. Hays and others that I approached ultimately won Darden's grudging acceptance of this undertaking. I was of less success in getting foundation funding for the school, although Hardy was himself most successful in raising the necessary financial backing. I hope I was of some assistance in that regard. I also was wrapping up my assignment at the Washington Psychiatric Institute, as my plan of action was being implemented. One amusing aspect of this was the calls I often received at my county office from the institute's director, Jack Durell, requesting some information. My assistant would call out to me, within the earshot of some constituents who were in the office for various reasons, "It's the Psychiatric Institute calling!" I wondered if the people of Mount Vernon might be thinking I was under psychiatric care.

This was a period of family bonding and community bonding. The boys were growing up fast, and Sylvia and I spent as much time as we could with them. I tried to make as many school events and sports activities as my schedule permitted. And over time Sylvia exposed them to sailing at a nearby marina that gave lessons. I also attended as many civic association meetings and other community events as I could. These included 4-H Club affairs, various holiday celebrations such as the Fourth of July, community center receptions, etc.

It was about this time that Brooks Hays, Frank Bane, and I started a tradition of meeting for lunch once a month to reminisce, and I regret very much I didn't have a tape recorder running to preserve these recollections of two of the greatest American public servants of the twentieth century. I spent much pleasurable time at George Washington's historic Mount Vernon estate, to learn more about the life of our first president. What impressed me most was his dedication to civility, and I frequently quoted his book on that topic. Every year at the Mount Vernon celebration of his birthday, I laid a wreath at his burial site and gave an address, about some aspect of Washington's life, such as his crucial role at the Constitutional Convention, his bravery in battle, or his modest determination that he not be granted kinglike powers.

I was of course delighted to represent a magisterial district which had been the home of the Father of Our Country. I was especially pleased that the Mount Vernon Democratic Committee had not been turned off about my being a candidate for that august position when I pointed out that I was a Jew and a civil righter, credentials that were not particularly valuable in a district with about 2 percent Jews and 2 percent African Americans.

I was aware that George Washington had referred kindly to the Jewish population of the new nation, especially writing to the congregations in Charleston, South Carolina, and Newport, Rhode Island. Washington visited Truro Synagogue in Newport and also exchanged correspondence with a synagogue leader, Moses Sexias. In that correspondence Washington said our government was one "that to bigotry gives no sanction, to persecution no assistance." Washington went on to write, "May the children of the stock of Abraham, who dwell in this land, continue to merit and enjoy the good will of the other inhabitants, while everyone shall sit in safety under his own vine and fig tree, and there shall be none to make him afraid." It was partially for such reasons as devotion to religious freedom and encouraging a pluralistic society that I urged Fairfax County schools to emphasize the contributions of George Washington and his colleagues who made our country the refuge of so many newcomers who added to its greatness.

By the summer of 1975—while I was in the midst of mounting a campaign for a full-term reelection against the same special-election opponent, Howard Futch—negotiations I had been having with The Brookings Institution came to fruition. Walter Held, who had succeeded Jim Mitchell as head of what was then the division called the Advanced Study Program (now Center for Public Policy Education), responded to a budgeting crunch he was suffering by releasing two permanent staffers and hiring me as a part-time consultant (really part-time employee) and conductor of educational programs. (The reader should understand that Brookings had four divisions, this one primarily on education and the other three, economics, government studies, and foreign policy, on research.) Even though I had a strong civil rights background, Held had to convince Acting President Gil Steiner that my being hired would comply with guidelines for equal employment opportunity. Held fought for me because he was convinced that my contacts in all three branches of government—executive, legislative, and judiciary —would be of great advantage to Brookings. When I put together a seminar on the budgeting process that included top Ford Administration officials and key congressmen from the appropriations and finance committees, I lived up to that promise.

It was a wild time as my election day approached. I had assembled an excellent team with Linda Golodner as my campaign manager and Mike McClister as my campaign consultant. McClister, who was with the Democratic National Committee, put together some wonderful campaign literature which was given wide distribution. I was proud that McClister agreed to help me, since he was a nationally renowned consultant who usually charged much more for his services than he charged my campaign. Golodner was equally outstanding and helped me put together a group of campaigners who enabled me to put my best foot forward. As I debated Futch at civic association meetings, I grew more and more confident that we would win quite comfortably. This confidence was reinforced by the fact that several key local Republican Party officials were quite friendly to me, even though I maintained a moderate-to-liberal posture. With State Senator Joe Gartlan on the ballot, I thought that would help me, but it turned out that I helped him, some evidence of my growing political strength.

There was an unpleasant development before election day regarding the area's volunteer firemen. I had made a passing comment that they should not solicit funds door-to-door, because the county paid for a full professional fire service and additional fundraising would constitute double taxation. (The volunteers were useful primarily to supplement the professionals.) Nonetheless, they became very upset about my comment. While I tried not to be confrontational, they seemed to want to target me for electoral defeat. The editor of the *Mount Vernon Gazette*, a volunteer fireman himself, did a front-page story with the headline "Cikins Meddling with the Fire Services." However, another prominent volunteer firefighter, Mike Keck, reached out to me, and he raised funds for a full-page ad defending my position. Soon, the matter got even further complicated by a death threat phoned into a newspaper, specifying the time I would be shot and some thought that it was a volunteer who made the call. The Fairfax police provided a private detective to accompany me on my political campaigning, although people were puzzled because he did not get involved in the process itself. At the appointed moment for the assassination, I was addressing a large group in a church in Lorton, with the detective on the platform watching the crowd. Nothing happened, and after a couple of days I told the detective I was ready to go it alone.

The whole episode upset Sylvia, and I was glad when it passed. The press was very cooperative about not writing about the threat, and so practically no one knew about the risk I was taking. When my board colleagues found out about what happened, they said if I had made the threat public I would have won in a walk; but I didn't want to be the most successful candidate in the cemetery. I later made my peace with the volunteers who decided to raise the money they needed by holding bingo games at the fire stations. When my good friend Bill Evans, the leading national expert on developing quality fire services, with an outstanding management consultant firm, offered to review the Fairfax system on a complimentary basis, my motion to do so was soundly defeated. Evans called me several years later, pleased that the county had contracted with him to do this study for a huge sum of money. His research contribution made it much easier for all parties involved to be reconciled and also to make the county operation more efficient.

Another matter that arose during the election was more central to my interest. Soon after I had become a supervisor, I had moved to have the board authorize legal action to have the Lorton Reformatory—a District of Columbia prison established in 1916 in what was then countryside—removed from Fairfax County. I did this in a gentle fashion, saying that the facility was very outmoded and should be replaced by several small facilities located in the District of Columbia that met modern penal standards. I recommended that the basis for our action should be the numerous problems of air, water, and other pollution, as well as the risk to public safety if there were a prison escape. I got unanimous support from my colleagues and a suit was filed in Federal Court. The U.S. senator from Virginia was Republican Bill Scott, against whom I had considered running for the House in 1970. Scott had been elected to the U.S. Senate in 1972 over the outstanding Democratic incumbent, Bill Spong, only because Nixon carried Virginia by a landslide. Scott now decided he would introduce legislation to oust the reformatory. I knew his legislation was designed to reward fat-cat land speculators who were aching to get their hands on the land, so I asked to testify. (I called for the land to be a public park.) The Democratic chairman of the Senate Judiciary Subcommittee handling the matter behaved like an ass in attempting to block my appearing, on the grounds that it would be political (since I was in the midst of an election)—as if the Congress never had witnesses with a political agenda. I shamed him into letting me appear, but he asked my opponent Futch to appear also, which was okay with me, since I knew one hundred times as much about the issue as Futch did.

I had a wonderful time blasting Scott for his being the instrument of greedy land speculators and not caring about the well-being of his constituents. Although some professional group had voted Scott the least competent Member of Congress—you will recall that he foolishly proved it by holding a press conference to deny the allegation—he showed some wisdom in this situation by not attempting to question me at all. The only questions I got were from the chairman, who (even as a Democrat) was doing Scott's dirty work for him; but he was almost as "competent" as Scott, so I didn't have any trouble making my case and demolishing his. The whole hearing was just a fraud, and I was pleased to undermine it. One good outcome from the hearing was that I won the admiration of the District of Columbia corrections officials who attended, a development that would have great significance at a future time.

This election evening in November 1975 was a most satisfying one for me. I won by a 55 percent to 45 percent voting margin, which was at least a thousand or two votes more than my adversary got, even though this election was only ten months after the first one, which I had won by about 70 votes. I had obviously made a good impression on my constituents in a very short time.

Chapter 6

Juggling Family, Health, and Public Service

During this period I had been gradually phasing out the clients that my consultant firm had obtained. Former Oklahoma Congressman Jed Johnson had taken over as director of the Former Members of Congress, a job he did wonderfully. I completed the work I had done for the Supreme Court and for the Federal Judicial Center. My work for the Washington Psychiatric Institute ended, as did my participation in the Voice of America programs. By the end of the year, I was pretty much occupied by Brookings and by the Fairfax County Board of Supervisors, and some additional professorial assignments. Sylvia decided that this busy schedule of mine meant less time for the two of us together, so she approached the Senate Committee on Commerce, Science & Transportation, which she had left some six or seven years earlier, about a position. Gerry Grinstein was gone, but Mike Pertschuk was chief counsel and he remembered Sylvia very favorably. There was an opening and she was hired. Addy Krizek knew a woman, Sara Ramirez, who could babysit the children, being with them after school and until we got home. Soon thereafter Bess Macomsen, whom Sylvia had found through the Virginia Employment Commission, succeeded Sara. On a visit to our home in Mount Vernon by my parents, I brought them to a Fairfax County Board of Supervisors meeting where my dad had a chance to address the board. It gave me great pleasure to have my parents see me in action at the board as they earlier had at the White House swearing-in of Brooks Hays.

Before the year was over, I had initiated a major new program at Brookings— seminars for newly elected Members of Congress. Since they had already been in office for several months when I first arrived at Brookings near the end of 1975, I decided the way to begin was not by holding a full-blown conference, but with dinner sessions at a Library of Congress meeting room on key topics before the Congress. Harvard had already begun a week-long "New Member" session held at the university in December 1974, (with only Harvard scholars involved); but I thought I could do a much better job on in-depth training by waiting until after the 1976 congressional election to hold Brookings first major session in January 1977. In the meantime, I focused on the dinner-session seminars, which were held in late 1975 and early 1976, exploring the topics of health care, foreign policy, economic policy, and criminal justice. I was able to invite the best scholars and practitioners to participate and attracted as many as fifty new Members for each of these sessions, usually of course, with some attrition. I was starting to make a difference at Brookings and getting more widely known in Washington.

It was appropriate to keep my three professional lives completely segregated—county supervisor, Brookings staffer, and university professor—and I made every effort to do so. The fourth life, my family life, did suffer somewhat, and I tried as hard as I could to spend time with Sylvia and the boys. Sylvia was back in the rhythm of working for the Senate, assisting Joe Fogarty, counsel to the Subcommittee on Communications chaired by Senator John Pastore of Rhode Island. Bess Macomsen, an African-American, had practically become one of the family looking after Dean and Neil in the afternoons before we got home from work, and we also got close to her family. To help simplify our lives, we changed temples from Rodef Shalom in Fairfax County to Beth El in Alexandria, which was only about fifteen minutes from home. We really missed Rabbi Berkowits and were not yet so comfortable with Rabbi Arnold Fink. The boys didn't relate very well to the Beth El environment because they were used to Rodef Shalom. Having grown up in hostile Dorchester, I didn't realize that Dean and Neil were so well accepted in our current communities that their identification with Judaism, while strong, wasn't as strong as mine had been. They recognized their Jewish roots, but as a great tribute to a county of comparatively little anti-Semitism, they felt religiously comfortable in whatever neighborhood we lived in and did not reach out specifically to such other Jewish children that might live in the area. While there would be some minor setbacks in that regard, with some occasional flashes of anti-Semitism, they had the wonderful childhood that I had been deprived of, but had learned to live without.

The year 1976 turned out to be one of achievement and sadness and horror. At Brookings as a part-time consultant, (but as I have already mentioned, really a part-time staffer), I was conducting many seminars and writing a number of journal articles. Even though I was in the education division, I also did considerable research. The Brookings staff of the other divisions wasn't too well-disposed toward my writings, which I had published in numerous journals other than Brookings, since these research divisions—economics, foreign policy, and government affairs—were quite arrogant when interacting on that level with my division. I couldn't have cared less. I was relating most successfully to senior officials in all three branches of the federal government, my seminars were wildly successful, and my articles were well received. I gathered dozens of congratulatory letters from the business and government officials who were my seminar students. I also became quite friendly with the distinguished public officials I invited to appear.

The year 1976 was also most satisfying to me as a county supervisor. I focused on (1) health care at the Health Systems Agency (HSA) and the Fairfax Hospital Association (FHA, later Inova), (2) promoting criminal justice, (3) coordinating the agencies involved in implementing the Fairfax County PLUS planning process, (4) operating as chairman of the Metropolitan Council of Government's (COG) public safety committee (dealing with region's police, fire and emergency preparedness entities), (5) creating seven Mount Vernon task forces on youth, (6) helping UCM grow, (7) assisting the residents of the mobile homes on the Richmond Highway Corridor improve their quality of life, and (8) meeting with the local ministry to create a ministerial alliance. This period was when I began working with Ventures in Community, another fine group of ministers and laypeople helping the community of Mount Vernon care for its homeless people.

During that year, 1976, my appointee to the Fairfax Park Authority, Glenn Fatzinger, reminded me that there was money in a bond referendum that could be used to create a recreation center for Mount Vernon. People were particularly eager for a skating rink, which surprised me, since we were in what was considered to be "the sunny South" where ice skating rinks would be scarce. Nonetheless, I threw myself into getting such a rink. Many enthusiastic citizens assisted me, especially Bruce Bolstad who functioned as one of their major leaders. However, there was much opposition, especially when the cost rose from $2 million (the amount provided in the bond referendum) to $4 million for the original design, because of runaway national inflation. Many supervisors also thought private enterprise should build the facilities, (even though no one was interested). Others thought a skating rink was impractical since it would be a money loser. Still others thought the design inappropriate. Given all of these obstacles I still was ready to proceed. I went before the Fairfax County Park Authority several times, with many Mount Vernon citizens accompanying me, but we were not successful in getting approval. On the fourth round, we brought in a scaled-down version that would keep the cost at $2 million. The chairman of the authority, Carl Sell, and the director, Joe Downs, were of great help in facilitating this proposed cost reduction, which would require altering many features of the building, but not the basic big-league quality of the rink itself. The authority finally approved this version and sent it on to the board of supervisors. The board then rejected my submittal on several occasions, using the opposition arguments already noted.

On July 14, 1976, I heard that my father died unexpectedly and I flew immediately to Boston to arrange his funeral. While I was still in mourning, I felt it crucial to schedule another rink vote for July 28 to keep up such momentum as I had achieved. On that very morning, my mother had a stroke, out of grief, and died herself, meaning that I left Virginia immediately and was up in Boston at the moment the vote was taken, and the Mount Vernon Recreation Center was finally approved. The vote was 7 to 1, with the only nay coming from a supervisor whose district feared competition to its own (privately owned) skating rink. What a wonderful testimonial to the board's confidence in me and kindness toward me. Losing both of my parents within a two-week period was a devastating experience, which still causes me great anguish to think about; but I had no choice but to go on seeing through my obligation to the people of Mount Vernon to get them a skating rink as the first step in the creation of a full-scale recreation center.

Another "Sneak Attack" on My Health

At the end of the year, there was a national scare about an epidemic of "swine flu," after a soldier at Fort Dix, New Jersey, died from a type of virus that the medical profession thought only swine could catch. The Centers for Disease Control and Prevention (CDC) urged everyone to get a swine-flu shot. What they didn't say was that they knew that "X" percentage of those who took the shot would be seriously adversely affected by it. A red flag should have gone up when the drug manufacturers refused to make the vaccine until Congress enacted legislation absolving them of all responsibility for any adverse reactions. That meant that any person hurt by the shot could only sue the federal government, an almost impossible undertaking. The statute also provided that civil actions would be heard only by a judge and not by a jury, another blow to anyone who was adversely affected. However, I am concerned that the CDC might well have deliberately withheld information about these matters on the understandable logic that people would not take the shot if they were at risk. In the end no additional cases of swine flu were reported while forty-five million people were vaccinated and many hundreds of them were adversely affected. Some were permanently paralyzed, some blinded, and some even died. My doctor was generally against even "normal" flu shots, as he had seen many harmful reactions, but he said that in this case, given the fear, I should get the shot, and I followed his advice. I did so partly to set an example to my constituents since President Ford had urged all Americans to take the shot. Unfortunately for me, exactly three weeks later, which I found out later to be an appropriate gestation period, I lost the complete sight in my right eye. When it happened, I was terrified, since I feared the other eye would also stop functioning and I had no idea why I had been hit with this affliction.

I rushed to my ophthalmologist, who wasn't sure what the problem was, but diagnosed "optic neuritis" and prescribed massive doses of cortisone. Because I had a delicate stomach which was the residual impact of three bleeding ulcer attacks, I also took massive doses of Maalox to coat the impact of cortisone on my stomach. The next few months were a nightmare, rushing from specialist to specialist—some of whom were real quacks— from New York to Florida, without much success. My right eye stayed totally blind for several months, but over a period of two years it slowly returned to relative normalcy. I was warned this ailment could return at any time. My physicians finally figured out that the swine-flu shot was the culprit, but they wouldn't go public with their views since they feared retribution. Over the years, with the cost of travel, physicians, and lost time, the whole incident cost me about $10,000, which of course was a tiny factor in the total horror I experienced. Mark Friedlander, whose wife introduced me to Sylvia, happened to be a leader in lining up victims to sue the federal government in a class action, and he agreed to take my case on a contingency basis. But there would be no swift outcome, because such cases move slowly, and this one didn't reach the courts until the first of the year 1981, a little over four years after I was afflicted.

In the meantime, I tried to carry on as I had done before, but with only one eye working. When I look back at that period, I feel the Lord must have been with me, because I drove to many meetings that took place during stormy weather, and I always made it in one piece. No one but Sylvia and my physicians were aware of my condition. Not long after I was blinded, I presided over a meeting of many dozens of my constituents dealing with the agendas of the seven task forces on youth I had created, and I kept wondering if I could complete the effort without dissolving into hysteria. I kept wishing that the right eye would snap back to normal, but it did not improve at all at that time.

One of the task forces carried the ball to get the recreation center completed on schedule. Many complications arose. For economy's sake, we were using an ersatz material, resembling white masonry, on the exterior; but many Mount Vernon architects preferred a brown color, which I thought was ugly, and I overrode their arguments. The figure skaters wanted windows, which we had installed, but later removed. The community wanted a small common room which was provided, at the loss of some locker rooms, which cramped the facilities for the skaters. It was feared that with all the penny-pinching, the exterior of the building would look ugly, so we managed to find about $35,000 to provide attractive landscaping. (Once again, I am very grateful to Carl Sell and Joe Downs for making this possible.) Ultimately, in February, 1978, we had a ribbon cutting. I had been very apprehensive that few people would use the skating rink, and I finally breathed a sign of relief when hundreds of people showed up for the opening night. Contrary to expectations, it was a moneymaker from day one, even though we provided for reduced entry fees for those who came from disadvantaged families.

While the "rec" center was under construction, Bruce Bolstad was organizing families interested in hockey, so that when the new ice rink opened, we could put together teams of young skaters to participate in regional hockey competition. He recruited me to work with the group of parents who were eager to have their children compete. While I had had a mild interest in the Boston Bruins as a boy, and I had been a pretty good ice skater myself, it was a whole new experience to mingle with neighbors who were so committed to the sport.

Once the rink had opened, my sons Dean and Neil learned to skate and soon became involved in the hockey club. I remember (not so fondly) getting up at about 4:00 a.m. to take them to practice sessions, often at the Tucker Road (Maryland) Rink; the trip was necessary since Mount Vernon had already become overbooked. With two players, with different schedules, it was quite a challenge to keep up with their needs, to say nothing of the cost of ice time, equipment, and travel. I was able to remain a member of the Mount Vernon Hockey Club board for about six years.

Back in 1976, the Mount Vernon Hospital had opened. As the Fairfax County Supervisor from Mount Vernon, I joined in the ribbon cutting but made sure that my predecessor, Herb Harris, also got proper recognition. As a member of the Fairfax Hospital Association board, I served on its finance committee. I practically broke my neck getting to its meetings held at Fairfax Hospital Association headquarters in the County, driving to the meetings from The Brookings Institution during the workday. At the beginning, the hospital had financial problems, and I did everything I could to help it become prosperous. I worked closely with Col. Sam Hinson (who had become a developer after retiring from the military) to get all the appropriate approvals he would need to construct what would become a series of rows of doctors' offices, close by the hospital. Slowly doctors gravitated to the area and the financial situation improved.

Fairfax County's record on hiring minorities was not a particularly good one, so I thought I should do something about it. I prepared a plan of action and moved at a Board meeting that the county adopt an affirmative-action hiring plan along the lines I had learned at the federal level. This motion led to quite an uproar. After the dust settled, some of the board engaged in a thoughtful discussion. I should mention that the November 1975 election led to Republican Jack Herrity becoming Chairman of the Board. Two other Republicans were elected, Marie Travesky and John Shacochis, both of whom I later became quite fond of, as well as Jack. Three Democrats, Martha Pennino, Joe Alexander, and Audrey Moore, often voted with Herrity. Thus there were only four members I could count on to vote favorably on this issue: Jim Scott, Alan Magazine, Martha Pennino (on issues of this kind), and of course myself, but I didn't know where I'd get a fifth one. Audrey Moore, who wasn't particularly civil rights oriented, had a son who was somewhat disadvantaged; and I had become quite involved in an organization for the mildly retarded set up by my cousin Ida Brown. I shared much of my knowledge of the general area with Audrey, and this helped us bond. While I certainly had no hidden agenda in our budding friendship, much to my pleasant surprise, Audrey provided the fifth vote. She later told me she took some heat from her constituents, but she stood by me and I was very proud of her for her willingness to help. My staff wanted me to publicize my victory, but I thought that idea unwise. The minority community knew what I had done, and the rest of the community would have mixed feelings. My philosophy of leadership meant that I would always try to do the right thing, but not in such a way that I might be committing political suicide.

In a number of other instances, I also worked to find middle ground without the community becoming embattled. In one, the National Park Service (NPS) and the people of Fairfax County had agreed that there should be a recreational path for biking or walking along the Potomac River. The problem was that everyone wanted the trail—just not running in front of *their* house, causing *their* lawns to be disturbed, or *their* doors to get knocked on by strangers. A logical, but not reasonable, solution would be to run the path down the middle of George Washington Memorial Parkway. The NPS asked me to be of help, and we held numerous joint hearings for the citizens involved. We finally came to the conclusion that the path could run down one side of the highway for some distance and then cross over a stone bridge to the other side for another distance before crossing back over at the Fort Hunt area. Not everyone was happy, but I was very pleased to see, some years later when I left office, that many people from both sides of the road came to my farewell party.

In another instance, a prominent resident of Mount Vernon, Gerry Halpin, was embroiled in a controversy with his neighbor, the American Horticultural Society (AHS), over the use of a common road to reach their properties. The Horticultural Society also wanted to build additional, higher buildings on the property, a project that was objected to by nearby residents. AHS threatened to move and sell its land to the Soviets, who were looking for a site for some of their ambassadorial services. I employed a technique that I used on a number of other disputes. I invited all the parties to my office to negotiate, and insisted that they stay until we found middle ground. In this case, the matter was resolved by giving Halpin the disputed access, permitting AHS to construct its own exclusive access and one building somewhat less tall than the one originally proposed.

During this time, I had begun discussions with my old friend Mark Cannon about Chief Justice Burger's interest in a judicial outreach from the Supreme Court to the Congress and to the Justice Department. Ever since Mark had become Burger's administrative assistant in 1972, we had occasionally met to compare notes on this idea. He was interested in the work I was doing at Brookings with outreach to Congress, helping new Members get better informed about the issues they would confront. We both thought a similar format might work for the chief justice's intentions.

Chapter 7

Groundbreaking Seminars for Congress and the Judiciary

In preparation for the new members conference in January 1977, still as a part-time Brookings staffer, I had built an alliance with the Congressional Research Service of the Library of Congress. It was decided that Brookings and CRS would take the Members to the Cascades Conference Center at Colonial Williamsburg in Virginia for a long weekend. BI and CRS coordinated with the Congressional leadership to get their blessing and arrange for an appropriate calendar slot after the Members had arrived in Washington. To make the whole effort possible I had reached out to many foundations and finally identified one that would underwrite the budget we had prepared. It was agreed that Members could bring their children and spouses, who would be invited to sit in on the instructional sessions or participate in a separate set of activities. A senior official from Amtrak, John Clarke, had joined our Brookings division as a senior member, and he and I came up with the idea of taking the group to Williamsburg by train, in separate cars from the rest of the passengers. The trip would enable friendships to be formed, with people moving about some of the time and later during the meal served on board. For me personally, these conferences were a wonderful vehicle to meet new Members, and as a result, I knew almost half of the Members of the House and one-quarter of the Senators by the time I was involved in my last program. There were ten of these seminars held over a period of eighteen years at the beginning of each biennial Congress.

Our first Williamsburg program was indeed a great success. About twenty-five new members agreed to attend. I had done a tireless marketing job, seeking out Members at their temporary offices. The train concept worked very well, with buses arranged to take Members and their families from a designated spot on the Hill to Washington's Union Station. When the train arrived in Williamsburg, officials were waiting to transport us all to our accommodations, where a welcoming reception was held.

The CRS and I decided on the format and the topics of the many sessions, which were generally well received. Each panel usually had three specialists, often a national expert on the chosen subject, and one expert each from the CRS and from Brookings. For example, Alice Rivlin, a prominent Brookings economist, presided over a session about the national economy, with presentations by two top former members of the President's Council of Economic Advisers, Herb Stein who served under Nixon and Walter Heller who served under Kennedy. Their comments represented the gamut of views held by top economists of a variety of persuasions.

In total, the families had a good three days together, which enhanced the value of the weekend. These newly elected members had been on the run for months, and we built in much time for them to enjoy the Colonial Williamsburg ambience. Among the attendees in 1977 were Representative Al Gore of Tennessee (later, of course, senator and then vice president of the United States), Representative David Stockman from Michigan (later director of the Executive Office of Management and Budget), and Representative Leon Panetta of California (later chief of staff at the Clinton White House). By the time we boarded the train for the return ride, everyone was pretty much exhausted, and there wasn't too much conversation.

Walter Held was very pleased with my performance and offered me a full-time position at Brookings, despite my eye problems, which some suspected but nobody really knew about. I readily accepted, because it was agreed that I could continue in my role as county supervisor, and earning, all together, an acceptable living. Also important was that, while I had health coverage with the county, Brookings would provide excellent retirement benefits, as well as additional health coverage. This decision did mean, of course, 100-hour weeks. I would continue for the next sixteen and a one-half years in the educational division of Brookings, holding many seminars, but also conducting wide-ranging programmatic efforts and writing numerous journal articles.

With Jimmy Carter now in the White House, I reinitiated conversations I had had with Mark Cannon about holding "Administration of Justice" seminars. We evaluated who might be interested. Attorney General Griffin Bell had appointed University of Virginia law professor Dan Meador as Assistant Attorney General for Administration of Justice, while House Judiciary Committee Chairman Peter Rodino had named House Judiciary staffer Alan Parker as Chief Counsel. Jim Eastland of Mississippi, chairman of the Senate Judiciary Committee, was not likely to be interested. Mark and I set up meetings with Meador and Parker, and we slowly agreed on a format to hold a first meeting in the beginning of 1978, also in Colonial Williamsburg, and also over a long weekend, at the Cascades Conference Center. Chief Justice Burger, Attorney General Bell and House Judiciary Chairman Rodino all agreed that it would be wise to exclude the Senate Judiciary Committee this first year. Each branch would cover its own expenses, at least for this first go-round. I was able to hold Brookings's expenses to about $3,500 through a lot of one-time maneuvers. As the years went on after the first meeting, the Justice Department agreed to make a grant to Brookings of about $25,000 a year to cover expenses.. These meetings continued until I retired in 1993 (some fifteen meetings in all).

During my sixteen-and-a-half years at Brookings (after the year

and a half as consultant or part-time staffer), I gave priority attention to a number of areas: the administration of justice; criminal
justice (fair sentencing); corrections (rehabilitation of wrongdoers);
the congressional process; governmental relations with religious institutions, foundations, and universities; drugs and AIDS policies;
direct outreach to companies in the Fortune 500, especially IBM,
DuPont, Exxon, and several others. I was also called upon to lead
programs that Brookings considered basic, such as exposing business
and government leaders to the major public issues confronting the
nation. Since I wanted to be creative and imaginative, I designed
numerous programs, and managed to raise the funds necessary to
implement them. This meant, on the average, obtaining about ten
to twenty grants per year, raising between $100,000 and $400,000
annually. By doing so, I gained a lot of freedom to "do my thing."
The three other divisions of Brookings, which were research-oriented,
generally raised less of their budget than was needed and had to get
allotments from the endowment income. In my own efforts, I generally raised far more money than was necessary to cover the expenses
of my programs, thus contributing significantly to the Brookings general fund. It is also relevant to note that, on the few routine programs
assigned to me, I made them popular enough with corporate and government attendees to be actual moneymakers.

The American Jewish Committee (AJC) asked me to serve as Secretary of the Washington Chapter, during this time of the AJC
becoming a more open active player in Washington public affairs. My
membership on the AJC Board ran from 1965 to 1983. It peaked
during my early Brookings years, 1975-80. Many of the most prominent Jewish professionals in the area served on the Board as well as
rabbis and community leaders. Forums were held on some of the most
significant issues confronting the Jewish community, and I found the
association most stimulating indeed. I developed associations at the
AJC that enhanced my Brookings seminars, especially on learning from
the AJC how religious inputs can be made in public policy formulation.

The same year that I began the judicial conferences, Mark Cannon nominated me for service on the national board of the Kennedy School of Government Alumni Association, and I was selected for such a position. This undertaking was a most rewarding one, since the group represented a cross section of Kennedy School alumni, from an Army general to an assistant secretary of a federal agency to a local government official. We got together fairly frequently, but I wasn't able to attend the meetings held in Cambridge, with all the other time demands I had. After about three years, I opted to drop out. It was partly because it was very difficult for me to try to recruit students to attend the Kennedy School, since in my own career, I saw first-hand how government officials were being mistreated by their political bosses—and the general public as well. I didn't have the heart to ask the best and the brightest to consider public service. Yet now, as I look back on my life as a government official, I wish I had paid more attention to fighting to reverse the denunciation of public servants and had encouraged others to do so as well.

It was during this time that I also became better acquainted with Chief Justice Burger, thanks to Mark Cannon; and it was very inspiring to learn how deeply Burger felt about bettering relations between the three branches of government. He also was profoundly committed to improving the lot of people in prison. He began by urging that inmates get literacy and job training, so that they could be rehabilitated before returning to society. I didn't realize at the time how deeply involved I would become as a lieutenant of the chief justice on both this matter and the improvement in the administration of justice. It was in Burger's office that I first met Ken Starr, later famous as the special prosecutor in the investigation of President Clinton, who was one of the chief justice's law clerks. Starr and I were to become close friends as the years went by, during which he became a senior Justice Department official and later he rose up the judicial ladder. Mike Luttig, today an influential judge on the Fourth U.S. Circuit Court of Appeals, was a research assistant to Burger at that time and also became more involved in our joint efforts.

Sylvia and I had been considering a move for some time, and we had periodically looked at other houses for sale, to no avail. When the federal government announced a significant salary increase for its employees, we decided to act quickly, before prices skyrocketed. We loved our neighbors but had outgrown our house. Two of our neighbors, the Tarpeys and the Norrises, had moved to a new subdivision known as Mason Hill. I liked the name, since the original owner of the section was George Mason, the intellectual father of the American Revolution. We were told that a house was for sale by its owner without use of a real estate agent. The owner had only been there one year, but was being transferred by his company. It did not take us long to decide that this was the house for us. We moved in shortly thereafter, but soon discovered that there would be problems with the neighborhood. We suspected that some local children had broken into our house and removed some items we had brought over in advance of the moving van. Before long, we came to recognize that some of the teenage boys in the neighborhood were juvenile delinquents. Dean and Neil found hostility, not friendship. Even the children of the minister of the church across the street from us (who lived on the church grounds) started a confrontation in our own backyard. Our sons found solace only with friends in our old neighborhood, which wasn't too far away. So much for going to a neighborhood that had more comfortable housing. This situation was troublesome for someone in public office, but I stood up to the minister who was clearly wrong in defending the misbehavior of his children, even though it was politically risky for me to do so; but I would not tolerate the intimidation of my own children. Fortunately, over the years the troublemakers moved away in considerable numbers and many outstanding new families moved in. We gradually became much more relaxed in the environment, which became wonderfully accepting, although it never quite reached the outstanding level of our prior neighborhood. Possibly our delight in the old neighborhood was influenced considerably by how wonderfully our children got along with all our neighbors.

My health was getting shakier during this period. The right eye was still giving me trouble. I had been having problems with my back as well, and it was getting progressively more painful; I started to find myself bending over slightly. Carol Ann Coryell, a dear friend and colleague on Fairfax County matters (I had appointed her to the Community Services Board, even though she was an active Republican), also had serious back problems and referred me to her orthopedic physician, Bill Hanff. Dr. Hanff took one look at me and, with great skill diagnosed my problem as spondylitis, a form of inflammatory disease similar to arthritis that usually results in the progressive fusion of all the bones in a person's back and also causes all kinds of skeletal problems. That diagnosis led to me embark on a series of physical therapy sessions orchestrated by the chief physical therapist at Mount Vernon Hospital, Liz Francis. Over time my back curvature became worse, and I developed serious hip and shoulder problems that threatened me with the need for surgery. It wasn't long after that I developed another ailment, colitis. While it is not universally accepted, many physicians believe optic neuritis, spondylitis, and colitis are all auto-immune diseases. With Sylvia's help and fine medical support, I rode out these difficulties and would not let them slow me down. There were occasions, however, for years to come, when I went to conduct conferences, not only in Colonial Williamsburg but all over the country, I was subjected to severe back pain or other skeletal pain The presence of chest pain was especially disconcerting and led to my having numerous electrocardiograms, which until 2004, proved not to reveal threatening health problems.

My schedule in 1978 continued to be hectic, despite my health problems. A leading community activist, Toni McMahon, brought to my attention that the 250th anniversary of George Washington's birthday would occur in 1982. I have always felt that Fairfax County did not do enough to recognize the incredible accomplishments of

Washington and the other Founding Fathers, or the Founding Mothers. At a board of supervisors meeting, I moved to create a special commission whose members, including myself, planned many events throughout the County to honor the occasion and encouraged the schools to teach their students more about the origins of our country.

At the same time, I began early in 1978 planning for the second biennial New Members of Congress seminar in Colonial Williamsburg, to be held in early 1979 (the reader will recall that the first meetings with new Members were in late 1975 and early 1976 and were dinner meetings in Washington, not a Colonial Williamsburg seminar). I worked hard to maintain a high enrollment, since the Congressional leadership seemed to tilt in favor of a similar program at Harvard, which had the support of Speaker of the House Tip O'Neill, in whose district the university was located, The Speaker was cooperative with us and did give our program his blessing, but his heart was with Harvard. The two programs had many differences, beyond that of Harvard's being a full week while ours a jam-packed three-day weekend. In addition to the ice-breaking train ride (nothing comparable done by Harvard), we invited the best lecturers from anywhere in the country, who represented a wide range of viewpoints, while Harvard relied solely on its own faculty. We encouraged family participation, while Harvard asked the new Members to come alone. Over the years, we received letters from Members who had attended both conferences, who stated flatly that ours was more informative and useful than the one at Harvard, and that the icebreaker atmosphere was very satisfying. Nonetheless, I always tried to keep the competition on a friendly basis, especially because I knew some of the people involved in Harvard's effort.

Also early in 1978, Brookings held the first Administration of Justice seminar. In attendance were about fifteen members of the House Judiciary Committee, led by Chairman Peter Rodino of New Jersey and Ranking Republican Robert McClory of Illinois; about fifteen jurists, led by Chief Justice Burger; and about fifteen senior Justice Department officials, led by Attorney General Griffin Bell. There were also some distinguished legal scholars invited to participate in some of the sessions, and a sprinkling of staff members. The planning committee had agreed that the seminar discussions would all be off-the-record, to facilitate the uninhibited free exchange of ideas. The committee also decided that the agenda for the first year or two would refrain from being excessively controversial, because the very idea of holding these joint seminars raised sensitive questions about maintaining the separation of powers. Later, as our stature grew, we took on any subject relevant to our interest. Some of the leading topics that first year were: (a) congestion in the Federal Court system, with some discussion of dividing the larger circuits; (b) proposals to eliminate federal diversity jurisdiction; (c) a push for a comprehensive plan to resolve minor disputes through the use of arbitration rather than the courts; and (d) recommendations to abolish obligatory jurisdiction on some matters.

Despite much trepidation, the weekend went very well, and we received many laudatory comments from the participants. They welcomed the opportunity for these problem-solving information exchanges, and the setting was perfect for that sort of communication. Since the family attended with me (all participant families were invited), our son Dean had the pleasure of having the chief justice, the attorney general, the chairman of the House Judiciary Committee, and the head of the FBI sing "Happy Birthday" to him during a coffee break. Mark Cannon and I reported in the *Washington and Lee Law Review* of Winter 1981, that Chairman Rodino said, "This is not just an experiment, it is an experience." Assistant Attorney General Maurice Rosenberg also said, "The overworked word 'historic' is exactly right in estimating the impact of the sessions."

Some time earlier, Jim Carroll, division director at Brookings, who had gone from CRS to Syracuse University and then to Brookings, suffered the loss of his brother who was murdered during a holdup.

Jim had responded to this terrible event in a remarkable way, by reaching out to the District of Columbia to assemble an informal group of distinguished citizens to help rehabilitate prison inmates. I was happy · to participate, especially since the Lorton Reformatory (the D.C. prison located in Fairfax County) was in my magisterial district. In about 1982, when Jim went back to become a dean of the Syracuse University School of Public Administration, I took leadership of this organization at his request and was able to formalize and strengthen it, incorporating it as a nonprofit (the Washington Correctional Foundation). It was now able to raise money for helping D.C. inmates get the education and training they needed not to recidivate. A number of committees were created to accomplish this objective, including ones on medical and dental health, mental health, budget and finance, vocational education, job development, academic education, public relations, foundation procedures, and legal counsel. I arranged for Chief Justice Burger to become the honorary chairman, and he stated in *our* information brochure: "I am pleased to note that the Washington Correctional Foundation is directing priority attention to providing literacy training and employment training to the inmates of Lorton Reformatory, crucial skills necessary to their returning to society as fully rehabilitated. This is imperative."

Since I kept up with Arkansas affairs, I was interested to note that Bill Clinton had been elected governor of Arkansas that year. While he was positioning himself as a liberal, he did invite former Governor Orval Faubus to be his guest at his inaugural dinner. So much for his projecting his civil rights image. In the book *No Surprises* by an Arkansas journalist, Paul Greenberg, the author writes: "The story of this on-again, off-again courtship-and-duel doesn't fit neatly into the self-constructed myth of Bill Clinton's having been a zealous advocate of civil rights during the Faubus era."

Leaving Elective Office

As much as I enjoyed my service as county supervisor, the

enormous demands on my time from my two major jobs and some university teaching were taking their toll. Sylvia and our sons Dean and Neil were not too enamored of my work schedule. For example, at Brookings I had received a sizeable grant from the National Institute of Corrections of the Department of Justice to hold a series of conferences for state legislators around the country to promote what was called at that time "Alternatives to Incarceration." It meant a great deal of preparation and some travel, and little time at home. The effort itself was a great success. With the help of contacts I had all over the country and the assistance of the National Association of State Legislatures, I identified key state legislators to attend the seminars. Significant changes were made by many state legislators especially from Texas to Utah. I teamed up with NIC to coauthor a report "Alternatives to Incarceration" in 1979. For political reasons, my grant was not renewed and I was not able to continue maintaining the momentum I had achieved. It was a sad setback, because I could not help the dozens of state legislators who called me for help for several years thereafter. The federal government is often fickle and does not carry through on initiatives that it supports at the start.

I had learned that foundations were much more reliable in certain circumstances. The second "New Members" conference was supported by the Ford Foundation and went quite well. Not only did we have about twenty House members attend, but several new senators agreed to participate. The train ride had become an attractive device to get participation and more spouses and children came along. The relationship with the Congressional Research Services was not always smooth (while I personally made some good friends), since there were differences both on the speakers to be invited and on the details of the logistics. But we soldiered on and the results were more than satisfactory.

Bowing to the pressures from my family, but extremely reluctant to give up my supervisor job, since I was making a major contribution to the Mount Vernon Magisterial District and to Fairfax County,

I announced in February of that year that I would not run for reelection. Before I went public, I asked Gerry Hyland if he were interested, but he said he wasn't ready. When I did announce, Sandy Duckworth moved fast to preempt the Democratic field. I did feel it was necessary for a successor to have ample time to mount an effective campaign, which was why I acted early. But I did feel I was overly dramatic in my announcement, which I made at the board, having researched a significant resignation in past history that I decided to paraphrase. As I put it, "I can no longer continue to conduct the awesome responsibilities of the office I hold without the support of the woman I love." That was my variation of what King Edward VIII said in 1936 at Windsor Palace when he abdicated the throne of England to marry Wallis Simpson. For the last six to eight months of my service, everyone called Sylvia "Wally." Duckworth won a close race with Farrell Egge, and I'd like to think that my support for her did make a difference.

On May 18, 1980, a major story appeared in *The Washington Star* by staff writer Thomas Crosby, entitled, "Grueling Hours, Lack of Privacy Causing Public Figures to Resign." Crosby interviewed numerous elected officials in the Greater Washington area who had chosen not to run for reelection. I was honored to be included in the story, since many of the others were quite distinguished public servants such as Norman Christeller of Montgomery County, Maryland, and Richard Hobson of Alexandria, Virginia. A number of psychiatrists and psychotherapists were consulted to explain why these resignations had occurred. The reasons the officials gave were varied, and the explanations given by the psychiatrists were even more varied.

When I was queried, I emphasized the great demands on my time. I was quoted as saying "the job was considered part-time but it was really full time. I spent 100 hours a week on two jobs." Crosby mentioned that I was a senior staff member at Brookings as well as a supervisor of Fairfax County. He went on to quote me as follows: "It became too much. It took its toll physically, it wore me down and I never saw my family." The psychotherapist said that "lives in official Washington subject public officials to an occupational syndrome that can affect local officials as well.... The incredibly long hours cause people to wear themselves out physically, more than any other city I've seen and the intensity of the stress is the same all day."

About the same time, Blaine Harden of *The Washington Post* wrote a long story about the demands on my time. He followed me around on a day in my life, starting from early every morning until about 9:00 a.m. at my Fairfax County supervisor's office, after which I made a half-hour drive to Washington for a full day of work at Brookings (calling my county office at lunch time), arriving back at the county after Brookings (having grabbed a sandwich at a fast-food place) to attend several evening meetings, and then concluding by 1:00 a.m. after reviewing materials at my county desk. As is obvious, there was little time for family.

Administration of Justice Seminars Hit Their Stride

In March 1979, after the New Members of Congress seminar in January, and after the announcement of my pending retirement as county supervisor (as of January 1, 1980), we held the second Administration of Justice Seminar. During the intervening year, the planning committee had met about a half-dozen times. The group comprised the chief counsel and minority counsel of the Senate and House Judiciary Committees, Mark Cannon and one or two assistants representing Burger, two assistant attorneys general, a senior staffer from the Administrative Office of the Courts, a senior staffer from the Federal Judicial Center, and me—about twelve people in all. These meetings were extremely valuable, since they were conducted on an amicable bipartisan basis, and all decisions on format and invitees were made on a consensus basis. Also many friendships were created, helpful on a range of other matters confronting the world of the judiciary (such meetings went on over the whole fifteen years of the seminars). Ted Kennedy of Massachusetts had become the Chairman of the Senate Judiciary Committee and his two senior staffers, Ken Feinberg and Steve Breyer, were extremely supportive. Not only did Kennedy himself attend the seminar, but also Ranking Republican Senator Strom Thurmond of South Carolina, Senator Howell Heflin of Alabama, Senator Alan Simpson of Wyoming, as well as some fifteen members of the House Judiciary Committee.

Four major matters were addressed at the gathering. The first was restructuring federal appellate jurisdiction through creation of a new U.S. Court of Appeals for the Federal Circuit by combining the Court of Claims and the Court of Customs and Patent Appeals. A vigorous discussion ensued about the balance needed between general and specialized courts. The second category covered issues of judicial discipline and tenure. Members of Congress cited instances of judicial misconduct, while the judges, not surprisingly, defended the good behavior of the judiciary (a frank discussion could never have been held if the meeting was public). The third major topic involved feedback on the Speedy Trial Act of 1974, a discussion that led to recommendations for corrective amendments to the law to expedite criminal trials. Lastly, there was an examination of recommendations for revision of the criminal code, as well as the possible creation of commissions to minimize disparities in sentencing.— without compromising judicial independence. This topic was of particular interest to me, because I had worked with scholars at the University of Illinois (Chicago Circle) and officials of the Minnesota Corrections Commission to develop legislation in this area. (The effort was later to go awry with the development of mandatory-sentencing guidelines that severely reduced judicial discretion. On January 12, 2005, the U.S. Supreme Court took corrective action in the cases *U.S. v. Booker* and *U.S. v. Fanfan,* ruling that the guidelines were advisory, not mandatory, with the appeals courts hearing appeals of the reasonableness of the federal judges' decisions.)

It so happens that the National Center for State Courts is located in Williamsburg, and Chief Justice Burger made sure we invited several state chief justices to each conference, to provide an opportunity for collaboration and sharing of information between federal and state arenas.

In further reference to the article that Mark Cannon and I wrote for the *Washington & Lee Law Review*, "Congressman Romano Mazzoli of Kentucky said he had never attended a conference where he used more of the information he had obtained than [at] the first Williamsburg conference, but . . . [that] the second conference was even better." Apparently Senator Kennedy didn't have the same experience, because he bolted the conference on Saturday afternoon to watch a basketball game on television. I may have been partly responsible, as I let Judge Elmo Hunter's presentation go on too long, cramping the time of several other presenters, especially Solicitor General Wade McCree who was such a thoughtful and amusing speaker. It was an overly polite gesture on my part not to stop Hunter, which I never let happen in future seminars, no matter how distinguished the speaker. My lapse may have been partially caused by the great back pain I was suffering from the spondylitis ailment, which forced me to sleep on the hotel floor part of the time. When I went to see my rheumatologist about my condition later in the year, he suggested I take Motrin for my pain—a serious mistake. It caused me to have significant internal bleeding, which led to my being hospitalized for about a week. I had two blood transfusions, and looking back, I feel lucky not to have become HIV positive, since AIDS was not well known then, and blood was not yet being screened. While I was very friendly with my rheumatologist, I decided to replace him.

Now that I was about to leave the Fairfax County Board of Supervisors, I was indeed quite wistful. My five years had been very productive, and I had felt that I was master of my fate more than any other position I had had. While Brookings gave me great latitude, I still felt like a "hired hand." Many people in Mount Vernon had expressed their appreciation for my service, and I felt that the occupation fit my capacities very well. Even while giving Brookings fifty hours per week, I had made another fifty hours available to solve many of the problems confronting my constituents. A number of them paid me what I considered the supreme compliment when they asked what I would do after leaving the board, not even knowing that I had been simultaneously working another full-time job. My frail health was not a factor in my decision to resign, but rather the strong wishes of my family. Unlike others in public life, I really meant it when I said family needs mattered most. At my last board meeting, I told my favorite retirement story, originally created by the great playwright George S. Kaufman. It's about a man who retires after fifty years of loyal service to his company. After several months, he misses the ambience of his old office and so he returns to the building to walk the corridors. A former colleague comes out of his office and looks at the man in some puzzlement. Then the light dawns and he says, "Ah yes, Carruthers, forgotten, but not gone."

After my departure from the county position, I felt some sense of decompression, even though I stepped up my activities at Brookings. As one example of my attempts at creativity, I had often wanted to indicate the interrelationship between economics and other disciplines or endeavors. One opportunity came my way totally fortuitously, walking down the street in Washington. I bumped into Tom Graves, who had been a senior official at the Executive Office Bureau of the Budget, and was now a consultant for the U.S. National Endowment for the Arts (NEA). He and I then concocted a method for enabling Brookings to relate the arts to economics. I received a grant from NEA to prepare a seminar on the value of cultural resources in enhancing regional economic development. One example of that would be the Wolf Trap Foundation for the Performing Arts in Fairfax County, which had been a significant factor in attracting major corporations to locate in the county. The U.S. Department of Commerce, then headed by Secretary Philip Klutznick, expressed a deep interest in the matter. We had a very successful seminar that included numerous prominent cultural and political figures from New York City, who emphasized that New York's being a cultural mecca contributed great economic value to the city. The Department of Commerce ultimately (December 8, 1980) issued a report entitled "Cultural Resources/Economic Development, Strengths and Limitations, A Roundtable."*

When I had first approached Brookings President Bruce MacLaury with the idea that Graves and I had formulated, he had some reservations, but ultimately became an enthusiastic endorser. In fact he urged me to think of additional, unusual ways that economics could be related to other disciplines. I then reminded him, tongue-in-cheek, that the arts connection was one area for which I had been able to get significant funding.

During this period, I also had increased involvement with the Washington Correctional Foundation and my university teaching. I served notice that I would be available for pro bono activities involving Fairfax County social service agencies, but only after a year or two of catching up with my list of things to do. My right eye was slowly coming back to usefulness, but I still could not read out of it. It sure did make my driving a lot safer! Our older son Dean had his bar mitzvah at the beginning of 1980, and he did a splendid job at the service. Sylvia was able to make some trips with me when I took Brookings groups to various American cities. She had become quite invaluable to the Senate Committee on Commerce, Science & Trans-

---

* Just to bring this matter up to date, I want to mention that the January 29, 2005, issue of *The Washington Post* had a feature in the real estate section about a very popular area of Northern Virginia called Shirlington. The article described the need for a better mix of culture and economic development to continue to succeed. Rod Irwin, a strategic projects manager in Arlington County's Economic Development Office, is quoted saying," We thought cultural amenities were a strong way to attract people. Moving the library there and relocating the Signature Theatre there became the draw." Such an effort would include the construction of about 650 rental units and for sale condos to attract more people to Shirlington from surrounding areas. Arlington County officials estimate that the library and the theater will draw an additional 200,000 people per year.

portation, and her job seemed quite secure for the future. I had become somewhat active on the County Committee of 100; and this year at a dinner meeting, I joined with one of my former interns at Brookings, Christopher Bright, in presenting a paper on the possibilities for productive and multifaceted economic development in the county.

My leadership of the Washington Correctional Foundation gained considerable attention in the nation's capital. The work of our board—made up of Congressional, religious, and business leaders; university officials, managers of private clubs; and individuals, such as Frances Humphrey Howard (Hubert Humphrey's sister) —led to many hirings of ex-offenders as well as increased job training at Lorton, especially in culinary arts. (Some Lorton alumni got impressive salaries as chefs and cooks in restaurants and clubs after being discharged from the reformatory, and none of them to my knowledge ever recidivated.) As I wrote in the foundation's brochure, "We are convinced that rehabilitation will work if it is really tried, and we are well embarked on a venture to make that philosophy a reality. A civilized world requires no less of us." Senator Arlen Specter of Pennsylvania, Chairman of the Senate Appropriations District of Columbia Subcommittee, was so impressed with our effort that he managed to get $40 million appropriated to the District of Columbia to reinforce what we were doing. But most of that money—which was administered under the new director of the district's corrections department, not our foundation—disappeared without a trace. Specter created an investigating committee to find out what happened to the money, with prominent attorney Richard Ben-Veniste (who recently served on the "9/11 Commission") as chairman and me as vice chairman. The witnesses so confounded the investigation that both Ben-Veniste and I resigned. The money was never found. Imagine how the inmates felt.

I was becoming more heavily involved in teaching for Nova University, which had numerous centers about the country. This meant traveling to cities such as Philadelphia, New York, Chicago, and St. Louis and to western Massachusetts, to teach from Friday evening through Sunday afternoon. I developed a technique of role-playing for the students in which they would be divided up on opposite sides of a major public issue. I remember focusing on the issue of public housing in one of those cities, where the students representing those who supported such housing nearly came to blows with those who opposed. It became too hot and heavy and I had to intervene. In another session—this one was in St. Louis—most of the students were associated with the Army Materiel Command, and the subject was the operation of the organization. They had written papers in advance, examining all aspects of the organization. The director of the Nova Center in St. Louis was the civilian "second in command" of the Army unit involved. When he told the students that I was staying with the commanding general of the Army center (who happened to be an old neighbor of mine, Jim Hesson), some of the students paled, because their papers had reviewed their commander's efficiency. I quietly assured them that their papers were kept in strict confidence, and their views would not be revealed to *anyone*—leading to many sighs of relief.

My regular lecturing for Nova University generally helped keep up my morale during times of stress. The assistant dean, Bob Baer, and I had bonded, and he assured me that the response of the students remained quite high. On the student visits to Washington, I generally shared the platform, in different time frames, with columnist Jeffrey Birnbaum, and our effort apparently not only was important intellectually to Nova but also financially, since the programs were quite profitable. As time went on, however, there were a series of changes at the top at Nova, and the Washington element lost favor and status. Gradually, the whole effort was phased down. While I had known many of the leading players of Nova in the 1970s; by the 1990s, that association had evaporated. It had been an exhilarating run, better in many ways than my teaching at both GW and American University, since Nova was an innovative undertaking that served as a role model for others. My final lecture was in 2004.

I took on yet one more role when Bruce MacLaury, the president of Brookings, asked me to serve on the Environmental Scan Committee of United Way of America, which was headquartered close to home, in Alexandria, Virginia. MacLaury was serving on the United Way board, along with many CEOs of major corporations, and each of these folks had nominated someone to serve on the this committee. The appointees were mostly company vice presidents for long-range planning, and I jokingly told them that I substantially dragged down the average income of the group. This was the beginning of about a dozen years of involvement, with meetings held quarterly, until the embattled president of United Way, William Aramony abolished the group for fear that its success would reflect badly on his failures. I think of my colleagues on the committee as "futurists;" who were a remarkable group of creative and thoughtful people. It was a great experience to become familiar with their thought processes, which were often quite unconventional, but also quite brilliant. We published a series of studies on a variety of long-range topics, such as ways the nation could make improvements in social service delivery, in a book entitled, "The Road Ahead," which made projections of future developments in the United States and their relevance to nonprofit organizations. These studies were sent to the hundreds of United Way affiliates and also sold to other nonprofits, thus bringing in a significant sum to the coffers of the national organization. I stayed on to the end, long after MacLaury had completed his time on the United Way board.

The third annual Administration of Justice seminar was held in the spring of 1980. The date was set to accommodate the chairman of the Senate Judiciary Committee, Ted Kennedy of Massachusetts, who was already gearing up to challenge President Carter for the Democratic nomination for president. But Kennedy dropped out of the seminar after we had already announced his participation. He went on the campaign trail, instead of living up to his commitment to us. His staffer Ken Feinberg was very apologetic, since Kennedy had assured him that he would be available. I think Kennedy made a political mistake anyway, because I can't think of any place he could have been that would have helped him more than the support of the attendees at this seminar. Because of this development, there was some reduction in attendance, because the timing was not as suitable for possible attendees. Another shock was the notice that Congressman Peter Rodino was withdrawing financial support for the seminar, because he was economizing to make ends meet for his House Judiciary Committee. (I later found out the committee ended the year with a substantial surplus.) Although we were getting some financial help from the Department of Justice, Rodino's action meant Brookings would suffer a loss; nonetheless, MacLaury graciously authorized me to notify all congressional participants that we would pay their expenses. These were the kind of roadblocks I would confront as the years went on, but I persevered for a total of fifteen years on this program, until I retired from Brookings in 1993.

To briefly review what took place at this third seminar, in addition to the greater exploration of our usual subject matter, there were two issues that deserve priority attention. First, there was an intensive discussion of the issue of judicial discipline, where it was made clear that the Congress planned to enact legislation. Legislation was indeed enacted later that year and very recently (2004–5) a study of the implementation of that act was initiated by the Judicial Conference (a key instrument of the Supreme Court) with Supreme Court Justice Stephen Breyer leading the review. The second key issue about which there was great concern was that of judges delegating too much authority to their clerks and other subordinate officials. In other words, this concern was expressed over the bureaucratization of the operation of the Federal Courts. I teased the group with a Brooks Hays story directed at Father Drinan, then a Member of Congress, when I cited biblical authority for the argument that judges should do their own thing, because the Bible says: "And Jacob leaned on his staff ... and he died."

In the 1980 election, Ronald Reagan became president and the Republicans took control of the Senate. Herb Harris—whose 1974 election to the House had opened my way to being a county supervisor—lost his seat in the Congress. And Bill Clinton lost his bid for reelection, appearing to be too liberal a governor for the people of Arkansas. It was quite interesting preparing for the fourth New Members of Congress seminar in such a political milieu, and I decided to make some changes. For a review of earlier Congresses, I invited Brooks Hays and Walter Judd to talk about the House, and Alan Simpson of Wyoming and David Pryor of Arkansas to talk about the Senate. For a change of scenery, the location this time would be a resort hotel in Virginia. Brookings was going to go it alone this year, without the collaboration of the Library of Congress or the American Enterprise Institute and with MacLaury managing to get the Ford Foundation to provide financial support. For reasons that I could not understand (I do know that Members of Congress, even new ones, are fickle), however, the number of attendees started to drop, from about sixteen to about eight; and MacLaury decided to pull the plug.

As the next year, 1981, began, Congressman Bill Nelson of Florida (today a United States senator) came to the rescue. He had enjoyed being at the preceding seminar and offered to host a "mini-seminar" at his Washington residence. Some eight new Members agreed to attend. The seminar went off very well, and we at Brookings were very grateful to Congressman Nelson for enabling us to continue the tradition we had established. In the future, these valuable seminars would be accomplished through an alliance of the CRS, Brookings and the American Enterprise Institute (AEI), a moderate to conservative "think tank" This coalition received financial support from the Henry Luce Foundation, contingent on having all three entities involved. When I reported that such an arrangement had been made, President

MacLaury objected, arguing that Brookings alone could do an even-handed job. When I told him that from $75,000 to $150,000 was involved, he relented. MacLaury's reversal reminded me at the time of a Brooks Hays story about the man who asked his priest to say a mass for his dead horse. The priest answered that he could not take such an action. The man then said that an Episcopal priest had agreed to offer appropriate prayers in return for a $100,000 contribution to his church, and the man started to walk away. The priest called him back and said, "Why didn't you tell me that the horse was a Catholic?"

I was especially proud of my part in keeping the program together over its eighteen years. There were many times that it looked like it would fly apart. It was a rather difficult arrangement for the three sponsors, since they each had strong ideas about how the programs should be conducted, who should be the speakers, and how we could encourage new Members of Congress to attend.

I was honored, after the eighth biennial seminar (of the ten we held before I retired), to receive a special thank-you letter (not the usual pro forma) from the Librarian of Congress, James Billington, who handwrote an additional comment, "You are very much the spirit of the meetings." An example of the challenges we faced occurred at the very last seminar, which was held in 1993. The chairman of the Joint Chiefs of Staff, Colin Powell, served on a panel dealing with military problems confronting the new president, Bill Clinton. Powell went on for some time expressing his profound opposition to the "don't ask, don't tell" proposal for dealing with homosexuals in the military. It was his opinion that homosexuals were a serious detriment to military efficiency. His comments led to others at the meeting offering a very delicate response to Powell, a man held in high regard, but civility was maintained.

Maintaining the Administration of Justice Momentum

Under President Reagan, William French Smith was appointed Attorney General, and I was delighted that Smith had named Kenneth

Starr as Counselor to the Attorney General. Because of our friendship, Starr worked hard to persuade Smith to continue supporting the Administration of Justice seminars. Smith allowed holdover Democratic Justice Department high officials to attend the 1981 meeting, even though they were going to be replaced shortly thereafter. This fourth seminar had considerable attendance from the Congress: fourteen Members from the House, led by Chairman Rodino and Ranking Minority Leader McClory, and four senators— Thurmond, Heflin, and Simpson, and Utah's Orrin Hatch. Other participants included six federal judges led by Chief Justice Burger, seven senior Justice Department officials led by Attorney General Smith, two state supreme court judges, and about thirty-five additional key people.

Judge Clifford Wallace led a spirited discussion of planning for the future of the judiciary, and a later revision of that report was crucial to the work of the Committee on Long Range Planning of the Judicial Conference and also instrumental in the creation of the Federal Courts Study Committee. Relevant to the 2005 debates concerning the appointment and confirmation of federal judges, back in 1981 Judge Abner Mikva discussed the long-term perspective for selecting and retaining judges, looking for ways to minimize conflicts. Among the other highlights of the fourth seminar: Judges Gignoux and Hungate reviewed the rule-making process; Ralph Kleps analyzed preemptory challenge legislation; Vermont Chief Justice Barney promoted the State Justice Institute as an important mechanism for enabling all levels of the judiciary to cooperate more effectively; and Ford Foundation officials urged greater utilization of alternative dispute resolution as a means of reducing the enormous overburdening of the Federal Court system;. Solicitor General Wade McCree concluded the seminar with an assessment of "ascertaining congressional intent," which is a serious difficulty because Congress, quite understandably, often deliberately enacts ambiguous provisions in legislation and leaves it to the courts to do the interpretation.

It was in this year, 1981, that the *Washington & Lee Law Review* published the article, mentioned earlier, that Mark Cannon and I wrote. We reviewed the Administration of Justice seminars and the historic effort at cooperation among the three branches of government. The seminars received a great deal of attention throughout the judicial world. Chief Justice Burger had risked the stature of the Supreme Court to undertake this innovation, and later, Chief Justice Rehnquist had strengthened our approach. The doctrine of separation of powers had not been tarnished and much good had been accomplished by these seminars.

Burger would later that year make a historic speech to the Lincoln, Nebraska, bar association in which he said that "factories with fences" should be created in prisons, enabling inmates to be trained in literacy and meaningful job skills. "When society places a person behind walls and bars, it has an obligation—a moral obligation—to do whatever can reasonably be done to change that person before he or she goes back into the stream of society," Burger told the group.

Not long after, Ted Koppel called Burger to ask him to appear on his new television program, "Nightline," to discuss prison industries. Mark Cannon and I were in the chief justice's chambers at the time and we urged him to accept. He reluctantly agreed, and the program that was soon aired was a most successful one, with Koppel asking the stations to extend their coverage for an extra half hour. This experience led Burger to be far more willing to make similar media appearances. (He had found he even enjoyed chatting live about prison conditions with several inmates who participated in the Koppel program.)

The Fire Still Burns to be a Public Servant

Congressman Tom Evans, a Republican from Delaware, who had attended a New Members seminar, and his wife Mary Paige, an accomplished artist and a Democrat, had become good friends of mine. Evans was cochairman of the Republican National Committee, although, ironically, his wife had been on President Nixon's "enemies list." Evans was the first Republican member of the House to endorse Ronald Reagan for president and had become Reagan's man in the House. After Reagan was elected, Evans agreed to assist me in getting an appointment to a Democratic position at a regulatory commission. Senator Simpson agreed to help on the Senate side. I had some interviews at the White House and thought things were progressing pretty well when an unfortunate development took place. Three Republican members of the House had gone to Florida in the fall, ostensibly to play golf or to go hunting or fishing. They were Evans, Tom Railsback of Illinois, and Dan Quayle of Indiana. It was discovered that a sexy lobbyist, Paula Parkinson, had shared a lodge with them. For Evans and Railsback, this marked the beginning of the end of their political careers. Quayle survived because he had just been elected to the Senate and did not face the electorate for six more years. Also his wife Marilyn said that her husband would prefer golf to sex anyway. So as events unfolded, with Evans now under a cloud, my outreach came to an end.

During early 1981, my civil action against the federal government for blinding me in one eye with the swine-flu vaccine had finally come before Federal Judge Albert Bryan in Alexandria, Virginia. In the 1976 legislation—insisted on by the drug companies before they would make the vaccine—a provision was included that restricted legal actions to actions against the federal government only, not the drug companies themselves, and to judge-only proceedings, with no juries. Clearly, my case would not be one of fact-finding by a jury of my peers. What's more, the only doctors who had the courage to testify on my behalf were British citizens, distinguished physicians, one practicing at George Washington University Hospital and the other at Georgetown University Hospital—who told me they wouldn't be surprised if they got deported. The "Justice" Department indeed tried to damage their careers and reputations. One doctor said that a representative of the department went to his superiors at Georgetown and made threatening comments about adverse actions that might take place if he testified. And the doctor from GW, who was attacked by the defense as not competent to be an expert witness, oddly enough was sufficiently competent to be part of the team that saved President Reagan's life when he was shot shortly after my case was heard. I had already sensed my case was dead in the water when the judge bristled at the obvious British accents of my two star witnesses.

The lead doctor for the defense was from the Wilmer Eye Institute of Johns Hopkins University. He testified that there was no causal relation between the swine-flu shot and my blindness, but then again, he was part of an institution that received substantial federal grants. Needless to say, the judge ruled against me. The Wilmer doctor could barely look me in the eye, so to speak, and the U.S. Attorney just shrugged his shoulders and said, "All in a day's work." Nowhere did I get the sense that anyone cared about justice, but only about winning. Some measure of the effort to find the "truth" was the admission in evidence of an expert's view that there was no causal relation between the swine-flu shot and optic neuritis and the rejection (on technical grounds) of the *same* expert's later finding that there *was* such a causal relation. I got the same feeling "about justice" when the three-judge circuit court panel—Winter, Phillips and Ervin—that heard the appeal also ruled against me. Apparently the words above the west entrance to the Supreme Court Building— "Equal Justice Under Law"—really mean "Pretty Much a Roll of the Dice." I now understood, at a personal level, the significance of Chief Justice Burger's statement that he once made to me, when he said that he thought that up to one-quarter of the legal profession might be considered incompetent.

The outcome was particularly ironic in my case, because I was naïve enough to have refrained from saying anything beforehand to any of the high-level people I knew in the judiciary or the Justice Department. To do so, simply to make sure that my case was fully understood and adequately reviewed, would not have been improper in any ethical sense; but I had not wanted to create the perception that I was seeking any favor—only that elusive "justice". This was a turning point in my life, with the court rebuff leading me to feel that I was ending any real chance for a political future.

Brooks Hays seemed to be failing that summer, but I just thought it was old age and didn't dwell on it. Some of his papers had already been given to the Southern Baptist Historical Library and Archives in Nashville and to the University of Arkansas, among other places. I had helped coordinate the donation of much of the balance to the new Kennedy Library in Boston. Dan Fenn, a friend of mine from Harvard and from the Kennedy years, was managing the library; and he arranged for Hays and me to fly to Boston (at our own expense, of course) to check out how the staff had catalogued the documents. Right before we were to leave, Dan called to say that he had just had a tooth pulled, and maybe we should wait a while to make the trip. I replied that it was "now or never," because it had taken a lot of planning to produce this window of opportunity. I am so glad I insisted. After Hays and I had viewed his documents at the Kennedy Library, I remained in Boston to visit my sick brother Abe; and Dan promised to get Hays to the airport. But Hays got lost once he was at the airport, missed his plane, and had to wait for the next flight.

Sometime thereafter, when Hays and Frank Bane and I were arranging to have lunch together, Hays suggested we gather at his house rather than the Cosmos Club, his usual favorite. Of course, Frank and I agreed. It was the last time I was to see Brooks Hays. The lunch was on a Wednesday and he died in his sleep that weekend on the twelfth of October. He had gone over his affairs with a family member the day before, and, later, those that knew him got the eerie feeling that Hays must have decided the time had come to go. I felt happy, at least, that I had insisted we make that trip to Boston in August. I flew to Little Rock for the funeral at the Second Baptist Church, Hays's beloved place of worship, and was amazed when Orval Faubus walked in and sat beside me for the service. Maybe he hoped this action would lessen the time he would have to spend rotting in hell.

The Continued Struggle To Maintain My Career

Although my vaccine-damaged eyesight was improving, other aspects of my health gradually deteriorated, but not enough to prevent me from meeting all my obligations, and even then some. My back was slowly fusing, become one bone. I dealt with the pain, which was sometimes very intense, through medication. Both my shoulders and my hips had ceased to be a problem, after I had been fearing replacement surgery for quite awhile. The continued curvature of my spine was the most difficult thing to adjust to, since it seriously affected my appearance and sense of self, and would cause many more challenges in the future. As I exercised and tried unsuccessfully to walk erect, I grew more and more upset. Sylvia and Dean and Neil were great, and acted as if nothing had changed.

I was determined, however, that I would continue to do everything I could in both my career and my pro bono contributions to society. I would create and develop significant programs at Brookings, moving ahead with the Administration of Justice programs and making an ongoing success of the New Members of Congress training sessions. I was able to help Fairfax County by serving on a number of its commissions and its related organizations for delivery of human services and by continuing to advise on appropriate land use development. My professional work on Nova University programs was receiving strong support from the students, and my involvement in criminal justice and community corrections activities was beginning to show even more meaningful results than before. Life still had much to offer. I maintained this affirmative outlook despite other setbacks, such as suffering a seizure in 1983—out of the blue and with no apparent cause—and the discovery that I had ulcerative colitis, which developed into Crohn's disease.

I discovered that one can do much to offset any setbacks one might have. My parents had confronted a very difficult world of economic depression and had not let it defeat them. While I might have done things differently from them, they served as a role model for survival against all odds. My mother was a major player in raising substantial sums of money for charity, especially for the Boston Jewish Memorial Hospital and the American Jewish Congress. My dad had been forced by circumstance to abandon his budding career as an engineer and was only able to make a modest living as a life insurance salesman—a capacity in which he went above the call of duty, assisting hundreds of people to find their way through adversity. Proof of that was the multitude of letters we received after he died from his clients, singing praises for his help and guidance.

The eighties was a decade when Sylvia and I watched our sons mature with great satisfaction. A source of pleasure was the bar mitzvah of Neil in 1982. He did a splendid job and showed close identification with his faith. Dean graduated from high school in 1984 with good grades and was admitted to both the University of Virginia and Virginia Tech (he chose Tech because he wanted to be an engineer; we had bought him one of the earliest home computers when he was fourteen). He did not even want to apply to Harvard, since he thought it was too "uppity" an institution. When I reminded him that his father was *not* uppity, he said I was just an exception. While Dean had a slow start at college, he came on very strong in his final years. I had little experience with fraternities, because they were banned at Harvard, so it was much to my surprise, that Dean became quite active in a fraternity at Tech and ended up living at the fraternity, which was an academic plus. The experience also taught him leadership and responsibility.

When Dean graduated from college, he managed to convince a prestigious firm, Allen-Bradley (later acquired by Rockwell) to hire him, even though his grades weren't the best. After his training period, he ended up in Pittsburgh, Pennsylvania. This was a wonderful coincidence, because Sylvia's hometown of Jerome wasn't too far away and Dean was already familiar with the area. After living with a college friend for a while, he was able to buy his own house (with a little help from us).

Meanwhile Neil graduated from high school in 1988. He was admitted to George Mason University, but to our surprise, put only on the waiting list at Virginia Tech—even though the high school's student advisor assured us he would be admitted. Having visited Dean at Tech—and having a pleasant experience being introduced as the "little brother" to the girls at fraternity parties much older than he—that college was his first choice. I happened to know the head of the alumni association, and I appealed to him for help. He said he couldn't change anything, but arranged a meeting with the admissions director who did not impress me at all, I must say. He was certainly an arrogant person, almost hostile, but finally he said that if Neil enrolled at George Mason and got at least a B in each of five very tough courses, he could be admitted to Tech for the second semester. Neil decided to live at home and worked as hard as I have ever seen him work. He was getting Bs and As in four of his courses, but he was sweating the fifth, calculus. We all celebrated when he got a B in that, too, and went on to a successful college career at Tech.

Sometime during the 1980s, Sylvia and I planned to go to London for a visit. Such a visit was particularly important to me, since I've always considered London to be the most "civilized" city on the planet. I've spent much of my life promoting civility, and I enjoyed the days spent in London on several trips where I could bask in the aura. The day before we were to leave, Neil was diagnosed as having mononucleosis, and we had to cancel. It was quite a scramble, as we had to cancel airline tickets and hotel reservations, among other arrangements. With letters from doctors, we managed to cope with everything, with only the loss of $150. By 1989, we were able to embark again and had a wonderful time in London and the Cotswolds. Among the sites in London, visiting the House of Commons is always a most special delight, because of my deep devotion to the legislative process and fascination with how the British conducted their affairs in this area. We never miss an opportunity to go there when we visit London (or for that matter the legislatures of about every other capital city we have visited, such as those in Canada, France, and Israel). We have frequently attended Old Bailey because it is where much of the British system of administering justice takes place. I am equally fascinated by how the British structure their legislative and criminal justice systems, and how different they have ultimately become from ours even though ours are rooted in theirs.

Then we headed out to the countryside. Sylvia did the driving, which is always a challenge in England since they drive on the left; but Sylvia was equal to that challenge. We went as far as Bath, where we stayed at a bed and breakfast run by a fine man, whose political view was that Maggie Thatcher was too liberal (as everyone knows she and Ronald Reagan were soul mates!). Sylvia left her purse in a cab we took inside the city of Bath one day, and we tried mightily to track it down, unsuccessfully. The quest lost us the time that we would have spent at Stonehenge. I thought I might meet Bath's mayor to ask his help before we left, but got involved in conversation with the manager of the B and B until it was too late. That turned out to be time well spent, because the manager ultimately located the purse and mailed it back to us in Virginia. I guess I would consider this result a good payoff for my strong commitment to building bridges, even to a person with whom I had very little in common politically.

We had another experience that was even more upsetting. Before we left England, we visited Bill and Barbara Ogden, relatives of our dear friends, the Lipsens. To be on the safe side, they led us to Heathrow Airport well ahead of the time of departure. But we found that our rental car agency had no office on the airport grounds, and to return it, we took ourselves on a hair-raising ride to the office in a nearby hotel. Sylvia had to make a remarkable maneuver across a triple roundabout to get us to our destination. Any American who has driven in England and has confronted triple roundabouts would understand how courageous that action was! As we rushed into the lobby, I stepped right into some fresh cement a worker was putting down on the floor, much to his consternation. After we turned in the car, the shuttle rushed us to the airport, and we made the plane with about five minutes to spare. We lost our original seat reservations, however, and to our horror, had to sit in the smoking section.

The leading club for "intellectuals" and related professionals in Washington was Brooks Hays's old haunt, the Cosmos Club. With the sponsorship of the director of the Mount Vernon mansion, Cecil Wall, and Jim Mitchell of Brookings, I sailed into membership in 1984. The membership chairman said my application was a "slam dunk," since I was a protégé of the revered Congressman Hays. Over time, I found that I made little use of the club. The meals were average, and the membership tended to be a bit older than I and not particularly relevant to my interests. The club performed one useful function—a place to spend the night when I couldn't get home because of a snowstorm. Another function of the club, which others told me was very crucial, was the "status" it conveyed in Washington; and that did not impress me at all.

By 1987 two events took place that precipitated my dropping my membership in the Cosmos Club. First, it refused to accept women and belittled members who tried to change that policy—only caving in sometime later because of financial strains. And I am both proud and humbled by the fact that I resigned at the same time as Supreme Court Justice Harry Blackmun, legendary for his pivotal decisions securing women's rights and autonomy under the law.

My other sense of outrage concerned an obituary that appeared in the club bulletin. It was for a senior Foreign Service officer, Loy Henderson, who was a well-known Arabist, hostile to Israel. The obituary went to great lengths to express pride in this member's strong opposition to President Harry Truman for having recognized the State of Israel when it was created by United Nations resolution.

·The obituary went even further, deploring what it termed Truman's caving in to political pressure from the American Jewish community. Of course, there was no thought of the world's obligation to save the remnant of European Jewry, after six million of them were murdered by the Nazis, to say nothing of the longstanding claim of world Jewry to its rightful place in this land. In my resignation letter I chastised the Cosmos Club directors for their insensitivity in allowing such inflammatory language to appear in the bulletin and urged them to carefully monitor this matter in the future. To their credit, I did get a decent letter of apology.

It was during this period that the founder of AIPAC (American Israel Public Affairs Committee), Sy Kenen, suggested I apply for a job as the director of this pro-Israel lobby. I had gotten to know him in the days when he came to see Congressman Hays. While I had reservations anyway, it was not entirely clear to me at all that this was a sort of tentative offer; but years later, he expressed his regret that I had not accepted his overtures. I received a more serious call from Paul Berger, a prominent Washington lawyer, whom I had met and who had befriended me long ago at the Kesher Israel synagogue, and while I was flattered, I just didn't think I was best suited for such an assignment. In hindsight, I may have been too worried about the role I would have to play and might have been able to negotiate an agreement where I could recuse myself on matters that I was uncomfortable with. (I am confident that AIPAC performed at least as well without my leadership that it would have if I had accepted an offer.)

During the 1980s, I was somewhat more active in the Reform synagogue my family was now attending, having become accustomed to the leadership of Rabbi Fink. Temple Beth El was right across the street from the Virginia Theological Seminary, and Rabbi Fink arranged for a dialogue to get underway between our temple and this Episcopal institution. He, the assistant rabbi, and I, along with seven other knowledgeable laypeople met with ten of the seminary faculty about four times a year from 1982 to 1986. We would have dinner and a discussion with each of the entities taking turns hosting the event. These were not simply brotherhood gatherings; we probed deeply into the supportive and divisive elements of the two religions. We had an advance agenda and required reading, and each meeting was led by a different set of participants. As time went on, we gained the confidence of each other, and the discussions became more and more forthcoming. Had these sessions been recorded, the sum total would have made a profound contribution to Christian-Jewish relations. On the other hand, the participants might have been more guarded if they knew they were on the record, but I think they would have been able to deal with that concern.

Here are two examples of how frank the discussions became. At one session, the reading was *Discerning the Way,* part one of a three-part series *Theology of the Jewish-Christian Reality,* by Paul van Buren, an Episcopalian priest and professor of theology. The author essentially argues that religions are on parallel courses that ultimately intersect (in the achieving of a universal spiritual life). One of the discussants argued that he could not accept this hypothesis. He said he was taught that Christ had come to save the world, not simply Christians, and that, while he respected and loved all of humanity, he could not believe that all religions were guided by the same truths. In the other example, we once made an exception and allowed someone beyond our usual group of twenty to join us—a visiting Episcopalian priest from Jerusalem. The result was disconcerting. He complained that all Jews were in lockstep, especially in the United States, and blindly supported whatever Israel did, right or wrong. I responded that that was not true, in that I personally had turned down the directorship of AIPAC, because I had disagreements with Prime Minister Begin. Furthermore, Jews listened to arguments from people like my former boss, Congressman Brooks Hays, who had honorably mediated Arab-Israeli differences, because he had demonstrated deep compassion for the plight of the Jews and thereby had

proven he had "clean hands." My comments pretty much silenced
the priest for the rest of the meeting.

While I had pretty much gotten out of politics, the fire still burned
in the belly. Meanwhile Congressman Herb Harris, who, sadly, had
lost his seat in the 1980 election by only about a thousand votes,
then lost a comeback effort in 1982 by about the same margin. A
member of the Virginia General Assembly, Dick Saslaw, made an
effort for the same seat in 1984, to no avail. Since I was an ex-officio
member of the Fairfax County Democratic Committee, I began to
think I might want to give a run for this office some consideration.
Sylvia was still opposed, but at least the boys were now a bit older
and did not need as much attention. A major drawback was the state
of my health, because my back was not in good shape; but I thought
I could overcome that problem. In both 1986 and 1988, I attended,
along with Sylvia, the meetings of the Democratic Party's Eighth
District Committee, where a candidate would likely be decided upon.
I honestly thought that if I had spoken up I would have been chosen.
But, very reluctantly, I did not, and others were chosen. In 1990,
former Alexandria mayor Jim Moran did speak up, was chosen by
the Democrats, raised more than a million dollars and beat the incumbent, Republican Stan Parris. He has held the seat ever since.

Bork Hearings, 1987

Over the years, ever since I began the Administration of Justice
Seminars in 1978, on behalf of Chief Justice Warren Burger, I had
become acquainted with about 125 federal judges who attended the
seminars. It was considered quite an honor to be invited to these
sessions, because Chief Justice Burger was their inspiration, and one
needed to have a "need to know" to be invited. One of the judges I
came to know well was Robert Bork. He was considered a conservative, but rational, jurist with an outstanding mind. He had been a
law professor at Yale and teamed up with a Jewish professor Alexander
Bickel who was quite liberal. He pointed out to me that his first wife

was a liberal Jew, who unfortunately died, and his second wife was a conservative Catholic, while he considered himself a moderate Protestant.

During this period I also became friendly with theologian and Professor Alan Geyer of the Wesley Theological Seminary, and we jointly developed a series of seminars to help theologians (mostly progressive) learn how to influence public policy. In one of the seminars I invited Judge Bork to address an evening session. He graciously agreed and was intensely challenged during the question-and-answer period. I was happy when the adjournment time came, but Judge Bork was quite willing to extend the period for some time, which we did.

One of the attendees was a progressive Southern Baptist minister who was a good friend of mine, but happened to dislike Bork intensely. Much to my surprise, this minister was able to testify against Bork's confirmation to be a Supreme Court Justice at hearings in September 1987. I was concerned when he claimed that Bork advocated restoration of prayer in the public schools. I was called by a reporter from *The Washington Post* who wanted to confirm this allegation. I stated first that the meeting was off-the-record and second that I had no such recollection of Bork's remarks. The reporter ran the allegation in the newspaper in any event. I was upset and wrote a letter of rebuttal to *The Post,* with a copy to Judge Bork.

Among the members of the Senate Judiciary Committee who questioned Judge Bork about that story was Chairman Joseph Biden of Delaware. As soon as that happened, Bork pulled my letter out of his briefcase and proceeded to read it. The core paragraph was as follows: "Whatever one's views are about Judge Bork's qualifications to serve on the Supreme Court, he certainly is entitled to a thorough and accurate review of his opinions. In examining my notes of that meeting, I find no reference to any Supreme Court decision, but only the comment that the current turmoil in constitutional law may force some revisions." This letter and a similar one from Rabbi Joshua

Haberman of the Washington Hebrew Congregation led the committee to completely drop this subject, one of Judge Bork's high points in an otherwise very controversial debate.

Another very pleasing moment, during these hearings, for me at least, was when Senator Gordon Humphrey of New Hampshire (not Hubert of Minnesota), a newcomer to the committee, queried Bork about my letter, and Humphrey mispronounced my name "Sikkens" rather than "Sykins." Most of the other members of the committee quickly corrected him; and Senator Strom Thurmond, a man I had disliked when he opposed Harry Truman, but had come to be very fond of when he had changed his views, rose in his seat and said, "I know Mr. Cikins—pronounced Sykins— well and he is a fine gentleman." Since the hearings were on national television, I got some ego-boosting feedback.

A fun thing happened to me in the middle of 1988. A top assistant to former Speaker Tip O'Neill, Chris Matthews, with whom I had become friendly since he often spoke for me at Brookings seminars, was making a splash in Washington. After heading a political consultant operation, he had written a book that became quite famous. It was entitled *Hardball*. The success of this book led to his ultimately becoming a leading political commentator on television. Sylvia and I went to his book-signing party at the Politics and Prose bookstore, and he greeted me very warmly. He wrote this comment in my copy of his book: "Thanks for giving me the chance to do my 'orals' on *Hardball* at Brookings." Being able to show this inscription to other politicians has given me the opportunity to prove that I am not a "babe in the woods" in the political arena.

Monitoring Harvard

When Neil Rudenstine became the president of Harvard, I was upset that he did not honor his Jewish roots (his family had converted to Christianity). He shrunk from even mentioning that his father had been a corrections officer at the Sing Sing Prison in New

York State. I would have thought he would have been proud of how far he had come and how proud of him his father would be. At one of our National Committee on Community Corrections meetings, I mentioned my displeasure to NCCC member Margot Lindsay, who was a member of the prestigious Coffin family of New England and part of the senior Harvard community; and told her that I was thinking of writing a letter to Rudenstine telling him how disappointed I was. She urged me to hold off on my letter, and I was glad I did. At the next NCCC meeting she brought with her a copy of the latest *Harvard Crimson*, the school paper, with a front page story of Rudenstine's visiting the Harvard Hillel House and expressing his great pleasure at what a great contribution it was making.

Several years later there was a letter in the *Harvard Alumni Magazine* denouncing a story in the prior issue that had lauded a professor who was teaching the Yiddish language and had noted how popular she was. It was so unusual that a "dying" language was getting something of a rebirth in dozens of universities. The letter writer, named Sterner, identified himself as Harvard '51. Since I was Harvard '51, I looked him up in our reunion booklets. Because the Harvard professor had identified herself as a Zionist, Sterner took the trouble to identify Zionism as related to Nazism, a well-known tactic of anti-Semites. In one of our Harvard booklets, he called for civility of dialogue, which he seemed to have no capacity to exercise. Then I found that he had worked for Aramco, was a leading member of a group of "Arabists" in the State Department Foreign Service, and he had been the ambassador to the United Arab Emirates. As I pointed out in my challenging response, it was very "modest" of him to omit these credentials in his tirade. I got a kiss-off letter from the magazine; but when I shared my letter with Rudenstine, by some great new insight, the editors decided to share my letter with the readers in the next issue.

Keeping a Political Hand In, Nationally and Locally

Since Brooks Hays and the elder Senator Gore had been good friends over the years, when the South had only about six moderate white political leaders, I had become acquainted with the younger Gore at an early age and later when he was elected to the House in 1976. He was one of the new Members who came to the Brookings seminar, and he was one of the few new senators who came to the 1985 Seminar (elected in 1984). I was happy to support Senator Gore when he ran, although unsuccessfully, for the Democratic nomination for president in 1988. He reciprocated by citing my presence at a major Democratic gathering in Fairfax County. Over the years Senator Gore spoke often for me at Brookings on protecting the environment and also on utilizing scientific resources to improve the country's well-being. I was very happy that Bill Clinton chose him to be his vice-presidential running mate and very disappointed that he was ruled as not having won the 2000 presidential election.

During 1987 I worked very hard, among many others, to help Gerry Hyland get elected county supervisor for the Mount Vernon District. The incumbent at that time was a Republican, Farrell Egge, and I believed that Hyland would make a fine supervisor, supporting many programs with which I agreed: for example, he was a past president of UCM. Hyland was successful in winning that election, and then, in a note he sent to me in November 1987, he wrote, "You have made this victory possible, good friend, with your sound advice, sage perspective, and total commitment to my candidacy. I have chosen to follow in your footsteps, Warren, but doubt that I can fill them half as well as you. Thank you my very special friend." I was pleased that the Mount Vernon Magisterial District once again had an able Democratic county supervisor.

Building Consensus

By the eighties and into the nineties, I became more and more involved in the world of improving the criminal justice system. Priority needed to be given to rehabilitation of those who had become criminals. When I spoke, I reminded Americans about what Dostoyevsky had said, "that a civilization will be judged by how it treats its wrongdoers." Ernest Lefever was an old friend from the CRS days and by then a senior staff member of a conservative think tank, the Ethics and Public Policy Center. When he asked me to chair a seminar on criminal justice at the center, I was happy to oblige. But I had one proviso—that I could invite at least one moderate conservative to serve on each panel. Lefever agreed, and I then asked people such as my old friend Mark Cannon and a senior official from the U.S. Justice Department, Rudy Giuliani, to participate.

The criminal-justice seminar turned out to be a considerable success, with people of all persuasions searching for middle ground. One participant, however, nearly derailed the effort. That was Ernst van den Haag, Professor of Jurisprudence and Policy at Fordham University—a renowned criminologist who believed in severe punishment for even the most minimal of criminal behavior. I was proud of Giuliani when he took on his old scholarly mentor and counseled moderation. I was also proud of Giuliani on a later occasion, when he was willing to challenge his boss, Attorney General Ed Meese (a person I consider an honorable conservative and a good friend who has championed the cause of prison industries), when he expressed disapproval of the ACLU (American Civil Liberties Union). Giuliani said that, while in many situations he strongly opposed the ACLU, it performed a valuable service, and if we didn't have one, we would have to create one.

Confrontation at Brookings

Policy and practice had changed at Brookings since I arrived there, and some of the research was farmed out to other places in the country, with the result that some of the books issued by the institution came from reputable scholars who had little or no direct association with Brookings. The institution decided to create a new category of staffer—the Nonresident Senior Fellow. Many of the in-house staff opposed this development, because it diluted whatever camaraderie managed to be achieved at Brookings. One of these new "nonresidents" was John DiIulio, at that time a professor at Princeton University, His addition to the Brookings nonresident senior fellow category was sponsored by Tom Mann, the director of our Government Division.

DiIulio was a protégé of James Q. Wilson, a distinguished professor, noted for influential works on government and criminal justice. DiIulio was now making his reputation as a hard-line criminologist, after being known as a moderate for some time. It was he who had who coined the phrase "super-predator" to identify young people, mostly black or Hispanic, who, he predicted, would overrun the country unless many more were imprisoned. An op-ed he wrote, emphasizing the super-predator menace and how valuable prisons were in controlling this development, was published in *The Wall Street Journal,* and DiIulio was identified as being with Brookings. In what I thought would be a defense of Brookings from such extremism, I wrote a letter-to-the-editor presenting a different point of view (although it was not published by *The Journal*), and had it distributed throughout the institution. When Tom Mann saw my letter, he erupted and called me on the phone, screaming at me for my temerity in challenging such an eminent nonresident scholar as his friend, the genius John DiIulio. It was the ugliest experience I had ever personally confronted, even worse than the behavior of Orval Faubus years before.

I then distributed my letter to about 125 prominent criminologists in the U.S. and found that at least 90 percent of them agreed with me. A number wrote to reassure me that I represented the mainstream, but Brookings didn't seem to mind being identified with DiIulio rather than me. It was then that I began thinking about finding a different milieu in which I could continue to make a contribution. The Center for Public Policy Education (CPPE) was always the least recognized of Brookings' four divisions, and I found that this situation was not improving, with our division being held in less esteem than others, no matter how hard I or my colleagues tried. Someone told me that the chairman of the board, Louie Cabot, said at a board meeting that as he traveled about the country, the Brookings name he heard mentioned most approvingly was mine. But I realized that his alleged comment did not help my cause. Such a citation would only spark the emotion of jealousy within the institution, which was counterproductive for me. This treatment is probably similar to how university researchers often hold in low esteem their colleagues who teach splendidly but do little research. I assume most Brookings scholars knew little about my research activities, or any other activities I was engaged in, for that matter.

There were many activities I engaged in, beginning in the 1980s that I found particularly rewarding. At the request of my neurologist, Dr. Jack Cochran, I joined the board of the Epilepsy Foundation of the National Capital Area and for seven years worked hard with other members to educate the public about this brain disorder and erase the stigma associated with having it. From 1989-93, I was a member of the board of the Urban Philharmonic Society, a wonderful nonprofit organization led by distinguished African-American conductor Darrold Hunt. The society is dedicated to taking performances normally heard only in major concert and recital halls and presenting them in the ethnic communities of the Washington area. It also provides performance and employment opportunities for highly gifted minority, female, and disabled musicians. I was most pleased to be able to help with fundraising which was so crucial to the survival of this organization.

In the early eighties, I met a remarkable official of IBM, Dr. Ramon Barquin, who created the Computer Ethics Institute (made up of IBM, Brookings, and the Washington Theological Consortium).

I was honored when Dr. Barquin asked me to serve as secretary. Our purpose was to try to head off unethical uses of computers, and we held several conferences to achieve that end. Among our accomplishments was the creation of a document called "The Ten Commandments of Computers." When producers at NPR (National Public Radio) became aware of our efforts, they asked us for an interview; and Ramon insisted that I do it, even though he was our leader. I was one of six coeditors of a book that included the best papers on the subject that were delivered at our seminars. That book was called, *New Ethics for the Computer Age,* published by IBM in 1986.

During the 1980s, the CPPE underwent a number of personnel changes. It had gone from the leadership of Jim Carroll to Lee Fritschler to Larry Korb. Each of them had a different concept of how the division should function, and I was grateful that they permitted me to "do my own thing." This kindness eased somewhat my frustration over the institution's underlying negative aura related to CPPE. Helping me continue on a steady productive course were three splendid assistants, first Ann Specht, then Donna Dezenhall, and finally Pam Buckles.

Among other activities of interest during this period was the focus on apartheid. I held a seminar on the Future of South Africa, at the behest of the Wingspread Foundation, getting many college presidents and other interested parties to attend. This meeting was held during the peak of national uproar over apartheid, and the Wingspread Foundation was most grateful that I could respond to their request for a high-profile assembly on short notice. We had a surprise visit from a group of senior South African businessmen who were working to end apartheid, at some personal risk, I might add. At this time, many college presidents were considering a plan to withhold investments in South Africa, but the Harvard representative, John Shattuck, had a better idea. Since South Africa spent little on the education of its black population, Shattuck recommended that the universities start sending teams of educators to South Africa to set up an infrastructure of education for its minority population.

Since I had been working with Chief Justice Burger on upgrading the office of Chief Justice and holding and attending seminars in that regard, I also wrote in the *ABA Journal*, January 1985, a review of the book by Peter Fish entitled, *Office of Chief Justice.* In this review I called for a commission to be created to overhaul the judiciary, similar to the Brownlow Commission of 1939, which led to the creation of the Executive Office of the President. Although Burger had recommended a tenth Justice for Administration to accomplish the same end, I felt that a range of alternatives should be considered.

I held many seminars on a broad array of health-care matters and then in 1985 coedited the Brookings book *Effects of Litigation on Health Care Costs.* The nation has been somewhat obsessed with this question since the 1980s, and the Congress has considered legislation, all the way up to the present time, to deal with this matter. Both my seminars and the book revealed that the problem is much more complicated than was generally assumed. One might say that there are at least three culprits in this matter. The first is the insurance industry, which is about the most unregulated industry in American and often guilty of generating excessive charges. The second is the medical profession, which seems very reluctant to police the profession and remove physicians who are clearly giving substandard health care and putting some of the population at risk. And third, is the legal profession, which to a certain extent is taking advantage of the situation to file excessive lawsuits. Yet looked at from a different perspective, recent analysis indicates that the number of lawsuits has been slowly declining, and the total amount of the awards is also declining. Finding an evenhanded solution to this problem remains a very difficult task.

I had worked closely with the Drug Enforcement Administration (DEA) on efforts to reduce drug use, with special attention to the DEA's focus on demand (as well as supply) for drugs, becoming friendly with both the administrator, Bob Bonner, and the assistant administrator, Bill Alden. They asked me to chair the DEA's twentieth anniversary meeting, which was attended by all the people who had been administrators of the DEA. It was very valuable meeting, demonstrating that the DEA was not simply involved in interdiction of activities related to smuggling drugs into the United States, but also in helping change the counterproductive habits of the American people. Understandably, they were especially concerned about young people and worked closely with the coaches of high school sports throughout the country.

At the same time, the National Institute of Justice (NIJ) of the Department of Justice was doing many creative things, under the direction of Administrator James K. "Chips" Stewart. We bonded on the issues related to prison industries, and he addressed many seminars at Brookings involved in trying to get prominent business leaders interested in this subject. (In addition, he asked me to serve as on an advisory committee to review a range of proposals submitted to NIJ for funding from research organizations all over the country.) Regretfully, we had little success. Business and labor tended to team up in what might be called, "an unholy alliance," to prevent prison inmates learning how to do a meaningful job. They supposedly feared unfair competition when, at the time I was involved in this effort, less than 100,000 people were employed in total in all the prisons in the nation, when the total national workforce was about 140,000,000. Certainly, the benefit from improvement in public safety and the quality of life for all Americans would be worth this "piddling" amount of competition. I am especially disappointed in organized labor, of which I am a card-carrying member, which has, in contrast, shown far more public spiritedness in other issues, such as civil rights.

The Administration of Justice seminar continued through the eighties into the early nineties, generally held every year. Chief Justice Burger decided to take a sabbatical after the sixth in 1983. Three years later he concluded his role at an extremely well-attended seminar in Annapolis, Maryland, just before he retired as chief justice to head the 1987 Constitutional Bicentennial Commission. He and I, of course, resumed our joint effort on prison industries a couple of years later. Maryland Governor Harry Hughes held a special reception for the seminar group at the Governor's Mansion. However the U.S. Naval Academy seemed indifferent to our presence, even though Strom Thurmond, a high-ranking member of the Senate Armed Services Committee, was in attendance. In November 1985, Burger had given me a copy of his book *Significant Supreme Court Opinions of Honorable Warren E. Burger*, which contained many of his legal opinions. On the flyleaf he had written, "For Warren Cikins—with appreciation for leadership in improving justice—and best wishes." He added a postscript, "A sure cure for insomnia." His issuing this book at this time might well have been a signal of his intent to retire in the very near future.

I was worried that the new chief justice, Bill Rehnquist, might not be interested in continuing this program. Two judicial fellows, Tom Baker and Doug McFarland, had continued on after Burger left, and they worked hard to convince Rehnquist of the value of this effort to the judiciary. I was relieved when he agreed to participate in the seminars. He emphasized that he wanted to be certain this would be an opportunity for him to get to know the members of Congress in attendance. I made sure that at each of the following seminars, there was a breakfast meeting exclusively for the chief justice and the members of the judiciary committees. By 1992, the Rehnquist-led seminars were well established, and the journal of the judiciary, *The Third Branch*, asked me to grant an interview, printed in February 1992, entitled *Warren I. Cikins: Bringing the Three Branches of Government Together*.

With regard to the new chief justice's reshaping the seminars, I pointed out in that journal that he had "reshaped them in a manner that appears to maximize their importance. The seminar at the beginning of each Congress is now the gathering for the principals involved, with the next year being the gathering primarily for senior staff. To enable all to participate fully in the deliberations, Rehnquist has urged the utilization of discussion groups on each topic discussed. He has indicated his satisfaction with the willingness of Congress to address the problems identified by the judiciary, and has gone on to emphasize that communications between the branches are open, free-flowing, and abundant."

After the March 1991 seminar, Congressman Bill Hughes of New Jersey, chairman of the House Judiciary Crime Subcommittee, had indicated that he was extremely satisfied with the benefits he had obtained by participating. He wrote me a letter that said, "I have told a number of people, including those at my hearing just yesterday, that the Brookings Seminar has done more to foster interbranch cooperation than any initiative that I am aware of." In his P.S., he added, "It was superb, Warren, Many Thanks!".

By the time of the fifteenth seminar in 1993, I was committed to retiring before the end of the year. Many new faces were present at the seminar, because Janet Reno, the recently confirmed attorney general had come with many of her senior staff. Also present was soon-to-be-named Supreme Court Justice Stephen Breyer. There was a sense of an era ending. At the opening dinner, Chief Justice Rehnquist presented me with a framed letter, which he read, that thanked me profusely for my "imagination and perseverance," and said that "... the Brookings seminar has become a term in the vocabulary of anyone who speaks about relations between the three branches of government. The seminars have helped change the conventional wisdom about how the branches can communicate with each other and helped those in each branch realize that there is more than one way to look at a problem and more than one legitimate perspective on the administration of justice." At the end of the seminar the chief justice asked all the attendees to hold hands in one big circle, while he led the singing of "Auld Lang Syne."

While it had been a tremendous ordeal each year to put these seminars together, I felt deeply committed to their making a difference in interbranch cooperation, and I regretted that health and other considerations meant that I would no longer be involved and the seminars might well be ended. It was very disappointing to later learn that after one or two half-hearted efforts by the Justice Department and the Congress to put together similar gatherings, this valuable type of outreach did not survive. This bridging mechanism could still be very important, as is evidenced by the occasional flare-up between the branches, for which there is no longer an ongoing vehicle to find reconciliation. With the nation confronting serious problems of preserving civil liberties in the face of terrorism, we are left with the three branches of government having little interaction without the existence of a regularized forum to find middle ground.

Chapter 8

Humanizing Criminal Justice

The administration of justice had not been the only priority for me at Brookings during the eighties and early nineties. In addition to all my other duties there, I focused attention on the related topics of criminal justice, community corrections, and prison industries. Chief Justice Burger, beside his priority concern about the Administration of Justice, was also anxious to do something more about conditions in prisons. Before he retired as chief justice, he decided to create a National Task Force on Prison Industries with prominent businessmen, labor leaders, distinguished criminologists, and senior officials of all three branches of government as members. Frank Considine, president of the National Can Corporation, agreed to be the chairman. The objective was to help educate the nation about the need for sensible actions that would reduce crime, rather than devoting the nation's energies to incarceration and warehousing of convicts. Chief Justice Burger wanted to reverse the attitude that prison industries didn't work to reduce recidivism. As he put it, "The fact that [rehabilitating offenders] is far more difficult than we had thought is the very reason we must consider changes and enlarge our efforts." We began to have a series of luncheon meetings at the Supreme Court. Burger was well aware that some industry and labor leaders opposed prison industries, and he was determined to respond to their objections.

233

Burger soon arranged a task-force trip to Scandinavia to observe how these countries handled their crime problems. About a dozen or so members went and were quite impressed. I did not go because I had already made firm plans to go on a vacation with my family, and I was determined to keep my promise. I regretted missing the opportunity to learn, as well as the opportunity to bond with the other attendees, but I would make the same choice again. Norm Carlson, director of the Federal Bureau of Prisons, came back from the Scandinavian trip and, believing he could show the group some examples of how well the U.S. also does progressive incarceration, he arranged a trip for the same group to Kansas. That one I was able to go on. We went to the Kansas State Penitentiary (now the Lansing Correctional Facility) and the U.S. Federal Penitentiary at Leavenworth, both of which had excellent prison industry programs. We also went to a private facility—a sheet metal plant called Zephyr Industries, whose creator, Fred Braun, hired inmates. Zephyr was not far from the prisons and was an excellent example of the "factories with fences" concept that Burger championed. It was quite an experience to walk the floors of the plant amidst workers who had been sentenced to prison for severe crimes. We talked to them, and they were all enthusiastic about the opportunity to learn a meaningful trade.

Back in Washington, Burger persuaded GW president Lloyd Elliott to create the Center on Innovations in Corrections and Dr. Judith Schloegel to be the director. Schloegel had previously run a very successful job-placement program called Liberation of Ex-Offenders Through Employment Opportunities. I would serve as liaison between the task force and the center, which went right to work designing plans to place ex-offenders with local businesses and industries in the Greater Washington area. Schloegel was later lured away to participate in a statewide Florida program called PRIDE, run by drugstore magnate Jack Eckerd—a member of our task force, dedicated to at-risk youth,—who had acquired a contract with the state.

In follow-up to this movement, Burger initiated the National

Conference on Factories with Fences: The Prison Industries Approach to Correctional Dilemmas. It was held at GW in June 1984, and between 100 and 150 people attended. There were sessions on how Congress, the Justice Department, prison-industry policymakers, the business world, and the community could become more involved. Panels included Members of Congress, high-level officials from the Justice Department, and the vice chairman of the board of the U.S. Chamber of Commerce, among others. About a dozen state correctional industries were exhibitors at the conference. The meeting, cosponsored by GW, the Federal Bureau of Prisons, Brookings, and the Supreme Court, received considerable national attention and gave impetus to the movement.

As I later wrote in *Legal Times*, "A high-water mark in the Burger effort to stimulate an informed debate about the appropriate role of prison industries in society was the conference at Wingspread (a conference center in Racine, Wisconsin, designed by Frank Lloyd Wright) in February 1985. Almost 100 participants divided into 11 committees to study the following areas related to prison industries: laws, executive orders and regulations, procurement, marketing, inmate compensation, staff training, offender input, education, inmate training and job placement, business and labor concerns, industrial management, research and evaluation, media and public relations. Each of these committees made an effort to give a full-scale analysis of their topic areas in order to be of significant value to the governmental entities that had responsibility for prison industries.

Priority was placed on controlling prison costs and establishing programs that would help inmates defray some of the costs of incarceration. Private industry representatives, corrections administrators, legislators, university personnel and concerned citizens chaired or reported on these committees' activities."

After leaving the Supreme Court in 1986, the chief justice gave less attention to prison industries. Then one day late in 1990, the director of the Bureau of Prisons, Mike Quinlan, called me for help because the prison industries program was under attack. A congressman had introduced an amendment to that year's crime bill to sharply restrict the industries in four key product areas: furniture, textiles, apparel, and footwear. Quinlan couldn't reach Burger, and asked me to see what I could do. I did find Burger, and he said, in effect, that we should get together sometime. When I emphasized the urgency, since the congressional conferees of the two Houses were meeting that day and the bill was close to passing, as Congress was about to adjourn that weekend, Burger suggested we have lunch that very day, and I, of course agreed. Soon a long limousine pulled up in front of Brookings, and Burger stepped out to greet me. That scene didn't hurt my status with my Brookings colleagues. We went to the Lawyers Club for lunch. Burger asked me if I had a draft letter to send the conferees, and I said I did. He asked if I had a list of the conferees, and I said I did. Later that day the Supreme Court courier brought me a copy of the letter Burger had sent the conferees, and he had toughened up the one I gave him considerably. He called the anti-prison industry provision an "astonishing proposal" that would be "an incredible setback to one of the most enlightened aspects of the federal prison system." We later found out that Senator Strom Thurmond informed his colleagues, in view of the chief justice's position, he could not accept this amendment, and that killed it. *The Washington Post* then reported that Burger publicly said: "My position on this is the most conservative one you can imagine. If you can take an individual and train him so he can do something a little more useful than stamping license plates, he's a little less likely to go back (into prison). This isn't for the benefit of the criminal community. It's for the benefit for you and me."

For a long time I had been giving some thought to exploring the cost-benefit considerations in utilizing more private prisons. While the federal prison system was well run, many states had serious problems. On the other hand, there were constitutional questions about allowing private entities to be involved in the incarceration of people.

I felt the courts should sort that matter out. When I had worked for TVA long ago, the federal government had justified its going into the production of electric power in order to serve as a yardstick for the private sector. The concept was that competition was good for all parties concerned. It was understood that public power would never become more than 5 to 10 percent of the total power produced. I came to the controversial conclusion that greater use of the private sector in running prisons made sense, if it was done under close supervision, and with the understanding that such prisons would never become more than 5 percent of the total. I also believed that the growth should be gradual, starting with minimum security inmates and graduating to medium security. It would probably best that the private sector never get involved with maximum security. I had the opportunity to have these ideas expressed in a 1986 article in the *Notre Dame Journal on Law, Ethics, and Public Policy,* entitled "Privatization of the American Prison System: An Idea Whose Time Has Come?"

From time to time I have written letters to the editors of numerous publications—from *The Washington Post* to *U.S. News & World Report* to *Harvard Magazine* to the local *Mount Vernon Gazette*—on the theory that, when possible, citizens should communicate directly with the public on matters they feel strongly about. I have done so in the hope that this method does make a difference. In the late 1980s, the United States faced many moral challenges that disturbed me and led me to believe that greed was gaining in public acceptance. I was worrying that Congress was losing its way. Charles Keating, chairman of the parent company of a California savings and loan association, was a major player in a huge financial scandal that ultimately cost the nation hundreds of millions of dollars. When Edwin Yoder, a columnist for *The Washington Post* and a person I respect very much, defended the actions of five senators who cooperated with Keating to varying degrees, I felt the need to respond. The central paragraph of my letter, which *The Post* ran on January 31, 1991, read:

Having worked on Capitol Hill for the legendary Congressman Brooks Hays (D-Ark.) and for Sen. Clair Engle (D-Calif.) and Sen. Ed Muskie (D-Maine), I can guarantee that none of them would have engaged in such activity as the Keating Five. I remember constituents of Brooks Hays making such requests and being stonewalled, whereupon they would assure him that they would seek help elsewhere. I would be surprised if any senior staff members on Capitol Hill would have any trouble distinguishing between the shady members of Congress and the "straight arrows" of which there are many.

Two senators who survived over time were John Glenn of Ohio and John McCain of Arizona, who were the least culpable. Nonetheless, the whole episode reflects the need to focus on promoting greater ethical behavior by members of Congress.

My involvement with the Federal Bureau of Prisons deepened during the eighties and into the nineties. I was asked to serve as the convener of the Summits on Prison Industries held in 1992, 1993, and 1998, which I did as a pro bono consultant in 1993 and 1998. With each of the directors over this span of time—Norm Carlson, Mike Quinlan, and then Kathy Hawk-Sawyer—I had the warmest relations. The same could be said for the directors of the Federal Prison Industries (FPI or UNICOR), Gerry Farkas, Rick Seiter, and Steve Schwalb—distinguished public servants all. During the first summit, we had about eighty participants, representing government, labor, and business. With the continued growth in the inmate population, it was most likely that prison industries would in fact grow, and so the meeting was to find alternative growth strategies—ways that would minimize adverse impacts on private industry and labor. But we acknowledged that if we could not find alternative growth strategies, we would find ways to expand the traditionally successful product lines— furniture, apparel, textiles and electronics. The participants were looking to first find common ground and then create an "implementation" committee to promote the summit's recommendations.

The Bureau of Prisons issued a major report summarizing the work of the 1992 and 1993 summits and a later report on the 1998 summit. I cooperated with the bureau in the preparation of these reports and was identified as the chairman of the summits. My comments below extract relevant portions of the findings.

As a result of the first summit, two work groups were formed: the Communications Group and the Growth Strategies Group. The first group was designed to enhance communication between FPI and all other interested parties. It would also examine potential changes to the guidelines for private-sector involvement in the development of new products. The second, the Growth Strategies Group, was divided into four subcommittees—Offshore, Services, Subcontracting, and Additional Strategies. They met for a year, in preparation for the second summit in July 1993. Each subcommittee presented its findings and recommendations. The Services Subcommittee suggested that FPI look at expanding into data services, equipment repair and rebuilding, printing, and other services such as textile repair, telephone support, distribution and mail services, and furniture rehabilitation. The Subcontracting Subcommittee saw opportunities in providing finished components, providing labor to manufacture items out of raw materials supplied by the customer, and performing simple or complex assemblies of materials supplied by the customer. The Offshore Subcommittee had met opposition from the labor sector and recognized that it would be difficult to find products or product components that were made entirely offshore; so it decided to focus on products currently being made in the large part offshore or being made using offshore labor. The subcommittee determined that using inmate labor would account for less than one percent of whatever was the domestic market share of that product family. The Additional Strategies Subcommittee identified two growth strategies—the recycling business and sales to nonprofit organizations.

After the 1992 summit I received a letter of appreciation from Mike Quinlan. He said that he was very pleased with the progress that was made and looking forward to a productive working relationship with the key stakeholder groups. He kindly noted, "This conference would not have been such a success without your expertise and guidance," and he made these additional observations: "The Summit is a landmark in the history of the Federal Bureau of Prisons. For the first time, Federal Prison Industries, Inc. [FPI] and major private-sector stakeholder groups will work jointly to develop a plan that will allow FPI to expand to meet the bureau's needs with as little impact on the private sector as possible. In addition, we can begin to resolve the communication problems that have caused misunderstandings in the past."

While I was working to eventually decrease the inmate population, John DiIulio was busy encouraging the jailing of more people. I was pleased that after *The Wall Street Journal* published his piece "The Value of Prisons," one of the most prestigious criminologists in America, Joan Petersilia, the director of the Criminal Justice Program at the RAND think tank, wrote a very thoughtful article in the *Los Angeles Times* arguing the other side of the story—"Building More Jail Cells Will Not Make Us Safer." About a year later, in December 1993, I myself had a relevant article, "Crime Hysteria in the United States," published in *On The Horizon,* the environmental scanning newsletter for leaders in higher education. I quoted John O. Haley, a University of Washington law professor, who had responded in *The Wall Street Journal* to DiIulio's "the Value of Prisons" article. In Haley's article, which was headlined "More Prisons, but Still More Crime," he said, "Professor DiIulio ignores the failures and the costs of our current attempts to prevent crime by warehousing offenders. In Washington State, public expenditures to maintain the current system of prisons exceed the total cost of a community college system of more than fifty campuses."

Despite the rebuttals, DiIulio's influence flourished. It is never too difficult to whip the country into a frenzy over issues of crime and punishment. Most candidates and elected and appointed officials are terrified, even liberal Democrats, of being called "soft on crime." The fact that I was a protégé of Richard Nixon's appointee as chief justice of the United States, Warren Burger, has given me something of a "Teflon coating" protection on that issue. Nonetheless, it should be noted that when I ran for reelection to the Fairfax County Board of Supervisors, I was known as someone who hoped to improve the lot of Lorton inmates, which was not a popular point of view, and still won a strong victory. I believe that if you talk sense to the American people, backed up with real facts—not doctored facts—you can find consensus for making progress toward humane criminal justice, and also strengthening public safety. The criminal justice legislation of 1984, however, brought from the states to the federal level some concepts and laws about determinate sentences, accompanied by so-called sentencing guidelines and sentencing commissions—which ultimately wreaked havoc with the proper treatment of wrongdoers. The most extreme manifestation of this excess was the creation of many dozens of "mandatory minimums" and ultimately the "three strikes and you're out" legislation that have created not justice, but enormous *injustices*. This legislation essentially destroyed the opportunity for judges to *judge*, since they simply became number crunchers of punishment charts. The ultimate absurdity came in the early 2000s, when a law was passed making it miserable for any judge who was courageous enough to give a sentence that was less than the guidelines provided. Chief Justice Rehnquist, to his credit, denounced that law in a public statement. Today, as I mentioned earlier, we are seeing a rising hostility to this perversion of criminal justice; and it should be again noted that the Supreme Court ruled that the guidelines are advisory, not mandatory.

It was in the midst of this climate, back in the middle 1980s, that the chairman of the U.S. Parole Commission, Ben Baer, put his career on the line by assembling a number of key people in the field of criminal justice to create the National Committee on Community Corrections. Its purpose was to offset the impact of the recent harsh legislative acts. Baer came to me for help, as well as to Donald Santarelli, former head of the Law Enforcement Assistance Administration, and ultimately, Santarelli was chosen to be chairman, I was named vice chairman, with Baer serving as the elder statesman. We got fully underway about 1985 or 1986. Among the first members were Federal Appeals Court Judge Ken Starr, former Attorney General Ed Meese, Alan Breed of the National Council on Crime and Delinquency, Jim Gondles of the American Correctional Association, Margot Lindsay of the National Center for Citizen Participation, George Keiser of the National Institute of Corrections, Professor Norval Morris of the University of Chicago Law School, Professor Donald Gottfredson of Rutgers School of Criminal Justice, Donald Murray of the National Association of Counties, Walter Ridley of the D.C. Department of Corrections, Harold Wooten of the Administrative Office of the U.S. Courts, Mary Shilton, leading criminal justice consultant, and several others. We have been meeting about every other month since then in sessions designed to help like-minded criminologists buck the national trend that has led to the United States becoming the highest incarcerator in the industrial world, a sorry "achievement" indeed. Having such a distinguished group representing the gamut of political ideologies, but working together for the common good, is crucial to preventing the so-called "hard-liners" from becoming successful enough to destroy any chance for reduction in the prison population or rehabilitation of inmates.

Fairfax County Activities

After a hiatus of two or three years from county affairs, to enable me to decompress from the enormous challenge of being a supervisor, I went back into the fray as a citizen volunteer. My first assignment was to serve on the board of UCM (United Community Ministries), the organization I had worked with as a supervisor, which was continuing its wonderful work helping the less fortunate in Fairfax County, especially the southeast area. When I was a member of the search committee, the person I had championed to become director was Sharon Kelso, and she had turned out to be a dynamo. I could not say no to her outreach, and I served UCM on its board for six years, until 1989. Among the areas I made a contribution to was the establishment of a policy for people with AIDS or who are HIV positive. Research I had done at Brookings, when ignorance of AIDS was at its peak, was of some assistance. From 1986 to 1991, I was also involved in an offshoot of UCM—Fairfax Fair Housing—where I worked with other dedicated people to find lodging for those who couldn't quite make it without a boost. In this area, my experience as supervisor was helpful, since I knew how to get a multiplier affect with limited resources to enable people to get affordable housing. This effort was severely damaged by the federal reduction in housing assistance during the Reagan years.

County Supervisor Gerry Hyland asked me to serve on the Southeast Fairfax Development Corporation (SFDC) in 1987, and I agreed to do that, too. At that time the Mount Vernon Council of Civic Associations was somewhat hostile to the SFDC's objectives and there was considerable friction at corporation meetings. Since I was respected at the council and had originally created the forerunner of SFDC with Supervisor Joe Alexander, I was able to work with both sides to find middle ground. This was the beginning of an outstanding upgrade of the Richmond Highway Corridor, also known as Route 1, that ran right through the county.

When the county created the Route One Urban Design Task Force in 1988, Supervisors Hyland and Alexander, Joe asked me to chair this joint effort on their behalf. Ken Doggett, the county staffer assigned to assist me, was outstanding. With his guidance, we did a major job of outlining a series of steps that would both help to beautify the corridor and make it more functional both as a thoroughfare and as a commercial district. The plan provided for planting more foliage along the corridor (which Mary Thonen took the initiative to accomplish), including on the median strip; putting in mast arms at intersections, to decrease the number of unsightly wires, and to provide for readable road and street signs; and devising a system for improved and regulated commercial and public signage, getting rid of eyesores. Doggett helped recommend many improvements to both the main street and the service roads to make areas more passable and safe.

The most demanding task Supervisor Hyland asked me to carry out was the periodic reviews of the comprehensive plan for Mount Vernon. As chairman of the task force, I did five of those reviews between 1989 and 2002. These activities took a great deal of time, but made me feel very good, since they were of major significance to people's lives and were still quite consistent with the original PLUS Plan that I had put together in 1975 as a supervisor.

One of the more significant assignments I embarked on was to serve on the special County Committee on Structural Reorganization that functioned during 1992–93. County Chairman Tom Davis named former Governor Linwood Holton as chairman and me as vice chairman. My connection to Davis was through Christopher Bright, who worked for Davis and for me in the past. This was the first time I had met Holton, who was revered as a courageous, moderate Republican governor, a person who had turned Virginia around on civil rights. He was suffering from shingles and in great pain. I was very happy for him *and* me when he recovered. The committee had four subcommittees to look at every aspect of county operations, and we were pleased to find that the county was generally in good shape. I was proud to point that three of the four subcommittee chairmen were elected supervisors in the next election—Kauffman, Mendelsohn and Connolly. We did recommend a major increase in supervisor pay, but that did not come to pass.

My relationship with my successor supervisor, Gerry Hyland, had always been a rather uneasy one. While he was friendly and did reach out to me on occasion, I did not feel completely comfortable with him. One example relates to my interest in serving on the school board, when there was an opening for a member from Mount Vernon. Although the process involved creating a committee to make recommendations (which really turned out to be a charade.), it was probably a strategic mistake on my part not to go to him directly and find out if he favored a particular candidate, The last time that Hyland had to make a school board selection, the committee had a large number of members including me. The results had not pleased Hyland, so he announced that this new committee would be small. He also said he would choose the new board member from among the committee's top three nominees. When I asked Hyland's staff members for their assessment of the overall situation, they sounded excited about my interest. The school board and the board of supervisors always seemed to be feuding, and in their opinion, I would be an excellent builder of bridges. They then showed me a list of nominating-committee members, and I knew them all well—about eight to ten people who would be friendly to me.

When I went to be interviewed by the committee, I was shocked to find the room full of people, about twenty-five or thirty of them, most of whom did not know me at all. I had received no notice of this change. My interview did not go anywhere nearly as well as I anticipated. Even so I came in third in the vote of the committee. Then the chairman of the committee—who worked in Hyland's law office—announced that he would choose from the top *two* candidates, and Kris Amundson, apparently Hyland's selection all along, was chosen. Amundson was clearly qualified to be on the school board, did a good job, and has gone on to be a fine state legislator. If Hyland had done what I would have expected of him—to call me well in advance with notice of his choice and his inclination and his procedural change, I would have dropped out of the process immediately. I regret deeply that he did not consider that option.

Possibly one of the reasons for Hyland's attitude was that in

March 1990, the *Mount Vernon Gazette* had written an extremely flattering portrait of my activities as a citizen volunteer. The headline was "Cikins: He Seeks Consensus." In this article, the writer, Christa Watters, cited comments of strong approval from many Mount Vernon politicians, Democratic and Republican alike, including Hyland himself. The paragraph I like the best went as follows: "Cikins himself says, 'I'm a Democrat who flies my colors, but my whole lifestyle has been outreach to bring together people from the full ideological gamut. I'm a bridge-builder.'"

Watters told me she went about the whole county and could not find a single politician who would say something unkind. Regretfully, as I write these words more than a decade later, Mount Vernon has become a microcosm of the current world, where mean-spiritedness has become a way of life; and I am not immune from being the target of unflattering comments. At least, in 1990, an effort was made to keep such comments under a rock. While I am of mixed emotions about even having the matter brought up here, I must say it does remind me of the Brooks Hays story about the boy who comes home from school with a black eye, and when his mother asks him what happened, he replies, "It all started when Billy hit me back."

Change in the Supreme Court

In 1991, the confirmation of Clarence Thomas to the Supreme Court came before the U.S. Senate. A key Republican senator considering the confirmation was a splendid friend of mine, Alan K. Simpson of Wyoming, who behaved in an uncharacteristically combative way, in what I thought unfair treatment of a witness, Professor Anita Hill, who testified against Thomas on sexual-harassment grounds. I became very angry at Thomas, and after the hearings, I wrote Simpson a gentle letter expressing my concerns. I felt that friendship meant little if one could not share ones views with that friend, no matter how highly placed they were. Let me review some of the remarkably thoughtful letter that I received back from Simpson:

I fully understand what you are saying. Let me share with you what I shared with the folks at the "Roast and Toast" in Cheyenne. It was not really an "apology" or an act of "remorse," as the press called it. Instead it was a "taking of responsibility." There is a difference.

Let me also share with you what I have shared with people who have written on that issue. I loved the phrase you used about how having an "equal devotion to moderation in political exchange would overcome very understandable partisan urges." I am afraid that I fall prey not to partisan urges—but instead I go off the rail when I see someone's personhood, their life's work, and their dearly earned reputation being destroyed. That is wrong—I need not get into that personally, but I always try to think "How would I feel if this were happening to me?" Many times that makes things too personal and too intimate.

Indeed, I consider you a true friend. You are a man of rare civility, kindness, balance and morality. I cherish our friendship—and I deeply appreciate the manner in which you expressed your feelings to me. It meant a great deal to me—and I mean that.

Having a man who had been second in the leadership in the Republican Party in the Senate write me such a letter "meant a great deal to me," too, since cross-party friendships were already on the wane. His letter helped soften my unhappiness over Clarence Thomas's being confirmed by the Senate and contributed to my continued effort to keep an open mind. This was especially important for me during the time when my attitude about Brookings needed the benefit of such an open mind.

The Hope That Springs Eternal

In the early nineties, when I began to foresee my retirement from Brookings, I looked toward the 1992 presidential election as a chance, should the Democrats win, to get a high-level position as the capstone of my career. The status of my health did worry me, but I was determined to push ahead with all the strength I could muster. Evidence of the impact of the spondylitis was the stooped posture and difficulty maneuvering both in walking and in driving a car. In 1991, and then in 1992 and 1993, I fell and landed on my head, each occurrence happening while I was at work. Sylvia took me to Mount Vernon Hospital in the first two instances to be stitched up, and I survived the third fall with only bad bruises and swelling. During this same period, I was growing more and more dissatisfied at how Brookings was treating me and my colleagues in the Center for Public Policy. The Brookings computer entry, the literature about the institution, and even the registry at the entry to the building, could all be interpreted as belittling the contribution of our division. I was reluctant to challenge the slights, since I was preparing myself to leave in any event and did not want my retirement procedure to be undermined in any way.

While I hoped for a 1992 Democratic victory, I was not too optimistic about the chances. One of the alternatives I considered was reaching out to several of the Democratic senators I knew to see if there might be a staff position available after leaving Brookings; I felt I still had much to contribute. My stature was rising in both the criminal-justice world and the health policy world, and my knowledge of Congress and its operation was widely appreciated. When my fourteen years of federal employment ended in 1969, my salary was about $28,000, the highest federal pay at that time. If I could add three years of service at a range of $80,000 to $100,000 per year, only a moderate salary in 1992, I would increase substantially my federal retirement fund. The congressional option, however, involved a major commitment of three years of full-time effort, that could otherwise be used in volunteer activities and continued pro bono professional duties. I finally decided that I should explore other ways of continuing to make a difference, especially through writing about civil rights and the contributions of Brooks Hays, as well as the administration of justice and the contributions of Chief Justice Burger, and forget worrying about my retirement living standards (with Sylvia mildly supportive of my newfound attitude).

I was aware that an organization within the Smithsonian Institution—the Woodrow Wilson International Center for Scholars—awarded residential fellowships to outstanding individuals for writing about activities of major public concern. My dear friend Mark Cannon had received one of these fellowships some time ago. And so I applied for such a fellowship, proposing as my topic the impact of the fifteen Administration of Justice seminars and the roles of Chief Justices Burger and Rehnquist. One needed three letters of recommendation. Chief Justice Burger and Congressman Bill Hughes of New Jersey wrote glowing letters on my behalf. The third letter, representing the Justice Department, came from Ken Starr, who was at that time the Solicitor General of the United States. Most of that letter is included here:

> Warren is well known to and much admired by me. We have labored together in the administration-of-justice vineyards over the span of almost two decades, first during my service as a law clerk to Chief Justice Burger in the mid-1970s, and then here in the Justice Department beginning in early 1981. More than any other individual, Warren has been the undisputed leader in forging links among the three branches in his shaping and guidance of the annual Brookings seminar program. Reform after reform has emerged from those deliberations, many of them duly enacted into law—quietly and without fanfare. The rich history of that program is eloquent attestation

both to Warren's vision and his staying power. He is brimming with ideas, yet he stays the course with a steady hand on the tiller. Patience, graciousness, civility and statesmanship round out his public policy skills, founded in creativity and high intellect.

But I should not overlook the most obvious aspect of Warren's background and attributes—his unwavering commitment to human decency and human dignity, as evidenced by this son of Boston leaving the comfortable precincts of Harvard and heading south at a difficult time and planting seeds there that continue to bear fruit. He was in the deep South during remarkable and turbulent times, capped by his experiences in the Kennedy Administration and his labors of love with the remarkable Brooks Hays of Arkansas.

Unfortunately the director of the center, Charles Blitzer, known to have friends at Brookings, was not impressed by Burger, Hughes, and Starr, and rejected my application, almost by return mail. I regret deeply that I was unable to benefit from a Woodrow Wilson fellowship. I tried as best I could to do the study of the Administration of Justice seminars on my own, but with other obligations and frail health, I did not succeed. I was cheered on in this failed effort by former Assistant Attorney General Dan Meador, who was now back teaching at the University of Virginia Law School. I was sorry to disappoint him since he had been such an inspiration in the early days of formulating the seminars—even though he had just been stricken permanently blind. In a desperate effort, I tried to get Judge William Schwarzer, head of the Federal Judicial Center, to provide me with some logistic support; but he refused, even though his staff director Russ Wheeler appeared to be for it. I went to the head of the Administrative Office of the Courts, Ralph Mecham, who was very enthusiastic at first, but backed off at the last minute. And so the definitive study of this historic effort remains to be done. Interestingly, a number of areas addressed several times by the seminars have resurfaced today, including judicial accountability and sentencing guidelines. For example an American Bar Association commission, with the support of Justice Anthony Kennedy, has called for changes in sentencing and incarceration. And Chief Justice Rehnquist has appointed Justice Stephen Breyer to chair a committee that will evaluate how the federal judicial system is dealing with judicial misbehavior and disability.

To refer back to the interview with me contained in the February 1992 newsletter of the federal courts, *The Third Branch,* I spelled out how the Administration of Justice seminars got underway and some of the program's successes. I indicated that while much of the agenda originally planned had been accomplished, new participants were becoming involved all the time. It was vital that the machinery to promote legislative achievements through reconciliation and compromise between the three branches exist. The agenda for the 1992 seminar was an example of the continued relevance. It included implementation of the 1990 Civil Justice Reform Act, the work of the new judicial discipline commission, the status of crime legislation, the work of the long-range planning committee, and the status of bankruptcy legislation. The interview ended with my comment, "There are those who moan that the congressional and judicial cup is half empty, but I exult that it is half full and rising."

As I review the many issues these seminars gave priority attention to, I recall seven recurring themes: aspects of the functioning of the courts; possible methods of delivery of justice; issues of judicial discipline and judicial tenure; concerns about amendments to the criminal code; sentencing and corrections matters (with some special attention to drugs); improvement of federal-state judicial relations; and problems of growing court workloads.

The Clinton Election

By the summer of 1992, I reached out to the Clinton presidential effort to offer my services to his candidacy. I contacted Bruce Lindsey, whom I had met during my Arkansas days when Hays ran for governor. Lindsey's secretary was very excited about my call and promised he would call back quickly. He never did, and I did not persist beyond one more try. By October I had decided to hold a Brookings seminar immediately after the election that would review whatever had happened. I took an enormous chance, because I scheduled the seminar to be held just two days after the election. I contacted major players for both candidates, as well as a few people involved in Senate and House races. I was pleased that Tom Mann had opted to join with the effort at the American Enterprise Institute, or elsewhere, and thus relieved me of any need to consider asking him to participate. When C-Span saw the array of top speakers I had committed to be on the program, they chose to cover my program rather than AEI's. When the time came, I had only one dropout—Clinton's campaign manager, Ron Brown, whom Clinton ordered to Little Rock. But I was able to get another senior player, Ron Klain, general counsel to the Clinton campaign and on his debate-preparation team, to take his place. I must have done something right, because C-Span played the program over and over again throughout the entire weekend.

My family decided we would go on a vacation to Switzerland in January 1993, getting out of town during the hoopla of Clinton's inauguration. Our son Neil had pretty much finished his college courses at Virginia Tech, but would not graduate until that spring. He and Dean—who was well rooted in Pittsburgh with Rockwell—had agreed to go along with Sylvia and me, as long as there would be good skiing and awesome nighttime entertainment. We researched and found that Davos fit the bill perfectly, also being a place where leading world economists gathered every year. We had a wonderful time there, and simply *read* about the presidential inauguration—something I had attended many times and had no desire to do again. When a German couple at the hotel restaurant overheard us make some disparaging remarks about Clinton, they were surprised to find out that we had voted for him and that we truly wished him well in his presidency. Upon returning to Washington, I considered again making a halfhearted effort to look into a possible position with Clinton, but decided not to pursue the idea. What I did do was see Mary Hope Davis, the administrative assistant to Senator Dale Bumpers of Arkansas, to ensure that Neil would solidify his hold on a Senate job in the Capitol. She immediately made the appropriate calls in my presence and Neil was assured of his position.

On the eve of the inauguration, Bill Moyers had made a major speech, "On Being Baptist," at the First Baptist Church of Washington. He made reference to Brooks Hays as one of his great heroes, saying that Hays losing his seat in Congress "won for him a place in legions of hearts." Sometime thereafter, Moyers had some heart problems, and I wrote to him to wish him well. I also told him about Hays being demeaned by some Arkansans. he sent a very considerate response :

Thank you for the good wishes. I am doing well and sense that the avoidance of a massive heart attack does indeed concentrate the mind wonderfully and summons a spirit of moderation I intend to honor!

As for Brooks, what you report is saddening. Faubus doesn't deserve the rehabilitation, nor does George Wallace who is being revived of late by the press as a populist rather than a racist demagogue. If I ever get around to my book I'll see to it that Brooks gets at least in one source the recognition he deserves for courage and witness to faith in public life.

An experience I had early in the Clinton presidency disturbed me very much. I bumped into Jed Johnson, Jr., who, in 1964, had begun a very youthful, albeit short-lived, career in Congress He was elected as a congressman from Oklahoma at only age twenty-four; (the constitutionally required age was twenty-five, but he managed by having a birthday by the time of his January swearing-in ceremony) and then was defeated at age twenty-seven. He wasn't hurting because he married the daughter of a distinguished Florida congressman, Syd Herlong, and oil had been discovered on land the family owned in Oklahoma. Back in 1974, when I was ready to leave the directorship of the USAFMC (U.S. Association of Former Members of Congress), it was appropriate for Jed to succeed me, and he went on to do a splendid job with this organization. With Clinton's election, Jed was eager to see if he could get a good job in the administration. At USAFMC he had become quite close to Brooks Hays and had grown to admire him very much. Jed had an opportunity to sit next to Clinton at some important official function, and thinking it would help his chances, he proceeded to rave to Clinton about the president's fellow-Arkansan, Brooks Hays.

At our chance encounter, Jed told me he was very bewildered because Clinton had just sat there stony-faced as Jed praised Hays. I guess I could have been more cautious, but I proceeded to tell him that Clinton had no rapport with Hays and had supported the Faubus candidate against Hays in the 1966 Arkansas election for governor, and that Clinton probably was uncomfortable with a man like Hays who radiated morality and decency. (I do think Clinton was a good President, despite the Monica Lewinsky scandal, but not someone I would ever see as a role model.) Jed Johnson blanched when I told him these things as we talked on the sidewalk in front of Brookings. He died of a heart attack a few months later, in December 1993, at a very early age.

Retirement Preparations

As I approached my targeted retirement date, I realized I would not have any place "to hang my hat" in Washington once I left Brookings—having been rejected by the Woodrow Wilson Center, the Federal Judicial Center, and the Administrative Office of the Courts. I had continued on as vice chairman of the National Committee on Community Corrections, and I was most grateful to Don Santarelli, the committee's chairman, when he offered me office space at his law office, without charge. This office was very centrally located, near the Mayflower Hotel. I never fully moved in, since I was uncertain how long such an arrangement could last. It did provide me with a resting place in Washington other than Sylvia's office at the Senate Office Building, once I had retired.

Before I left Brookings, the folks at the Bureau of Prisons asked me to help them on a matter precipitated by Vice President Gore's new campaign called NPR (National Performance Review, later known as the National Partnership for Reinventing Government) to review government efficiency, contract procedures, and hiring policies. I had already met with several young men on that agency's staff to give them ideas on what this new initiative could accomplish. It appeared that somehow, between the first preliminary draft and the final issuance of NPR's original report, enemies of UNICOR had managed to slip in a provision seriously damaging the ability of prisons industries to function. I immediately contacted the Gore office, and a meeting was arranged in the office of the Deputy Attorney General. Everyone there, but me, was an official of the Executive Branch. They were all milling about so I called the meeting to order and presided. I found it refreshing that a citizen with no public office could do so. The end result was that Gore's people said that they couldn't take the provision out for obvious reasons, but that it would have very low priority and never be enforced.

Meanwhile I persevered in challenging John DiIulio's outpourings from Brookings, which called for massive increases in incarceration and length of punishment. I couldn't believe that Brookings could countenance such nonsense, but it did and gave

DiIulio even greater recognition and exposure. Tom Mann, of course, continued to shower his "affection" on DiIulio and "deep anger" on me. My only satisfaction was the many letters of approval I steadily received from the criminal justice community around the country, but I felt more and more alienated from Brookings.

While I still had the chance, I raced to have several articles published in significant journals. I was pleased when the Advisory Commission on Intergovernmental Relations asked me to write an article, "Community Corrections," which appeared in its Spring 1993 issue of *Intergovernmental Perspective*. The University of North Carolina environmental scan newsletter, *On The Horizon* ran more articles of mine that year, among them "The Clinton Administration Impact" and "President Clinton's National Service Proposal." By this time I was amused that over the years, Brookings had agreed to publish only three books that I had coedited, books on health care and criminal justice matters, but no journal articles written during my Brookings years, while about twenty of my articles had been published by other entities. I think a fair-minded person would say that some of my articles received a far wider readership than some Brookings articles did and that, in addition, my ability to write had been established when I was twenty-one years old, by Harvard's publication of my paper on the Council of Economic Advisers. Ultimately I would write or edit some fifty journal articles and seven books while living a very full life of government service and part-time university teaching.

In April I announced my resignation in a letter to Brookings President Bruce MacLaury, who had always treated me kindly, apparently unaware of the battering I had been receiving. He immediately wrote back to me:

> I must say that I was taken by surprise by your decision
> to retire as of July 1, 1993. You have been such a stalwart
> in the Center for Public Policy Education that your

departure will leave a gaping hole. At the same time I respect and admire your decision to make more room in your life for your interests. Your network of friends and admirers has been an asset to Brookings. Your own dedication to the best in public policy and government service has been an example to all whose lives you have touched. And your insistence on integrity and ethical behavior has set a standard for all of us.

After being asked if I would agree to having a farewell party. I went to my division director, Larry Korb, to request that he discreetly inform MacLaury that I would feel like a hypocrite to do so. At such a party, by way of professionally inclusive invitations, people would attend who had done me harm as well as those who had been supportive, and I did not feel up to dealing with such an arrangement. I guess that goes with the territory at any think tank, but I am naïve enough to expect better of mankind. Most of the people at the institution had been decent individually, but collectively the atmosphere was stifling. I was proud to be at Brookings, to use the name to accomplish the things I did, and to distance myself from those who I felt were lacking in qualities I hold dear. I guess one could say, quite properly, that Brookings had been very good to me for many years, and that the deterioration of that treatment simply represented a microcosm of the nation, where integrity and civility and bipartisanship were on the wane.

Thus I did not have a formal Brookings retirement event. I continued to carry out my responsibilities, ranging from the fifteenth Administration of Justice seminar to the second Federal Prison Industries summit—a conference that was actually held after I retired, but which I continued to work on and presided over. Sometime after the summit, the Bureau of Prisons prepared a publication entitled, *Factories With Fences—The History of Federal Prison Industries*, for which I prepared the dedication to Chief Justice Burger.

I was honored to receive one of the first copies printed, with an inscription from Attorney General Janet Reno, "To Warren I. Cikins, thank you for all you have done to advance the prison industries program."

In addition to his earlier response to my letter of resignation, Bruce MacLaury wrote me a fine letter of commendation, which said:

> There have been so many strings to your bow that it is hard to select just a couple for special note. But I shall always associate the Seminar on the Administration of Justice, and the Seminar for New Members of Congress with the Cikins name. You helped to develop them, and participated in their evolution over the years. They have made great contributions to successive administrations, chief justices, and congressmen. And that does not begin to touch the hundreds of lives that you have yourself touched in other programs you have conducted on behalf of the [Brookings] Institution.
>
> Brooks Hays stories were your signature. But they were more than reminiscences; they constituted a philosophy of life, for which you were a living example. Your concern for others was evident to all, not only in your professional activities at Brookings, but also in your political and volunteer lives as well.

MacLaury and his gracious wife Ginny invited Sylvia and me to a farewell dinner at the Cosmos Club and then, as is the Brookings tradition, presented me with a Brookings chair. It is similar to my Harvard chair with appropriate institutional identification.

As head of the CPPE division, Larry Korb, held a farewell dinner for me for the senior members of our division staff. He was extraordinary in the glowing remarks he made about my service, saying I was a role model for the division. I found this especially pleasing, since he had been a senior official in the Defense Department under President Reagan. But even more moving was another event. My faithful assistant Pam Buckles led me to a meeting at Brookings on a ruse, and when she opened the door to the meeting room, all the support staff of CPPE was there for a surprise party. It was wonderful to be recognized by those who themselves often weren't "recognized" for the crucial work they did. And, finally Sylvia and I decided to have our own retirement party for me on Capitol Hill, at La Colline Restaurant. We invited well over a hundred people and scheduled the event for a Friday so both our sons could attend, recognizing that this would reduce, if not end, any congressional attendance, since they typically went back to their home districts on Friday.

Our son Dean served as master of ceremonies and showed great presence. A number of my colleagues, each representing some organization or aspect of my career, were asked to say a few words. Sharon Kelso, head of United Community Ministries, represented my outreach to the underprivileged; Mark Cannon represented my lifetime of concern for issues of criminal justice and administration of justice, and my religious community; Lee White, former assistant special counsel to the president, represented the Kennedy White House; Walter Ridley represented the D.C. corrections community; Ken Starr represented the Justice Department; Congressman Amo Houghton of New York represented the Legislative Branch; Dr. Valerie Earle of Georgetown University represented my academic community; and Virginia State Senator Joe Gartlan and Fairfax Board Chairman (now Congressman) Tom Davis represented the Commonwealth of Virginia. Davis presented me with a plaque from the County which had many "whereases," an example of one being "whereas, while on the Board of Supervisors, as in his other endeavors throughout his life, Warren Cikins was acclaimed for his constant striving for a strong public policy founded upon consensus." The final whereas said that on the occasion of my retirement from Brookings, I was to be recognized for my "pronounced and profound role in the development of this historic County into the preeminent place to live and do business in the United States."

Chief Justice Burger was unable to attend the event because of ill health, but sent a letter that said:

> Through our work together on prison reform and other matters, I have come to recognize that you have always been imaginative and thorough in the projects you undertake. Your role in the development of the Administration of Justice seminars was crucial. The seminars, which were created with the goal of improving the administration of justice by building bridges of understanding between the three branches of government, did much to strengthen the administration of justice in America. Although the seminars' success is now well recognized, in the beginning it took ingenuity, courage and determination to undertake such an undefined and difficult project.

The next year was one for catching my breath. Sylvia and I did make a visit to Europe—to Milan and Florence and to Provence and Paris—where we had a wonderful time. Back home, I continued to promote the cause of reason and sanity in society's dealings with wrongdoers and to challenge those who advocated "locking them up and throwing away the key." I shared my concerns over the work of John DiIulio with many people, since he was working to cancel whatever good Chief Justice Burger and I were doing. My letter-writing agenda included Judge Abner Mikva, whom I had known originally as a congressman from Illinois, who had great judgment and integrity, and who was White House counsel to President Clinton in 1994–95.

This was a year when I tried, usually unsuccessfully, to set some records straight. I was upset over the treatment of Jonathan Pollard, who was excessively imprisoned for giving some secrets to the

Israelis, *our allies*. I wrote letters to numerous influential people and discussed the matter with congressmen and staffs, all of whom seemed to be very skittish. While I know little of the case, it seemed that the secretary of defense under Reagan, Caspar Weinberger, had it in for Pollard (even though he did eventually agree the punishment was too severe). Weinberger had a Jewish grandfather, and I wondered if the Jewish streak in his blood made him cringe at Pollard. I also thought the Central Intelligence Agency "club" defended Aldrich Ames, who had done enormous harm to the country as a double agent spying for the Soviet Union, and tried to blame Pollard for Ames's sins. Judge Aubrey Robinson, an otherwise splendid judge, also was too harsh, because he felt—perhaps because he was an African-American—that Israel was doing too much to help apartheid-embattled South Africa. All in all, Pollard was never able to get beyond the symbolism that many felt was necessary in punishing him (he remains in jail until this day). I was proud of Larry Korb, who also did all he could to get Pollard to have fair treatment.

At about this time Pulitzer-prize winner David Maraniss wrote a book about President Clinton. When I read the book, *First in His Class*, I noted several errors about Clinton's early political years—years I was quite familiar with. I both called and wrote Maraniss, but he avoided me and did not respond. I contacted about six people I knew at *The Washington Post* who knew him, and he then replied that he would be happy to meet me. Of course he made sure that never happened. I would have told him that Clinton's backing of Attorney General Frank Holt for governor of Arkansas was not a pro-civil rights action, but rather a perpetuation of the ideals of Orval Faubus and the racist establishment. Now that Clinton appears to be a genuine supporter of civil rights, it seems necessary to create revisionist history to make him always such, even though he was at that early time, at best, an opportunist.

My brother Milt became quite ill during this period, and a remarkable development took place. The medicines for his physical ailments conflicted with the medicines for the deep depression he fell into. He gradually sunk into a grave condition that took its toll on his devoted wife, Marnie. After many treatments at the best hospitals in Boston, he was sent back to his retirement home on Cape Cod, to just "make the best of it." A doctor at Cape Cod Hospital, Johnny Backman, would not give up on him and tried to find a formula to get him out of his funk. He would call me periodically to report on progress. One day, Sylvia took the call in my absence and thought the name sounded familiar. She asked him if he came from Jerome, Pennsylvania, and he said yes. Sylvia knew him and his family! His father had been brought to Jerome by the coal-mining company to serve as the local doctor, and he was the only Jew in town. He married a local girl and Johnny was their son, a graduate of Harvard Medical School. Backman got Milt back on his feet, and my brother lived reasonably well for a number of years more. This experience reinforced my belief in predestination and a grand design for the world.

Ebb and Flow in the 1990s

Warren Burger died in 1995, and this was a huge loss to those who cared about progressivism in dealing with criminal-justice matters. When *U.S. News & World Report* wanted to interview someone about his achievements, I was very grateful to have the chance to recount some of them:

> Burger wanted to bridge the gap between courts, Congress, and the Executive Branch. It was a risk, because some colleagues believed judges are on Mount Olympus and shouldn't rub shoulders with anyone else. But he was determined that leaders of the three branches discuss common problems, and that began in 1978. It helped produce a judicial accountability law providing discipline short of impeachment.

Another notable result of the sessions convened by Burger was to blunt a campaign in the 1980s to restrict court power over controversial issues like busing and school prayer. Robert Bork, before he became a judge, gave an impassioned speech against restricting courts. The talk—heard by conservatives like Strom Thurmond and Attorney General William French Smith—had a big influence on cooling down the push.

Burger tirelessly promoted work for prisoners—a concern since he visited a prison as a Boy Scout and saw warehoused inmates. He led prison tours with congressional, business and union leaders. In 1990, when members of Congress aligned with labor tried to gut federal prison industries, he fired off protest letters and single-handedly stopped it in its tracks. He was tough on crime, but he believed that some criminals had qualities that could be salvaged.

I wrote an additional tribute to Burger for *Legal Times*, a prominent Washington weekly newspaper, in the July 3, 1995 issue. It was called "Warren Burger's Quest for 'Factories With Fences,'" a modified version of which was included in a Bureau of Prisons book on prison industries of the same title. I told of Burger's great heart and great dedication to prison reform. In his quest for inmate rehabilitation, he had a special quality of spirituality; and he is sorely missed by prison officials, inmates, victims of crimes, and the general public—especially in an era of strong punishment (which he advocated) without the countervailing willingness to welcome home a reformed prodigal son.

Ironically Orval Faubus also died in 1995 and I had written an earlier piece about him in *Legal Times*, week of January 2. As I put it in the article, entitled "Lest We Forget—Orval Faubus, Brooks Hays, and the Little Rock Crisis," Faubus was a good leader on matters of education, health, and industrial development; but he will be and should be judged by what everyone agrees was his defining moment. Since there was a two-term tradition in Arkansas, he was very doubtful that he could be re-elected. As I explained it, "Faubus did not want to leave the governorship. So he moved to the right, as defined in terms of racial policies at that time. He found an issue that rallied the people to his side and persuaded them to break with tradition by re-electing him. In other words, when the governor raised the flag of insurrection in 1957, he deliberately and calculatingly stirred the latent racist emotions of his constituency to preserve his political ambitions."

Further on in the article, I reviewed the role of another person: "As we look back at the events of 1957 and judge the motives and merits of those involved, there is one person to whom insufficient credit is given and insufficient stature is attributed, and that person is not Orval Faubus. That person is Brooks Hays... In the fall of 1957, Hays became involved in attempts to defuse the Little Rock crisis. You might say that this was *his* defining moment. Later, when asked why he intervened—for he took considerable political risk—Hays replied simply, 'I could do no other.'"

Meanwhile the *U.S. News and World Report* had an article in the July 3, 1995, issue called the "The Era of Collective Repentance," referring to the recent apology from the Southern Baptist Convention for its longtime proslavery stand. I wrote a letter that *U.S. News* ran on August 14, reminding readers that the Southern Baptists had elected a lay president, Brooks Hays, the congressman who had intervened during the 1957 Little Rock crisis to try to get Governor Faubus to allow black students into Central High School. Hays had called on his fellow Baptists to obey the law. The Baptists reelected him their president in 1958, and it would have been nice, in 1995, if they had expressed their pride in Hays's action.

About this same time, Ken Starr was once again in the public limelight. He had been appointed Independent Counsel at the

Department of Justice to investigate Clinton's possible financial misbehavior, known as Whitewater, and was living in Little Rock. I wrote
him a note of congratulations. He immediately answered: "Greet-
ings from your old stompin' grounds in Little Rock. Visions of Central
High, Orval Faubus, and Brooks Hays must immediately spring to
life as soon as the lyrically named capital of this lovely, little state is
mentioned. It's a most pleasant and congenial spot (in contrast to
the 1950s, as you will all too vividly recall). It's not Camelot, to be
sure, but it's darn nice." I think the tenor of this note shows how far
away Starr would get later from his earlier approach to his assignment, as he would gradually become such a nationally controversial
figure.

A few years later, January 29, 1998, to be exact, I decided to do
something (if it would be at all possible) to ease the national tensions about the uproar over President Clinton's dalliance with Monica
Lewinsky. I wrote letters to many newspapers and political leaders
that I knew, hoping that my views might be of some value. The key
letter was to Ken Starr, whom I felt was being pressured to take dramatic actions by the prosecutors on his staff, who came from the
Justice Department. After a preliminary expression of my respect for
what he was trying to do, I stated:

> I have defended you with Democratic friends, and have
> taken some hits for that attitude. I might add that I really
> wish you had not taken the job, which is thankless at best
> and reputation-damaging at worst. I believe strongly in
> bipartisanship . . . [but] I fear the current situation has
> driven an enormous wedge between the parties.
> Perception is as important as reality, and the widespread
> perception that this has become a partisan investigation
> has done enormous harm. I guess I feel very strongly that
> a president should not be brought down by sexual
> indiscretion. You know me well enough to know that I
> abhor sexual misconduct or lying or subornation of

perjury, but they should be evaluated in this case in terms of their damage to the nation. They are not the stuff of criminal prosecution or impeachment proceedings, regarding sexual behavior. Getting overzealous in pursuit of such indiscretions only drags the pursuer into the gutter along with the pursued.

Starr answered me very graciously and quite quickly. "Thank you for an exceptional letter. It was thoughtful of you to express your earnest and heartfelt concerns. I will always welcome your good counsel and your friendship."

I regret very much that my efforts didn't do much good. Sadly, Starr's stature was somewhat adversely affected by his role in the investigation and the reaction to the report he wrote.

Our son Neil decided, after several years of being out of school and working as an intern at the American Bar Association Criminal Division and as a Senate Capitol staffer, that he would like to go to law school. There were two logical options, Nova University where I could use my professional status to assist in admissions, or Duquesne University in Pittsburgh, where he could live in the home of his brother Dean, thus easing the financial pressures on Sylvia and me. Neil made application to Duquesne with strong letters of support from Sylvia's boss Kevin Curtin, Vice President Gore's staffer Goody Marshall (son of Justice Marshall), and Bill Diefenderfer, a prominent Republican and a member of the Duquesne board. Since Neil's grades were not too strong, he was put on the waiting list.

One day, when Neil was working on the Senate floor, Senator Simpson came over to ask what he was doing lately. When Simpson found out that Neil was on the law school waiting list, he offered to help out. This is the heart of the letter he wrote Dean of Admissions Ronald Ricci:

Neil is just one outstanding young man. I have known his

family for many years and they are all remarkable people—true believers in the old adage that "Democracy is not a spectator sport." They have always participated fully and actively in the life of their community... It has been my experience that "the apple doesn't fall far from the tree," and Neil is no exception! His fine parents have shared with him the importance of hard work, determination, persistence, and always giving your best. This is his heritage... I have long been impressed by Neil's outstanding abilities—and potential! He is one of those rare types who has successfully combined his thirst for knowledge with an uncommon degree of common sense and a wonderful, warm personality. He is a well-rounded individual who has now set his sights on pursuing a degree in law. I have a hunch he'll be a fine lawyer some day.

Needless to say, once this letter arrived at Duquesne, Neil was soon admitted.

DiIulio Rears Up Again

Being quite intelligent and knowing how to play the game, John DiIulio—after changing his spots numerous times— had decided to continue feeding the national terror over crime as a means of enhancing his status. His "scholarly" positions, designed to increase incarceration, had attracted much attention from the media. I had kept Naftali Bendavid of *Legal Times* informed on this issue, and he decided to write a full-scale analysis of DiIulio's influence. His article was a front-page story on February 12, 1996, entitled "A Bull In Crime's China Shop."

Everyone wants a piece of John DiIulio Jr. these days.

Conservative lawmakers regularly quote the thirty-seven-year-old crime expert in floor debates and consult him on legislation. Sen. John Ashcroft (R-Mo.) hosted a breakfast recently so senators could hear him speak. He has twice addressed the House freshmen. President Bill Clinton has invited him to a White House dinner. New York Gov. George Pataki brought him to Albany.

So far in 1996, DiIulio's articles have appeared in *The New York Times* and *The Weekly Standard*, and he has been quoted at length in *The Washington Post* and *Time* magazine—which, for good measure, threw in a photograph of DiIulio in a tough-guy pose against a graffiti-drenched wall.

"I happen to have an influence on crime policy that I myself sometimes find frightening," DiIulio confesses.

There's only one problem: DiIulio is vehemently denounced by many criminologists. Several leading scholars say he manipulates figures to reach foregone conclusions. Others complain that DiIulio is a former moderate who has remodeled himself as a conservative to win the praise of politicians and the homage of reporters.

"He is getting a lot of attention, but he enjoys a terrible reputation in the academic world," says Kenneth Schoen, director of justice programs for the Edna McConnell Clark Foundation, which dispenses crime research grants. "They just sneer at the guy. Everything he does is crummy. The thing that bothers me about John is that because he is bright and articulate, he is dangerous."

"I do not think highly of his scholarship," concurs Norval Morris, professor of law and criminology at the University of Chicago and coeditor of *The Oxford History of the Prison*.

"It's a tribute to the superficiality of our analysis of crime that he gets such notoriety. He preaches what people want to hear in a field where myth far outruns reality."

The article includes a score card of DiIulio statements, headed "The Flexible DiIulio." Bendavid had found quotations in different publications in which DiIulio managed to answer both yes *and* no— to the following questions: Does Rehabilitation Work?... Does Intensive Parole Work?... "Is Crime Going Down?... and Are Prisons Inhumane?... Bendavid observed, "A review of thirty-eight DiIulio writings dating back to 1987 suggests his message has shifted significantly to the right, and taken on an increasingly strident tone."

Although DiIulio likes to call himself a Democrat, the article had a subtitle, "DiIulio Emerges as GOP's Favorite Crime Guru." He has, in fact, become the darling of conservatives such as William Bennett and William Kristol.

After the article appeared, DiIulio engineered much hostile reaction. I myself seemed to be "safe," because while I had been willing to suggest sources for Bendavid's research, I had endeavored to keep my name out of the article. But when Bendavid told me he had become somewhat embattled, I relented and wrote a long analysis. I agreed he could use elements of if it, if they would help him. Much to my surprise, the next issue of *Legal Times* ran an entire page of my analysis, entitled "DiIulio Article Was Fair, Not Inflammatory." That really set off DiIulio and his champion at Brookings, Tom Mann.

However, Marc Mauer, Assistant Director of The Sentencing Project, a nationally recognized organization for criminal justice reform, wrote to me in March: "This is just a fan letter regarding your letter in *Legal Times* on the DiIulio affair. I thought it was right on the mark, and a fine combination of substance and passion. I thought the original article was quite good, and fair, and if anything understated what many people in the field would say. I haven't seen the Mann letter [to the editor], but I gather it didn't contain much in the way of a substantive refutation of anything in the article."

At the same time, I became very disappointed with the leadership of the *Legal Times*. For whatever reasons, but probably bowing to the pressures mounted by DiIulio, the newspaper began running items that contained lies about me. DiIulio submitted a letter-to-the-editor, which was prominently displayed and headlined, "DiIulio: Here are 5 Things to Know About Cikins' Letter." Each one of those things on his list was at best a half-truth or distortion. *Legal Times* ran another prominently displayed letter, "Cikins Letter Was All Wrong About DiIulio," claiming that my statements saying Governors Christine Whitman and Tommy Thompson had been badmouthed by DiIulio were untrue. In response, an eminent criminologist, Dr. Mary Shilton, wrote to the paper: "Let me quote from John DiIulio from the *Pittsburgh Post-Gazette* of January 14, 1996 (as reprinted from *The Weekly Standard*), 'It is most disheartening to learn that Republican Governor Tommy Thompson of Wisconsin has established a commission to study 'alternatives to incarceration' and has declared he will build no more prisons. New Jersey's Christine Todd Whitman is busy consorting with national anti- incarceration advocacy groups." (You will note that Whitman and Thompson have served in George W. Bush's cabinet, not liberal extremists.)

Legal Times did run Shilton's letter debunking the pro-DiIulio letter, but in the least noticeable part of the paper with a meaningless title, "Selling the Sizzle, Not the Steak." When I demanded the right to reply to the falsehoods about me the paper had prominently showcased, contrary to the article I had originally written in their paper which was entirely true, the editor flatly refused, saying enough had already been written—thus giving DiIulio the last word. I protested to Bendavid, because I had been blatantly lied about in a situation where I was trying to protect him, but he said there was nothing he could do. Bendavid, in fact, would leave *Legal times* not long thereafter for a job with *The Chicago Tribune*.

This is far from the end of this story. William Rentschler, a longtime reporter for *The Chicago Sun-Times* who was a prominent Princeton University alumnus, wrote a personal letter about DiIulio to the *Princeton Alumni Weekly*. It was published on April 17, 1996, with the headline "Crime and Punishment":

> When the history of this final quarter of the 20th century is writ, we may well be remembered as the society that built prisons instead of schools and put punishment ahead of lifting the spirits and answering the cries of our people. If that becomes our sorrowful legacy, a goodly share of the "credit" for this vengeful and counterproductive agenda will accrue to Professor of Politics and Public Affairs John J. DiIulio.

> With Princeton as his prestigious platform, DiIulio ranks high among the advocates of the most drastic, indiscriminate, incredible costly, and thoroughly inappropriate degrees of punishment for all but the truly violent, dangerous, and chronic criminal offenders. If they don't look like us, smell like us, act like us, and they commit a crime, any crime, blow 'em away or lock 'em up forever. This only slightly exaggerates DiIulio's stance, and it has been at the core of our failed "wars" on crime and drugs for more than two decades.

> DiIulio's desire to increase dramatically our reliance on prisons endears him to the political hard right and the powerful "prison–industrial complex," which has made prisons our fastest-growing industry. Many ordinary people have been brainwashed into believing the U.S. is "soft on crime," when in fact, and by a wide margin, we have the highest rate of incarceration and impose the longest sentences of any industrialized nation.

A conservative tax slasher and an ex-officio trustee of Princeton, New Jersey Governor Christine Todd Whitman, states flatly that the problem of violent crime can't be solved by building ever more prisons. As she said last summer, "As resources become increasingly scarce, corrections must not be about punishing harder but punishing smarter. In fighting crime, prevention and early intervention are the only proactive responses. Everything else is reactive—after the crime occurs—and is less effective."

DiIulio replied in the *Weekly* of May 8, 1996, lashing out in all directions, in a threatening manner, which was not surprising. Among other things, he wrote: "*Princeton Alumni Weekly*'s decision to publish Mr. Rentschler's letter raises certain fundamental questions about its editorial standards and motivations."

I quickly called the editor of the *Weekly* to express my concern and he assured me that DiIulio's effort to get him fired (as he has tried and sometimes succeeded with other opponents) would not succeed. He told me he had a faculty editorial board of about a dozen professors and they all approved the running of the Rentschler letter, giving him plenty of protection.

The word spread about Brookings that Mann and DiIulio would like to silence me, which would be difficult, since I was already retired. All of this furor spooked the University of Pennsylvania, which had been prepared to give DiIulio a senior professorship. Penn backed off for a few years before hiring him in a lesser professorship.

DiIulio's next move was to consider advocating the role of religion in helping inmates become rehabilitated. A prison in Texas had become a role model for this effort, bringing DiIulio into the orbit of the state's governor, George W. Bush. When Bush was elected president, the rumor mill mentioned a place in the administration for DiIulio. A reporter for *The New York Times*, Elizabeth Becker, called me to ask what I knew about him. I answered, "I will not become a DiIulio to tell you what I think of him." I then gave her four or five names and phone numbers of people who supported DiIulio and equivalent number of contacts for those who opposed him. Shortly thereafter Becker's story appeared in *The Times* reviewing DiIulio's record and the results of her interview with him. He told her that he had an epiphany while sitting in a Catholic Church in New York City and now regretted being the champion of the theory that the country would soon be awash with "super-predators."

In early 2001, Bush appointed DiIulio director of the new White House Office of Faith-Based and Community Groups. *The Washington Post* of February 5 ran an op-ed by Vincent Schiraldi, president of the Justice Policy Institute, with the headline "Will the Real John DiIulio Please Stand Up":

> In the heat of the controversy over the creation of the Office of Faith-Based and Community Groups, John DiIulio, the office's director, has been lauded as a man of intellect and science. But for those of us who have followed the politics of crime and punishment for the past decade, no single person has been more closely identified with unsound crime analysis and punitive imprisonment policies than John DiIulio.

> The 1990s were a punishing decade for America, with nearly as many people added to our prisons and jails as in America's entire history prior to 1990. These policies were particularly devastating to the black community as one in three young African American males was put under criminal justice control and states shifted funds from higher education to prisons. Fittingly, the number of adults and juveniles locked up in America topped the 2 million mark at the decade's end. While many politicians

competed for top honors in the tough-on-crime sweepstakes, academia's acknowledged king of crime hype was John DiIulio. In 1996 he authored an incendiary report warning of a "rising tide of juvenile superpredators" waiting to engulf America. Bob Dole picked up on the "super-predator" epithet in a radio address during his presidential campaign. Rep. Bill McCollum (R-Fla.) dubbed legislation that jailed juveniles alongside adults "The Violent Youth Predator Act of 1996."

Turns out the tide never rose as high as DiIulio expected. The number of homicides committed by youth in America dropped by 68 percent between 1993 and 1999, and youth crime is now at its lowest in 25 years.

After the backlash against his gloom-and-doom proclamations, DiIulio wrote several pieces toning down his rhetoric. He began working with churches in inner-city communities, claimed that he never intended for young people to be incarcerated with adults and urged a stop to prison growth. These were startling turnarounds from a man who provided the intellectual backing for the largest prison expansion in our history, most of it at the expense of the inner-city blacks he was coming to embrace.

All of which leaves me cautious. Is DiIulio the man who called our young people 'fatherless, godless and without conscience' and who wrote in the National Review, 'All that's left of the black community in some pockets of urban America is deviant, delinquent and criminal adults surrounded by severely abused and neglected children, virtually all of whom were born out of wedlock?' Or is he the John DiIulio who has expressed hope for inner-city blacks, a hope that presumably does not include even larger numbers of them being funneled into the prisons he once so loudly espoused? Before a major federal initiative is put under his aegis, those are important questions to answer.

DiIulio lasted about seven months on the job. He clashed with many colleagues in the White House. The gossip about the matter in Washington was that challenging Karl Rove, Senior Adviser to the President, and Bush's chief political strategist, was not a good idea, and that the White House could only deal with one superego at a time.

Chapter 9

A Return to Life in the Community

Positive Developments in Fairfax County

Meanwhile, back in Fairfax County, I had been spending much of my time since 1997 continuing to chair the periodic update of the Mount Vernon portion of Fairfax County's land-use plan. During this period, the county began focusing on areas that needed some extra help; and I therefore also cochaired the Richmond Highway Revitalization Committee (created by the board of supervisors), which covered the Mount Vernon and the Lee magisterial districts. The committee's work ran from 1997 to 1999. The Southeast Fairfax Development Corporation (SFDC), really came into its own during this time and played a major role in the recommendations made by that committee. The SFDC, under the chairmanship of Sy Berdux (and later Rick Neel) and the staff directorship of Becky Witsman (with her deputy Stephanie Landrum), it put together innovative plans that would facilitate more rapid investment and economic development along the corridor.

SFDC put out a brochure listing about twenty-five development actions that were pending on the corridor, among them new restaurants, businesses, social-service centers, housing centers, and assisted-living facilities. Efforts were being made to demolish blighted

276

entities. As the brochure pointed out, "In the past 13 years, over $467 million in private investment has been made, equally $5.66 million in Fairfax County real estate taxes alone and creating or retaining 4,000 jobs. Since 1990 alone, more than $185.75 million has been invested. Projections for current and future projects equal $141.7 million."

On June 4, 1998, *The Washington Post* ran an article entitled "Study of Route 1 Corridor Gets Underway: Task Force Meets on Redevelopment." According to writer Michael Shear, "Cikins said that the focus of the group will be on two broad areas: how to develop viable commercial centers, known as nodes, and what to do with the areas between those nodes. It will be a mix of land use and beautification. We're talking about efforts that will take many, many years—you've got to start somewhere."

Shear said that I referred to the task force's goal as that of "luring high-quality businesses and jobs to the area." I was quoted as expressing pleasure as co-chairman, that "officials and activists in the Lee and Mount Vernon Districts [who] have not always seen eye to eye about how to improve Route 1 [Richmond Highway Corridor] are [now] working together."

I went on to say that "It didn't seem to make sense without having both sides of the corridor in one grouping. We agreed we would take some of our best people and put them on a joint task force."

The article noted that bigger and taller buildings than usual would be permitted to lure developers and promote area revitalization. I recognized that getting consensus would not be easy, but was crucial for a successful future.

I was always pleased to play a role in keeping all the different factions that make up SFDC working together with goodwill, even though there were many philosophical differences about increasing development versus limiting growth—swinging hard one way or the other decade by decade. Environmental concerns must be addressed without stifling intelligent growth, both commercial and residential;

and the county has gradually moved toward a more balanced approach.

After the task force completed its work in August 1999, I received an extremely laudatory letter from Supervisor Hyland. As he put it:

> Your commitment and interest was undaunting. You listened to many proposals brought by the development community, you heard from residents and their concerns and suggestions; then you considered each and every item and not until that was completed did you make an informed recommendation. That was no easy task!"... "Your work will revitalize this historic region, the strategically placed community business center with housing between demonstrates your methodical work and how much you truly understand our community's needs, wants, and desires. Your work will long be remembered by the general public, the neighbors and the business community.

Hyland concluded with a penned message, "Thank you good friend for *all* you have done for Mount Vernon." Would that his sentiment had prevailed into the future.

A New Approach to Prison Industries

In the midst of my work on Fairfax County's Richmond Highway Revitalization Task Force, UNICOR (the Department of Justice's prison industries division) asked me to chair a third National Prison Industries summit to be held in May of 1998. Attorney General Janet Reno was the keynote speaker at this meeting of nearly two hundred policymakers, practitioners, and experts. She opened the forum telling participants, "I believe very strongly in prison industries... for the prison itself and for the inmate and his future," and she asked the group to explore new and resourceful ways to utilize inmate labor, to "help America and not be an impediment." Several other

distinguished public officials and scholars also participated in enlight-
ening the forum members, pointing out the resistance to helping
inmates learn how to do meaningful jobs must be addressed in a
constructive manner. They attempted to show that a win-win result
was possible for all parties concerned—the inmates, business, labor,
and the public.

The monthly newsletter, *Detention Reporter*, covered the event;
and editor Rod Miller was kind enough to include my entire remarks,
a key paragraph of which stated:

> Issues of competition with the private sector and with free
> labor [have] made prison industries a contentious matter.
> Such considerations themselves collide with concerns
> about the societal value of literacy and job training in
> rehabilitating inmates and returning them to an open
> society with a fighting chance not to recidivate. As we
> gather to pursue a complete paradigm shift—a possible
> view of prison labor as a national economic asset—we
> hope to move away from the conventional wisdom that
> has thwarted all efforts to date to find permanent common
> ground.

I went on to evaluate the successes and the disappointments of
Chief Justice Burger in his efforts to make a difference. I ended with
a series of recommendations to the attendees: get away from traditional fears and suspicions, work to lessen adverse impacts, have
prison labor be regarded as a national economic asset, and recognize
that incremental change was all that could be expected.

A Potpourri of Family Events and Pro Bono Activities

The year 1998 was a great one for our family. The summer before his last year of law school, Neil married Traci Bechtold, and Dean
announced his engagement to Andrea Michael. Neil and Traci's wedding was in Pittsburgh with close to two hundred guests. The

complication was how to have a suitable marriage ceremony that could merge the bride's Catholicism and the groom's Judaism. It was finally resolved by holding the wedding in a Catholic church with a priest who was progressive enough to have Sylvia and me play a significant role in the ceremony. Father Ted was a wonderful collaborator, and we developed a great bond.

I delivered a family homily that reviewed the religious roots of many of those present. I said I was "one who has deep roots in Judaism, who once trained for the rabbinate, but who believes devoutly in the universality of human spirituality and goodness."

I went on to point out that Sylvia had a mixed religious background and had converted to Judaism, that one of my brothers was an ultra-Orthodox Jew, that the other brother married into the family of a Union Theological Seminary dean, that Neil's godfather was a Baptist and his godmother was a Catholic, and that one of my college roommates was Greek Orthodox, and a roommate from my early days in Washington was Mormon. Most of my close relatives, of course, were Jewish, including my eighty-six-year-old aunt who was present. (Sylvia's ninety-six-year-old aunt was also there!.) In closing I said:

> I would like to leave with Traci and Neil some biblical injunctions from both the Old and New Testaments that Brooks Hays and I shared. My favorite which is most relevant to budding lawyer Neil is from Micah 6:8, which says, "What doth the Lord require of thee but to do justice, love mercy, and walk humbly with thy God." My next is from the great spiritual Hebrew leader Hillel who proclaimed, "If I am not for myself, who shall be for me, but if I am for myself alone what am I, and, if not now, when?" Congressman Hays was a great conciliator who achieved many compromises of national significance in the Congress, and his biblical advice can also serve newlyweds very well. He often quoted Paul as saying in

Ephesians 4:15, "Always speak the truth, but speak the truth in love." In the same vein, he quoted Paul avoiding extremism by proclaiming in Philippians 4:5, "Let thy moderation be known to all persons." And, so to Traci and Neil, I wish eternal love, moderation, human caring, justice, mercy, and humility. That is the definition of a truly religious life.

Sylvia spoke to the congregation about why the groom—and in this wedding, the bride as well— stomps on a glass at the end of the ceremony. While there are several interpretations, we believe that the most likely is that the action is meant to remind Jews, as a sobering concern, of the destruction of the ancient Temple in Jerusalem.

Sylvia and I were able to take a vacation to western Canada that year, visiting Vancouver. It was a splendid opportunity to learn more about Canadian life and government, as we toured the facilities of Victoria, the capital of British Columbia. I had a health emergency on this trip, unfortunately—with some food stuck in my throat— and had a firsthand opportunity to observe the efficiency of the Canadian hospital system. Being there, I was reminded that I have long advocated a system of "single-party payer" of health-care costs. The U.S. pays about $130 billion per year on paperwork to deal with its myriad payers, as compared to Canada, where no more than ten percent of that total is spent by the government on a per-person basis. I was provided with excellent care as well. (As a noncitizen, I paid a flat fee which was reimbursed back in the States by my insurance company.)

Both 1998 and 1999 were busy years for me with a myriad of professional and volunteer activities. I was asked to join the Advisory Board (for fundraising) of the Rachel Schlesinger Center for the Arts at Northern Virginia Community College, where former Secretary of Defense Schlesinger donated a substantial sum in memory of his wife, who had served on this board. This activity helped me keep up my contacts in the business and professional worlds of Northern Virginia. At the same time I was involved with the Center for Community Corrections (the nonprofit arm of the NCCC), both as team leader for a new plan of action and as the coauthor and coeditor of a publication, *Partnerships in Corrections: Six Perspectives.* I wrote the chapter on the role of the judiciary in implementing criminal justice laws. While Congress had restricted to a considerable extent the ability of judges to exercise discretion in sentencing, they still had some room for flexibility, if inclined to pursue it. I pointed out where that flexibility was and expressed my concern that judges were not availing themselves of these opportunities. Unfortunately, sentencing commissions and sentencing "guidelines" for mandatory sentencing had worn the judges down. Later, I welcomed the letter I received from Judge Frank Coffin who had been my friend when he was a Member of Congress and who is now on the Federal Court of Appeals, and now commended my effort to encourage judges to act creatively. As mentioned earlier, the Supreme Court has acted in 2005 to help judges regain their ability to truly exercise judgment.

Rick Seiter, who had been a UNICOR Director, was now editing a journal entitled, *Corrections Management Quarterly*; and he welcomed an article I submitted (for the Winter 1999 Issue) entitled "Corrections Legacy of Warren Earl Burger." This article was an effort to shed light on the roots of Burger's later, priority concern over enabling inmates to rehabilitate themselves. I elaborated on earlier analyses to trace in detail how Burger had grown in sophistication and achievement in promoting prison industries and related corrections activities. Burger became a major player in influencing the direction of corrections back in 1971. President Nixon had directed Attorney General John Mitchell to convene a National Conference on Corrections after the unfortunate riot at New York's Attica prison. Burger keynoted the conference and called for the creation of a National Institute of Corrections to do four things: (1) coordinate research in corrections; (2) improve professional training in corrections; (3)

provide a forum for the exchange of knowledge and the promotion of technical assistance; and (4) enhance the professionalism of the corrections field. (Soon after this 1971 conference is when I met Chief Justice Burger for the first time and found we had very much in common.) The follow-up creation of a sixteen-member advisory board to NIC of a cross-section of major policymakers in corrections gave this field a significant push forward. As I put it in my article, "The Berger influence clearly was reflected because he emphasized the need to build bridges between the public and private sectors." The chief justice was dedicated to an honorable and progressive, national corrections policy.

As the year 2000 approached, the head of UCM (United Community Ministries), Sharon Kelso, asked me to review the history of this agency for the delivery of social services. I responded with an article in the *UCM Newsletter* of July–September 1999 entitled "UCM—At the Millennium Crossroads." I pointed out that Fairfax County had grown from a population of 50,000 in 1950 to almost one million. By the end of 1970 UCM was pretty well launched by a relatively small group of dedicated people and soon moved from a trailer to a modest building rented to them by the county. (While a county supervisor, I blocked all efforts to raise the rent so the then-director, Eleanor Kennedy, could use her limited resources to help as many people as possible.) I noted that by now "UCM was admired by the entire nation and United Way cited UCM as a role model for the nation." To this day even though Sharon Kelso has now retired, UCM is an entity that all the people in Fairfax County, especially from the magisterial districts of Mount Vernon and Lee, are united behind, despite whatever other differences they may have.

One day Dean called to ask if we would mind if he married Andrea in Bermuda that May in what is called a "weddingmoon," where marriage ceremony and honeymoon are combined. Naturally I answered that that was a "no-brainer." As Dean said, it isn't often that a bride and groom stay in the same hotel as their parents after the wedding. (They did stay another week in the bridal suite once the wedding party departed.). A fun time was had by all that came.

Once again, though, we confronted the problem of what kind of religious ceremony to have. It worked out to be similar to the arrangement for Neil and Traci's wedding. An Anglican minister agreed that Sylvia and I could share in the ceremony. He was a splendid person, and the ceremony was beautiful at a special spot on the island overlooking a very blue ocean. Appropriate to the location, the minister wore Bermuda shorts. In my sermon, I said that Sylvia and I "are great believers in the Lord's hand in bringing people together (as He did us) and we are completely convinced that this is the case today... Fortuitous is the coincidence that Andrea and Dean have the same birthday, making it easy for us to remember, January 27, just three days away from Franklin Roosevelt's, January 30, Dean's middle name being Franklin."

In my remarks, I went on to put my religious views in perspective:

Those of you who know me know that my Jewish roots and life experience compel me to look to the Old Testament to find guidance in leading a moral and productive life. So let me quote to you one of my favorite passages from Isaiah 58:12, which calls on all of us to be "healers of the breach." While this phrase can have several interpretations, I see it as setting a tone for life, urging us to reach across religious differences as well as societal differences. And so I call on Andrea and Dean to serve as role models of such healers, by continuing to build bridges between different social, economic, and racial groups; and I am convinced they are equal to the task. They have Sylvia's and my deepest love and devotion and full support in their journey through life. May their marriage be at least as long and loving as those of their two sets of parents. Amen.

Sylvia then performed the same role that she had performed at Neil and Traci's wedding, by telling the reasoning for the breaking of the glass, at the end of the ceremony.

Soon thereafter Neil graduated from Duquesne Law School. It was an especially impressive graduation for us. Neil's dean, John Rago, had indicated some months earlier that they were looking for a distinguished commencement speaker. Neil got in touch with former Senator Alan Simpson, who was now director of the Institute of Politics of Harvard's Kennedy School of Government, and he agreed to accept the assignment. Simpson came with his delightful wife Ann, and we had a wonderful precommencement dinner with them. His address was outstanding and extremely well received. It was carried on C-SPAN and friends later told me how impressed they were. What was especially kind of Simpson was raving about Neil in his introductory remarks (and including nice words about his parents) and embracing him when he was handed his degree. It wasn't long thereafter that Neil got a job in the legal department of Crown Castle International—a major owner and operator of technologically advanced, shared wireless infrastructure—working (among other things) in the field of cell-phone towers, which involves many complicated real estate issues.

To conclude a wonderful year, that fall Sylvia and I made yet another trip to Italy. This time we contacted the Acitelli family, Sylvia's relatives that we had gone to meet on our honeymoon in 1964. At the Rome airport, we rented a car and drove to Tivoli to see the remains of Hadrian's Villa, built two thousand years ago by an emperor who was notoriously anti-Jewish. We then went on to L'Aquila, the capital of the province of Abruzzo. (Interestingly, I learned from a history book that in the 1500s and 1600s, this was the most anti-Semitic province in Italy.) There we met a cousin of Sylvia's, Sandro, who was only fifteen years old when we first met him thirty-five years earlier. Fortunately we had been taking Italian lessons, since he spoke practically no English. He proved to be a wonderful guide and spent several days with us driving all about the region. A very special site was the Hotel Campo Imperatore, high in the Gran Sasso d'Italia area of the Apennine Mountains, where Mussolini had been held in 1943 after his overthrow. (He was rescued by German soldiers in gliders—saving him from death, for a couple of years.) But the most significant place we visited was Assergi, a small, walled village in the mountains where Sylvia's dad had been born. We enjoyed meeting many of the people, including several who were distant relatives. We then went back to Rome, where Sylvia's relatives gathered to wine and dine us at the home of Sandro's mother, Rosa. As you might expect, she fed us very well and refused to let us take her out to dinner. It was a sorrowful moment when we had to leave, because it was unclear if we would ever meet again. (Later, back at home, we sent a cowboy hat to Sandro's nephew, who had said he liked to watch westerns.) We ended this great vacation at the romantic places of Sorrento and Capri, with a side trip down the Amalfi Coast.

As the year ended, a group of influential citizens in Mount Vernon met with me at the appropriately named Romeo and Juliet Restaurant, reminding me of Sylvia's and my recently concluded visit to Italy. They included Sy Berdux, John Lynch, and Becky Witsman from SFDC and Jon Hass, a local developer. They had plans to construct a one-stop social-service center on the Richmond Highway Corridor and were seeking my help. I immediately agreed to do whatever I could to make this happen. They gave me a complete briefing on their plans. I then went to see Supervisor Hyland, who had previously expressed some reservations. I provided him with the strong justifications for what was planned, and he thanked me for bringing him up to speed.

In January, 2000 I testified before the Fairfax County Board of Supervisors at the hearing in support of what was to be called the South County Government Center for social services. Here is some of what I had to say:

"With many services now scattered up and down the corridor,

the citizens are put to great inconvenience and expense to simply obtain needed services. Coupled with this difficulty is the stress on county staff, which wastes millions of dollars per year in traveling up and down the corridor to carry out needed service delivery.

"When I was county supervisor from 1975 until 1980, I was concerned about a similar problem and consulted with Supervisor Joe Alexander about the matter. We thought we had made a major contribution when we centralized many services at the location next to the Chuck E. Cheese Restaurant on the corridor, calling it a one-stop center for social services delivery. Before long, as the corridor population increased, the needs also increased, especially since more of the center's low- and moderate-income housing was located on the corridor, these additional needs were so significant the development of more facilities spread down the corridor. And so here we are twenty years later facing a similar problem.

"I see this project as an enormous contribution to the revitalization of the Richmond Highway Corridor. As you know too well, there is great need for such an effort in this area. It will benefit *everyone* on the corridor, service user or not, because it will contribute substantially to the economic expansion of the corridor, serving as a yardstick for others. As one who has worked in the world of public-private cooperation, I am convinced the success of this outreach will motivate many more private enterprises to consider location on the corridor."

I have indeed been proven a prophet since the center has been a great success and many more outstanding economic developments are taking place.

Dean had been out of school for about ten years, and Sylvia and I were proud to learn that he had applied to the University of Pittsburgh's Katz Graduate School of Business (we suspect with the prodding of his wife Andrea) and was admitted. He embarked on a three-year night school program that would turn out to be very demanding, especially because he would continue to work on his regular job full-time. Since Andrea was a dental hygienist and Dean was a salesman for Rockwell Automation, their lives were considerably impacted by Dean's schooling, but they adjusted very well.

Family Losses

My brother Abe resided in an assisted-living facility in Boston, A prominent member of his synagogue had been of great help gaining Abe admittance. And I was especially grateful to the facility's Irish director who looked after my brother, who, needless to say, was a very difficult person to deal with. It seemed that the world had come full circle, since the Irish who had made his life difficult as a boy now kept him alive as an older man. That summer Abe was hit by a car (the same kind of accident that had afflicted him when he was nineteen years old) as he crossed the street in front of his building. After the accident, Abe was taken to the Beth Israel Hospital for treatment. He had numerous surgeries, was moved to a nursing home, and continued clinging to life. Meanwhile my oldest brother, Milton, was also ailing. He too was in a nursing home. He had been slowly fading and died on October 19, 2000. Sylvia and I attended his funeral at a military burial site on Cape Cod, where he was laid to rest with full military honors, being a World War II veteran. This ended a very difficult period for his wife Marnie who had tended to him faithfully.

Sylvia and I had already made plans for another trip to Italy which we embarked on shortly thereafter. After visits to Verona and Venice, we left for Geneva, Switzerland, planning to see the son, daughter-in-law, and two grandsons of beloved neighbors, the Tarpeys. Because of a tunnel blockage in the Alps, we had a hair-raising experience getting from Milan to Geneva, having to travel across about half of Switzerland and changing trains five times, often on a dead run, carrying baggage. We finally made it and had a delightful visit with the younger Tarpey family.

From Geneva we went to Lyon, France. I had, for a long time, wanted to visit the city that spawned the Nazi murderer, Klaus Barbee. What we found, however, was a wonderful remembrance museum that paid very respectful homage to the Holocaust victims. And, of course, we had some wonderful meals. We concluded our trip with a visit to Paris. I had gotten into the habit of calling home to check phone messages, and one day there was a message saying that my brother Abe was seriously ill and was back at Beth Israel Hospital. The next day the message said he was getting better. The next day it said he had died. This was November 10, about three weeks after Milton's death. There was no one but me to make arrangements for the funeral, which had to take place very fast, in accord with Jewish law. I embarked on a series of phone calls to the funeral home, the cemetery, several rabbis, the assisted-living facility, the nursing home, and numerous other places. I am extremely grateful to everyone that I talked to for cooperating so fully. While my phone bill was astronomical, the final cost of arrangements was moderate, and all was done properly. Very few people were able to attend the services. One who did was the Irish director of the assisted-living facility. Sylvia had tried to get us back from Paris to Boston in time, but that was just impossible. It was a very traumatic ending to the year.

Births and Honors in 2001

In a not unusual pattern of cyclical events in a lifetime, the next year was very upbeat. I had been nominated by Robert Greiser, a federal prison industries senior official, and then approved to receive the prestigious James A. McLaughlin Award of the Correctional Industries Association (CIA), an affiliate of the American Correctional Association. (Chief Justice Burger had received this award shortly before he died.) I was then invited, along with Sylvia, to attend the 2001 winter meeting of the CIA at Opryland Hotel in Nashville, Tennessee, to accept the award. Kathleen Hawk-Sawyer, director of the Federal Bureau of Prisons, made the presentation on behalf of CIA President Paul Petit and Executive Director Gwyn Smith Ingley.

Since Director Hawk-Sawyer pretty much covered my whole career in the field, I will try to sum up her remarks. She reviewed my lifelong role in contributing to fostering correctional work-training programs and honored me as a "tireless, honest broker" for correctional industry issues. She commented that "his career epitomizes the ideal of the McLaughlin Award," and noted:

> Three simultaneous events made 1975 an exciting time in Warren's life and a very good year for prison industries in America: First, Warren began a direct personal association with prison industries issues when he was elected to the Fairfax County Board of Supervisors in Virginia, representing an area of the county which included the District of Columbia corrections facilities at Lorton; second, Warren began a second career at Brookings Institution; and third, he began a twenty-year collaboration and friendship with Chief Justice Warren Burger, working on prison industries matters.

She warmly added, "I am very proud of our association and friendship with Warren and invite all to join me in congratulating him for his well deserved recognition".

Just over two months later I was again honored, this time by the Fairfax County Federation of Citizens Associations at its annual dinner, with the granting of a Citation of Merit. My former colleague who had been chairman of the board of supervisors, Jean Packard, read the award language:

> Warren Cikins is the senior statesman in Fairfax County. Whenever a community issue needs leadership or consensus building, Warren gets a call. He is respected and admired regardless of anyone's political persuasion.

One example of this was the sale of the Woodley Hills property, which would have left hundreds of families homeless. He was able to develop alternatives that included building trailer lots as well as maintaining the property for parks and future development. There was a lot of anger in the community over the original proposal, and Warren was able to find a way to bring calm and acceptable alternatives to the concern.

While serving as Mount Vernon representative on the board of supervisors, Warren put into place several citizen groups which continue to be a major force in getting things done and assuring citizen participation. One of these is the Route One Task Force, which continues to operate twenty-five years after its formation. This task force has been responsible for many initiatives, chief among them the affordable health clinics, the shelters for the homeless, the Mount Vernon Hospital, the Mount Vernon Center for Community Mental Health, and the George Washington Recreation Center.

She concluded by reviewing all my citizen activities in the county after I had left the board, noting that she and I had probably done much more than other former supervisors to improve the quality of our communities. While some of the language she used wasn't exactly accurate, the overall thrust of the citation did deal with the essence of my contributions.

The greatest event of the year, however, was the birth of twin granddaughters, Emme Leigh and Tori Alyn, on May 8, 2001. Sylvia and I got to Pittsburgh in time to be there when Neil and Traci brought the girls home. Their names were ones that I found in a book of Jewish names, although their parents probably had no idea of that fact when they named them. Emme, of course, is a variation of Emma, which is identified with the great Jewish poet Emma Lazarus, whose stirring words about welcoming the "wretched refuse of your teeming shore" and "your huddled masses yearning to breathe free" appear on the Statue of Liberty. And Tori has the Hebrew meaning of "turtledove." Their other grandparents, Bill and Donna Bechtold, who are very good Catholics, and who had become very dear "relatives" of ours, participated in a christening, and Sylvia and I held a Jewish naming. We got a book written by Anita Diamant that provided the procedure for carrying out the ceremony of the *brit bat* covenant for a daughter. Through the Internet, we obtained Certificates of the Covenant which we had appropriately filled out and framed. Neil and Traci had very wisely arranged to have not one, but two, doulas to provides Traci with physical, emotional, and informational support. These two took turns helping the new parents through the evenings and nights for eight weeks. We, the new grandparents, stayed for three weeks, also to be helpful—Sylvia much more than I, since I was mostly a "morale booster."

That year was also the fiftieth reunion of my class of 1951 at Harvard College. Sylvia and I went to Cambridge but did not participate in too many of the ceremonies, although we did march with my class on commencement day. My interest was largely in seeing my college roommates, most of whom I had known since age twelve or thirteen. There were others that I had known in those college years as friends, as well as several I had met recently in Fairfax County and elsewhere. It was great visiting with old and new friends, and so I didn't want to put in much time at formal reunion activities.

I spent much of the year working on the completion of the Mount Vernon section of the county land-use plan. There were some controversial proposals that led to some rather heated exchanges, but civility was maintained. We completed the revision with a series of recommendations that reinforced the revitalization outreach we had been promoting.

Meanwhile I had noticed that the Wakefield Recreation Center had been renamed in honor of Audrey Moore, a former supervisor for the magisterial district where it was located. I was somewhat surprised. In 1994, I had sent Supervisor Hyland, my successor, a document reviewing how difficult it had been for me to get the Mount Vernon Recreation Center launched with an ice skating rink. When I mentioned the possibility of my name being bestowed upon the facility, Hyland had intimated that a person had to be dead for such a step to be taken.

By making such an inquiry, I guess I wasn't living up to the role model of humility set by Brooks Hays, but I was reminded, and also angry, of how the people of Arkansas were overlooking the great achievements of his courageous career. There were so many revisionist historians that were attempting to demean his efforts to get his state to obey the law of the land. It would have been nice if the people had recognized his great contributions instead of shrinking from identifying with them. The only gracious action they took was electing his son Steele to the Arkansas Supreme Court. And so somehow I felt that it was not inappropriate for me to fight for recognition for the enormous struggle it took to gain success with the recreation center—a much greater struggle than I am sure Audrey Moore had to make to get her recognition. And, I might mention, Moore's successor as supervisor, Sharon Bulova, went all out to get her this deserved honor.

Difficulties on the Local Scene

At the end of July 2002 I went to my family doctor about some ailment; and he happened to tell me that a member of the Inova Health System board and the chairman of the medical staff of Inova Mount Vernon Hospital (IMVH), Dr. Khosrow Matini, had expressed some concern about the future of the hospital. He arranged for me to get a copy of a letter Dr. Matini had written his fellow board members the past November raising many questions about the status of this medical facility. I was already planning to see Supervisor Hyland to report the final results of the task force on the revised land-use plan, and so I brought Dr. Matini's letter with me. Hyland told me he thought the hospital was getting along very well under the splendid leadership of its administrator, Susan Herbert, and sent me to see her. She in turn thought Inova was handling Dr. Matini's concerns appropriately, but suggested I talk with my former board of supervisors colleague, Jim Scott, who was now a senior official of Inova and also a Virginia state legislator. Jim and I met, and ultimately it was agreed that a task force would be created, with representatives from all the key organizations in the Mount Vernon and Lee magisterial districts, as identified by their respective supervisors, Gerry Hyland and Dana Kauffman. In hindsight this was a great mistake; the issues should have been worked out between the doctors and the hospital administration. Nonetheless, a get-acquainted meeting was held in the fall of 2002, but the first working session wasn't until February 2003.

Before I left the meeting with Hyland, I brought up the 1994 memo I had sent him about possible recognition for getting the Mount Vernon Recreation Center underway. Hyland admitted that being dead wasn't a prerequisite. But he said his park authority appointee, Gil McCutcheon, was against my getting any recognition and thought Herb Harris should be considered. Herb was my predecessor as supervisor and had arranged for the land to be available for a recreation center, for which I always gave him due credit, but his struggle was as nothing compared to the effort I had to make to get the facility built. It started out as a plan for an ice skating rink and, in the end, also accommodated a swimming pool and an exercise center, as well as additional multi-purpose rooms. Anyway, Herb had just been recognized by the naming of a U. S. Post Office in his honor and would possibly have the hospital named for him someday. Hyland said he would never take an action that would overrule an appointee, which I thought was ludicrous. Numerous times he had changed recommendations made by committees I had chaired for him, without ever even discussing the matters with me. I also knew of several task forces in Mount Vernon District that he had over-ruled on issues of some significance. In principle, I have no objection to this sort of leadership, but Hyland's explanation of his position on renaming the recreation center struck me as simply using McCutcheon to prevent my getting anywhere.

I wasn't worried because I thought Herb Harris would support me strongly, and how wrong I was about that. When I called him, he gave me every reason to believe he supported me. But when I wrote him memo after memo asking him to take some supportive action, I never heard back. When I turned to my former board colleague Joe Alexander, he promised to lead a citizens group to help me, but after his talking to Harris and Hyland, he faded away. By this time I was getting mad. I sent a copy of my 1994 memo on the rink to 150 leading citizens in Fairfax County simply telling them what I had done. On my list was every current member of the board of supervisors. In response to my letters I received many favorable comments. One example was from Supervisor Penny Gross, who responded with a very gracious thank-you note. She said she enjoyed reading this "wonderful narrative" and reflecting on the "struggle you took on in its development." She went on to note that "it's hard to imagine the level of opposition at the time, but I guess it's always easier to say no rather than work to build for future generations. I'm certainly glad you stuck to your guns." A Mount Vernon School Board member, Isis Castro, called me to say that she was eager to create a commit-tee to have the center named for me, but after she talked to Hyland, she, too, faded away. As the year came to an end, I was almost rec-onciled to forgetting the whole thing.

By the beginning of 2003, I had received a letter from Knox Single-ton, the president and CEO of the Inova Health System, asking me to serve as chairman of what was being called the Southeast Fairfax Health Planning Task Force. The letter said he was also writing on behalf of Supervisors Hyland and Kauffman. When I originally supported the idea of creating the task force, I had said emphatically that I did not want to be chairman and had recommended by-then-retired State Senator Joe Gartlan. But when this letter arrived, I was hard put to say no, in view of my longtime record of pro bono service to Fairfax County. In view of my recent strained relations with Hyland over the Mount Vernon Recreation Center, I was surprised that he would want me to be the chairman of this sensitive group. I reluctantly agreed to serve, and this very wrong decision, however well intentioned, would seriously jeopardize my health, partially because of the great stress.

A get-acquainted meeting had been held in the fall of 2002, but the first working session of the task force wasn't until February 2003. At that meeting, I brought along a copy of George Washington's book on rules of civility, which I hoped would be our guide. This turned out to be a very counter-productive move. There was no chance in the world that there would be civility, with some seventeen task force members plus several other major participants, drawn from a cross section of community leaders, having about forty controversial agendas. Most of the rules for successful task forces were quickly broken. Among those were commitments adhering to a procedure that requires civility, not playing to the press, not furthering political agendas, working to strengthen trust rather than driving wedges, and focusing on a factual agenda rather than clouding the real issues. It became very clear that some of the task force members had no intention of observing these procedures. They preferred widespread early confrontation and widespread early publicity. For example, they invited the press to attend these meetings. Even so we had reasonably successful February and March meetings, identifying between sixty and seventy key items to review, including the legitimate concerns of the community about the hospital's future.

At the May meeting, to try to maintain the momentum that had been generated, I called for a closed session to deal with some sensitive matters that Inova officials had called proprietary. I have spent a lifetime in quiet diplomacy, and many congressmen, judges, and senior Justice Department officials have participated in off-the-record sessions that I conducted. I am totally committed to ultimate full disclosure, but sound public policymaking requires an intelligent dedication to timing. However, here in Fairfax County, the politicians present rose in protest (one was overheard saying "Now's the time to go!") and spent a great deal of time with the local press outside the meeting room. The local newspapers then wrote screaming headlines, saying that Inova was going to close Mount Vernon Hospital, and the task force was "hidden from the community and barricaded." That was a little absurd, since the task force represented all elements of the community. Senator Joe Gartlan was quoted as calling my views on policymaking "hackneyed," a somewhat disingenuous point of view, since he had participated in numerous closed sessions of the Virginia State Senate.

At a later meeting of the task force, I put the matter of closed versus open sessions to a vote. The tally, with two members absent, was six for all closed, nine for a mix of open and closed (as I preferred), and *none* for all open. I repeat, *zero* voted for all open—and that includes the politicians.

It had been clear to me after the May meeting that any chance for the task force to succeed in finding middle ground was severely damaged. I wanted to resign on the spot and suggest that the task force dissolve, leaving the matter to the physicians and Inova to resolve, but I was talked out of it. I regret now that I didn't leave then, because I would be a lot healthier now if I had.

I did talk to Leef Smith, a reporter for *The Washington Post*, who, by the way, said she couldn't care less whether the meetings were open or closed. In the May 22 edition of *The Post*, she described me as the "one-time county supervisor who helped open Mount Vernon [Hospital] in 1976." who said, "There's no way on God's earth they'll close the hospital—they won't get away with it." In a follow-up story on June 12, Smith quoted me again: "The issue is what kind of hospital it is going to be and how will it maintain some semblance of financial stability—does it stay specializing in certain things or be all things to all people? That's a big part of the question." The words unfortunately did little good in a situation already out of control.

Around the same time the task force got underway, a few supervisors had approached the Fairfax County Park Authority to do something on my behalf about renaming the recreation center. Also, Gale Curcio wrote a story in the *Mount Vernon Gazette* of February 27, 2003, headlined, "Pioneer's Work Applauded and Remembered." She quoted me as saying that we came close to not having this wonderful recreation center: "Everybody told us nobody would use it."

Curcio went on to note that part of the agenda I ran on in the special election had been "providing wholesome recreation for the children of Mount Vernon." After reviewing the history of how the community got the recreation center underway and its opening twenty-five years ago, she concluded the story by quoting me: "The rink was a success from the start and for many, many years I have had the great pride in driving by the facility every day."

Just a few days before the ceremony honoring the recreation center's twenty-fifth anniversary, I got a call from the chairman of the park authority, very coolly inviting me to the event. There had been little notice, and there were few attendees. A few park authority members came, including Gil McCutcheon, who made a "show" of friendship. Gerry Hyland read from a plaque that said, "The Mount Vernon Ice Skating Rink would not have become a reality without the tireless support and effort of Warren I. Cikins." The center's director, Trina Taylor, graciously told me the plaque would hang in the facility, she being genuinely appreciative of my efforts. Of course, a plaque on the wall does not equal a name above the door.

Retirements and Advancements

In the spring of 2003 I conducted my last class for Nova University. The assistant dean with whom I had worked, Bob Baer, was leaving, and there was evidence that university officials were prepared to shut down the Washington-area operation, even though it had been very successful for the school, both professionally and financially. I was ready to end my involvement anyway and did not make any effort to keep the program alive.

After many years of struggling with Alzheimer's, Sylvia's mother, Mary Acitelli, died in March. We were all saddened by her passage and participated in the funeral service. Our sons were great in describing the times she had looked after them when Sylvia and I were on vacation, and. I recalled how wonderfully she had treated me, both when I was courting her daughter and after Sylvia and I were married. Sylvia read from the famous passage in Proverbs, 31: 10, about the worth of a good woman, which is a price above rubies. It was uplifting to know that Mary had been beautifully cared for by the nursing home in Berlin, Pennsylvania, where she had lived her final years.

On the bright side, that June, Dean received his M.B.A. degree from the University of Pittsburgh, with honors equivalent to Phi Beta Kappa, called Beta Gamma Sigma. We had a wonderful time at the ceremonies with Judy and Bob Michael, Andrea's parents, and were very proud of Dean's achievement and dedication. Much credit goes to Andrea for her support and encouragement.

That fall, the Health Care Advisory Board of Fairfax County held a hearing on the situation with IMVH, and I was invited to testify. I covered much of the development of the task force, and the heart of my report was as follows:

> I think it's fair to say that everyone wants the Inova system and Inova Mount Vernon Hospital to survive and prosper, but the approaches are vastly different, and I

maintain some well-meaning activities of confrontation have been counterproductive. What have we seen in Mount Vernon? (1) great fear in a community which has been traumatized; (2) great upset in the nursing and related staff (which upset I see on my visits); (3) the medical staff going through the throes of disarray; (4) prospective patients having doubts; (5) civility lost; (6) some character assassination; (7) loss or credibility of some community leaders; (8) Inova itself damaged; and (9) [the] private Hospital Corporation of America encouraged.

On the bright side, there have been some task force accomplishments, contrary to the many criticisms. They are as follows: (1) key issues have been brought front and center; (2) the medical staff has been pushed to get its act together and set out its priorities for public review—Dr. Cleve Francis deserves much credit for constructive inputs; (3) Inova has hired the distinguished health consultant, Lewin Associates, to review relevant facts and views; (4) George Barker has provided the task force with invaluable information regarding the possible strengthening of Inova Mount Vernon Hospital and the deflection of HCA; (5) Inova has gained considerable insight into the attitudes of key Mount Vernon participants; and (6) an effort is being made to get assistance from DeWitt Hospital.

I concluded by indicating that my health was frail and saying, "My wife thinks I need another medical examination—from a psychiatrist, for ever accepting this assignment in the first place."

It was not long before I resigned as chairman. To add insult to injury, the *Mount Vernon Gazette* reported *very* erroneously that I was resigning because I had caused controversy, and then refused to run a letter I sent telling the truth about the situation—probably the first time in that paper's history a letter from a former supervisor was rejected.

January 12, 2004 was a great day and a troublesome day. Our daughter-in-law Andrea gave birth to Maya Francesca, a very beautiful little girl indeed. The name Maya appears in my name book as a modern Hebrew name based on a Roman mythological goddess. We were so happy and feeling blessed. At the same time, I went to my cardiologist, Dr. Cleve Francis, for a routine checkup and found that my echocardiogram signaled trouble. I was immediately put on several medications and scheduled for a catheterization to check on the possibility of clogged arteries.

The catheterization was done a couple of weeks later by Dr. Narian Rajan at Inova Fairfax Hospital in Falls Church, Virginia, and the recommendation was that I have a heart bypass operation because of some clogged arteries. Sylvia sprang into action, and her research discovered many problems with such a procedure being done on someone with spondylitis. I proceeded to make a list of twenty-seven concerns. The three major ones involved intubation problems, chest expansion problems, and difficulty in recovering from splitting the breastbone—necessary to do the procedure.

While I was still in the hospital, however, I almost was wheeled into the area to prepare for the bypass when, fortunately, Dr. Francis intervened. Back home, I did further research on the latest developments in bypass surgery and found that The Cleveland Clinic seemed to be "at the cutting edge," so to speak. That does not mean that Inova Fairfax Hospital isn't outstanding, but that possibly The Cleveland Clinic is more innovative. In any event, I am continuing to look into the matter, since chest pains persist. In the interim I have had an angioplasty procedure, and Dr. Rajan inserted three stents, one of which is coated with a protective drug.

Several months later, I developed swollen legs and gained fifteen pounds in less than a week. When I saw Dr. Francis, an echo-cardiogram showed fluid around the heart, and he immediately checked me into IMVH. The next morning Dr. George Besch performed a procedure called pericardiocentesis, which to a layman meant he inserted a device into my chest and pumped out about a liter and a half of fluid. There was fear of a very serious cause of this condition, but tests showed that it was probably a virus. There was still some fluid in the lungs, but it drained out in a couple of weeks. All in all, medically speaking, it was a pretty hectic period of time, and I still don't feel that I'm out of the woods.

Dean and Andrea did us a great favor by driving from Pittsburgh to Mount Vernon in the early spring so we could see Maya. We had the same naming ceremony that we had for the twins. She's a wonderful little girl with much dark hair, of course, and I marvel at being the grandfather of three little girls. I am one of three boys, we had two boys, and now the tables have turned. We were fortunate to get up to Pittsburgh for the third birthdays of Emme and Tori. They are making great progress and are a delight to us all. I certainly hope to recover enough to watch all the girls grow up.

By the middle of 2004, the work of the Southeast Fairfax Health Planning Task Force was pretty much completed, with only a watchdog role remaining. Those who wanted to promote expanding Inova Mount Vernon Hospital into a full-service hospital had prevailed, handily, calling for the expenditure of considerable funding. There was expectation that another Healthplex would be built in Lorton, similar to the existing one in Springfield, except that it was assumed that this one would feed many patients to IMVH. There are those who still wonder if this was the wisest resolution, over the long run, of the differences that existed. Would a better solution in the long run have been a two-hospital package, with Mount Vernon continuing quality services in such areas as cardiology, emergency needs, psychiatric care, rehabilitation, and joint replacement, and then a new state-of-the-art facility provided for all other health needs, located more centrally (based on demographics) with transportation from low income areas made available?

Regretfully the money for that option will apparently now go to Loudoun County Hospital, as it merges with Inova to create a new state-of-the-art facility. There are many other questions left unresolved. Only time will tell whether the money spent on IMVH will be most effective for providing high quality services, whether the facility will continue to attract enough patients to stop the red ink from flowing, whether the Healthplex will contribute to that result, and whether young doctors can be attracted to the community. These questions reinforce my opinion that the task force mechanism, which I recommended, turned out to be the wrong way to build consensus, rather than contributing to the wedge-driving that took place. I paid a high price personally for this misjudgment, since my health was seriously impaired trying to build bridges and find middle ground. Some factions of the medical profession, the political spectrum, the press, the community, and other interested persons preferred combat, a disturbing micro example of the national (and international) trend towards divisiveness.

Since I was no longer carrying out any professional duties and was not involved in any county committees, I thought the time had also come to resign as vice chairman of the National Committee on Community Corrections. When I made the announcement at the April meeting, I reviewed my twenty years of involvement. I got a laugh when I pointed out that federal incarceration had only gone up from 30,000 to close to 200,000 during that period while I was trying to reduce it. "Think how bad it would be if I hadn't worked so hard."

NCCC Chairman Santarelli, who had been an outstanding leader from the beginning, announced that he would hold a party for me at his home in Alexandria on June 25. This was only one of many gracious acts he had performed over the years, including paying for all the excellent meals provided at our meetings. Quite a few of my favorite criminologists gathered for the occasion. Don Murray of the National Association of Counties (NACO), although he was called away and could not attend, arranged that I be presented with the Bombay Company's mahogany memory box .The inscription read: "To Warren Cikins, from NACO. With profound appreciation for his many contributions to progressive county government in America."

The highlight of the event was the remarks of Edward F. Reilly, Jr., the current chairman of the U.S. Parole Commission, who presented me with a framed "Certificate of Parole." The conditions of my parole were described. "You will continue to contribute to the cause of bringing justice and fairness to offenders, and you will agree to accept the praise and admiration of all those who have had the good fortune to work with you." He had prepared a letter to me, which he read aloud:

> I wish to express my deepest gratitude for your years of service in the cause of justice. Your vision, along with that of Parole Commissioner Benjamin Baer, created the National Committee on Community Corrections, and your energy and commitment led the committee for nearly twenty years. Under your leadership, the committee stood as a beacon showing the way to a more humane criminal justice system. You have been one of the strongest advocates in this country for the use of community corrections, and you can be justifiably proud of the role you have played in promoting the fair administration of justice.
>
> I hope you have the opportunity to write and publish your views so that all of us can benefit from your insight. Along with so many others, I hope we can continue to benefit from your vast knowledge and experience. The National Committee on Community Corrections will miss having you in the role of vice chairman, but we will undoubtedly continue to turn to you for guidance.

It has been a great struggle to live up to the sentiments expressed by Chairman Reilly.

As I reflect on the ups and downs of my life, I think I identify with a statement of a fellow New Englander, Ralph Waldo Emerson: "The purpose of life is not to be happy. It is to be useful, to be honorable, to be compassionate, to have it make some difference that you have lived and lived well."

Epilogue

When I was a teenager, I read Herman Melville's *Moby Dick* and was so impressed by his writing that I read several of his other books. The one I remember best to this day *Billy Budd*, is about a young man whose well-meaning behavior challenges the established order of society. The representatives of that society are envious of his success and popularity and turn on him—leading him to a disastrous end. This book made a different kind of profound impression on me. It solidified my decision to dedicate my life to public service, but taught me to keep my back to the wall. I became extremely admiring of Franklin Delano Roosevelt. I identified with Harvard's greatest president during the last half of the twentieth century, James Bryant Conant, who called himself "a hard-boiled idealist." But I recognized that such a life would be a bumpy road. As I later told my wife-to-be, she should not expect me to seek riches, but that life with me would not be dull. I think I've lived up to that promise. I recognized that attempting to make a difference in society would not necessarily lead all people to welcome me with open arms but that some might make my life quite difficult.

I learned quickly that this would indeed be the case. My youth was incredibly stressful, but saved only by a loving immediate family in the depths of the Great Depression. Since I knew that getting a great education was the key to my escaping my environment, I threw myself into that effort with complete concentration—putting on hold all other objectives or possibilities. It was at Harvard that I met Mark Cannon who brought me to Chief Justice Warren Burger, and Brad Westerfield who brought me to Congressman Brooks Hays. It took a while to establish great rapport with Burger, but I had instant chemistry with Hays. Such success as I have had in my professional life is owed to these men.

Hays and Burger taught me to build bridges between people and warned me that such an effort was not for the short-winded. As this book emphasizes, such contributions that I have made have usually involved two steps forward and one step back. Even with the additional warnings that I taught myself, I still have a pretty trusting nature, which has often led to my being burnt.

Despite these ups and downs, I believe strongly that there has been divine guidance in my life. Not to get profane, but I remember when Brooks Hays was embattled in the Little Rock Crisis he received a telegram from a minister friend that read, "Blessed are the peacemakers, because they catch hell from both sides." Without that divine guidance, I could never have overcome that "hell." I recognize that I have not had the dreadful results inflicted not only on Billy Budd but also Prime Ministers Yitzhak Rabin of Israel and Anwar Sadat of Egypt, who took greater risks than I. I hope I will be forgiven for making any comparison with such great national and world leaders, but I believe I have been motivated by the same instincts as Hays and Burger and Rabin and Sadat. Hays and Burger have suffered from revisionist history that demeans them, while I have been the victim of many rebuffs throughout my life.

The years 1955, 1975, and 1990 have been the major turning points in my life: 1955, when I arrived permanently in the Washington area—working with Hays, then Engle, then Kennedy, then Muskie, and then Johnson; 1975, when I was elected supervisor, started working with Chief Justice Burger, and joined The Brookings Institution; and 1990, when I started the process of initiating retirement, so that I could give all my time to pro bono public service.

While I would like to look back and say that I had never made any opponents, which I can't, I can only defend myself by telling again the Brooks Hays story about the little boy who came home with a black eye, and when his mother asked what happened, he replied "it all started when Billy hit me back." I have never knowingly started any confrontations. I have been willing to take a stand in the face of strong opposition unlike Robespierre, a leader in the French Revolution, who was purported to have said, "The mob is in the streets, I must find out what direction they are headed for I am their leader." I would prefer to be identified with the British political leader Edmund Burke, who emphasized that a public officeholder should be totally devoted to the wellbeing of his constituents; but he should not simply reflect their momentary whims, rather he should exercise his conscience and his judgment.

Those who know me know that I am a great list maker. When I make the lists of those who have helped me, as compared to those who have hurt me, the helper list is much more significant, if not longer. Professionally, Hays (through Westerfield) and Burger (through Cannon) are central. The personal list starts with my wife Sylvia and our two sons, Dean Franklin and Neil Winston, and includes all other family, especially my daughters-in-law Andrea and Traci, and my cousin Ida, who was my away-from-home mother. I am still close to my four high school friends—Ed, Dave, Joe, and Mike—and I cannot omit Rabbi Laszlo Berkowits, who saw Sylvia and me through the necessary steps to sort out our religious needs and then married us forty years ago. There are too many others to list here, but I salute them all. Most are mentioned in this book.

It has been my privilege to witness many historic events in my fifty years in the Washington area. And I have been a player in some of them and even a significant player in a few. While I sometimes despair at the breakdown of civility and kindness and integrity and goodwill that is reflected in most walks of life—from politics to the media, to the clergy, to the business world, to government operations, and many of the professions—I detect signs that tell me that there will be a better future. I am confident that the One who watches over us will enable us to see a better day.

Index

A

B